RIVER FEVER

Will Bagley steering the *Phillip W. Bell* near mile 813, the River Styx buoy, on October 16, 1969. Courtesy Martha Goodale Pretzer.

RIVER FEVER

ADVENTURES ON THE MISSISSIPPI

1969 – 1972

A MEMOIR

WILL BAGLEY

SIGNATURE BOOKS | 2019 | SALT LAKE CITY

For Suzanne

Cover design by Aaron Fisher.
Map by Jason Francis.

FIRST EDITION | 2019

LIBRARY OF CONGRESS CATALOGING-IN-PUBLICATION DATA

Names:	Bagley, Will, 1950– author.	Francis, Jason, 1976– cartographer.
Title:	River fever : adventures on the Mississippi, 1969–1972 : a memoir/Will Bagley; map by Jason Francis.
Description:	First edition.	Salt Lake City : Signature Books, 2019.
Identifiers:	LCCN 2018049037 (print)	LCCN 2018052954 (ebook)	ISBN 9781560853541 (e-book)	ISBN 9781560852780 (pbk.)
Subjects:	LCSH: Bagley, Will, 1950–	Mississippi River—Description and travel.	Rafting (Sports)—Mississippi River.	LCGFT: Autobiographies.
Classification:	LCC F355 (ebook)	LCC F355 . B34 2019 (print)	DDC 917.704—dc23
	LC record available at https://lccn.loc.gov/2018049037

CONTENTS

ACKNOWLEDGEMENTS

What profit hath a man of all his labour which he taketh under the sun? One generation passeth away, and another generation cometh: but the earth abideth for ever. The sun also ariseth, and the sun goeth down, and hasteth to his place where he arose. The wind goeth toward the south, and turneth about unto the north; it whirleth about continually, and the wind returneth again according to his circuits. All the rivers run into the sea; yet the sea is not full; unto the place from whence the rivers come, thither they return again.

—Ecclesiastes 1:3–7

"So many people helped us," Suzy recalled. This is for all those who made this adventure happen: Howard Amend, Martha Goodale, Suzanne Cooper, Nan E. Cooper, Richard Stockton, Mario Marioncelli III, Diana Harvey, Eric Wood, Ward Stanger, Pedro Castro, Kim McKay, Andy Fuhrman, and Wendell Wright. I owe the people who made me a historian—Floyd A. O'Neil, Virginia Petch, Michael Landon, Chuck Rankin, Bob Clark, Elliott West, Michael W. Homer, and Laura Bayer—more than I can say. Special thanks to artist Curtis Jensen, who converted James Ney's photo into a vivid line drawing of our intrepid crew on the dismal morning of September 24, 1969 as we began rolling down the Mississippi. My appreciation for the dear departed, Abe Solomon, John Adams, Roger Pretzer, Joseph Hazard Van Gale, B. Carmon Hardy, Kenneth N. Owens, David L. Bigler, Brigham D. Madsen, Harold M. Schindler, and Larry and Margene Bagley, knows no bounds.

BY WAY OF A PREFACE

This book began long, long ago, as it was happening. Ninety percent of what you have in your hands was typed by 1975 and digitized via a Wang word processor ten years later. It began as a non-fiction novel and has evolved through variations as a novel and as straight history, but it's actually a young man's memoir. Since 1985 I've tinkered with it about once a decade, but only after attending my fiftieth high school reunion in October 2017 did I read through the entire opus. Rather than replace the arrogance of youth with the wisdom that allegedly comes with age, it mostly stands as written. I have added events such as the account of the May 1969 People's Park march to try to capture the spirit of the times. Experience compels historians to be suspicious of that willful trickster, memory. Messing with this manuscript has demonstrated that if the mind can't remember some ancient event, it will make it up to fill in the details. Rather than remake this as an old man's book, I have tried to limit revisions to essentials and park new prose in the afterword. Revisiting this forgotten lore made me wonder if I remembered anything at all about being Bill Bagley, a name I haven't used for forty-three years. Reading the manuscript indicates I recall more than I thought.

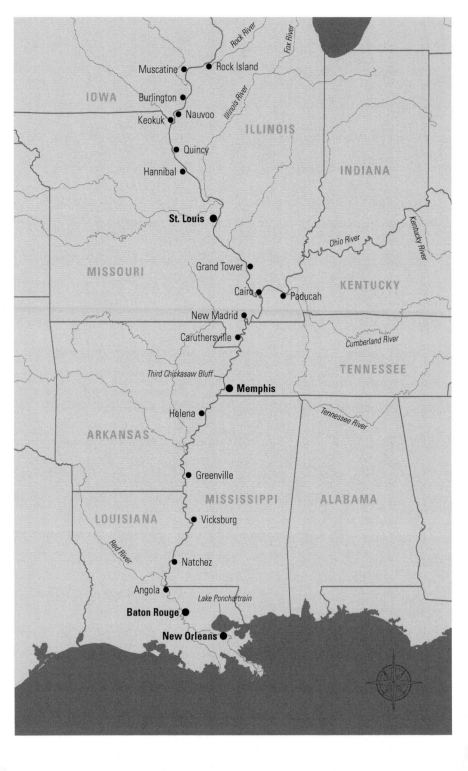

THE FISHERMAN

I suppose that Fred got out of bed that morning, fed his dogs, and ate breakfast. I wonder if he ate fish. He probably listened to the radio and heard the latest body counts from Vietnam or another glowing account of the triumphal march of Richard Nixon toward reelection. I'm sure he got in his black 1962 Ford pickup and drove down to the river. There he loaded his gear into a battered sixteen-foot aluminum skiff, cranked up his venerable Evinrude outboard, and set off into the dim dawn light on the Ohio River to check the lines and traps he'd set the previous night.

It was early March and a layer of bone-penetrating fog clung to the surface of the water. A tornado had just swept up the valley, and the river was in flood, so fishing was off. The rising light revealed a colorless day. The sky was a flat gray from horizon to horizon, the river was the color of steel, and the winter-naked trees lined the bank like skeletons, black and gray with no promise of the spring that was soon to come. A thick morning smell hung on the river, heavy with swamp and rot.

There was a small leak in Fred's skiff. When he returned to the landing, he hauled the boat out of the water and turned it over. He built a driftwood small fire and dug up an old coffee can. He began to melt tar in the can.

About this time my dog and I showed up. I was drifting in a twelve-foot wooden boat, keeping in close to the Illinois shore, looking for a place to land and build a fire. I pulled into the landing without seeing Fred. My dog leaped ashore and I dragged my boat up the bank so the wakes from passing towboats wouldn't swamp her. Fred was hunkered over his fire, stirring the can with a stick. I walked over to talk to him.

"What're you up to?" I asked.

"Melting tar to patch this skiff," he said. Fred was about thirty-five and had short black hair under a duckbilled cap, liquid black eyes, and water-weathered gray skin. He was so thin he seemed lanky, though he wasn't very tall. "I oughta use tin and solder, but this will hold it for a while."

We watched the tar begin to smoke and bubble in the pot. It crackled as it heated up.

I'd landed at one place already that morning and been run out by an old man who threatened to have a coronary if I didn't disappear straightaway, so I asked Fred if this was a public landing.

"It's a town park," he said.

"What town?" I asked.

"Olmstead. Illinois."

There wasn't much to the park—a boarded-up bait shop, a broken concrete boat launch, some elderly picnic tables, and a barbecue pit. The roof over the barbecue caught my eye. Several wet spring days had inspired a profound theory that in a storm any roof over your head was better than no roof.

It looked like it might storm, so I asked Fred, "Do you think it would be all right if I stayed around here for a while?"

"There's nobody to mind. You come a long ways?"

"From the Kentucky Dam."

"Where you going?"

"I dunno. Natchez or Baton Rouge."

Fred chuckled. "You don't have a motor on that boat, do you?"

"No," I said.

He laughed softly and shook his head. "That's a long row," he said. I laughed.

We stood by the small fire and I warmed my hands. "Make your living fishing the river?"

"I try," said Fred.

"Been at it long?"

"All my life," he said, and again, quietly, "all my life." He looked out over the Ohio and then across the park. "Is that your dog?" he said, pointing at Thor, who was pissing on trees and investigating garbage cans. I called him and Fred looked the animal over. Thor was a large yellow dog, a benign mix of German shepherd and golden retriever, big as an ox and dumb as a dinosaur. He'd just gotten his full growth, but he had yet to learn how to handle it.

"I like a good dog," said Fred. He started patching up his boat and said if I needed a ride into town later I could go with him. I unloaded my gear under the barbecue roof and cooked ham and eggs. I asked Fred if he wanted something to eat, but he turned me down.

I'd gained lot of respect for fishermen in the few days I'd spent in my boat. I'd seen them checking their lines in the early morning chill and knew that it was a cold, wet, dangerous job. The material rewards were hardly princely, either: every fisherman's truck I ever saw could have been the same work-worn black Ford. I felt foolish in front of somebody like a fisherman who actually made his living from the river. They knew how dangerous the river was: they knew that anyone who did for pleasure what they did for a living was stupid or crazy and probably both.

Early in the afternoon, we got into Fred's truck and climbed up from the river through the late-winter hills. "You're not from around here, are you?" asked Fred.

"I'm from California," I said.

3

"My daddy lives out there now. He retired out there."

"Where's he live?"

"Sacramento. He's got a house trailer."

"I was through Sacramento, six, seven days ago."

"He likes it in California. Says the weather's got this all beat. He even says the fishing is better."

"What's he retired from?"

"He was a fisherman."

What there was of Olmstead, Illinois, spread out over rolling hills, the homes far apart like a town that has grown up amidst farms. The houses were covered with aluminum or asphalt shingles, and stood hopeless and shabby, as if it were futile to resist the combined assault of weather and poverty. Olmstead reminded me of towns I'd seen in the Appalachians and the Ozarks, places where everybody was root-hog-or-die poor. I'm sure the tag end of winter made the place look sorrier than it was.

The town proper was clustered around a single corner dominated by an old general store. I bought some milk and crackers and asked Fred if there was any place to buy beer. He said sure, and we drove out to a roadhouse on the edge of town. The place was as big as a church and about as quiet. "You ought to see it on a Saturday night," said Fred. "Men get killed out here on a Saturday night."

On the way back to the river Fred stopped at his house and went in. It was a tight, tidy house with new white aluminum siding and a box freezer on the front porch. Fred wasn't getting rich, but he was pulling enough fish out of the river to make a living. From what he said when he got back in the truck it wasn't enough of a living to keep his wife happy. It looked like he'd stopped to check up on her. During the rest of the ride he cussed his wife and told me all his troubles. It's strange how when you're traveling alone you run into people who'll tell you their deepest sorrows. They'll tell you things they wouldn't tell their best friends.

We parked next to the Ohio and the talk returned to dogs and fish. "I've got awful luck with dogs," said Fred. "I can't keep a good dog these days, they're always getting run over, but a few years back I had a bluetick that was a real hound dog. I left him tied up to the house one Friday afternoon and took the family over to my brother's place in Kentucky. It's about ninety miles away. Come Sunday afternoon we were headed out the driveway, starting home, and here comes that damn bluetick, loping up the road with his footpads all tore up. How he crossed the river, I don't know."

I offered Fred a beer, but he declined. We watched the massive Ohio slide by, gray and swollen under the dark sky.

"How is it making a living off the river?" I asked.

"It gets tougher all the time. There aren't nearly the fish there used to be."

"Is the pollution killing them off?"

"That, and the damn telephone lines they run under the river. The lines kill more than anything else. Now my daddy, he used to catch some fish in this river. Some big fish."

"Damn," I said, thinking about the Good Old Days.

"Yep, there used to be fish that could swallow you whole and not even burp. But then, there might be fewer fish, but there's a lot fewer fishermen, too."

"How's that?"

"Son," said Fred, looking me square in the eye. "It don't do to be out in the river with all the towboats they've got now. Those towboats will kill you."

Towboats, yes. I'd seen enough of towboats to make me queasy.

"If one of those things were to run you down, you'd be a dead man."

I asked Fred how he sold his fish. He laughed. "Oh, I don't hardly sell any fish. The damnedest thing about the fish business is that when you're catching a lot of fish, everybody's eating hamburgers, but when they stop getting themselves caught, everybody wants fish."

We talked and I drank my Blue Ribbon. "Y'know, I don't see many people going down the river this early in the year."

I understood why. "The mosquitoes aren't so bad this time of year."

"Yeah, they're all froze. Some boys come through here from up in Canada last December. Had a canoe. They were walking around saying how fine the weather was, in December."

"You see a lot of people going down the river in the summer?"

"All kinds. Lots of people come through on rafts built out of oil drums. I met some boys last summer who were going down in inner tubes."

"Inner tubes?"

"Big diesel truck tubes. They had paddles they'd sort of scull along."

"Inner tubes," I said. "Jesus."

We watched the wide Ohio, the waters flat and smooth in the now-still afternoon. I'd always heard that the Ohio was supposed to be blue, but so far the river had always been gray, the color of the sea in a storm.

"You know what," said Fred. "Sometimes I've got half a mind to just cut loose and go down the river myself. Leave all this behind. But I don't reckon I ever will."

We sat a while longer, hypnotized by the broad river. I asked Fred what I owed him.

"Nothing," he said. "Just be careful."

II

THE RIVERS OF AMERICA

The next morning Fred was out on the river before I was out of my sleeping bag. I got up, ate some canned peaches, fed Thor his kibble, packed up my gear, coaxed Thor into the boat, and rowed out into the current. A storm threatened but never materialized, and it was warming as the sky cleared. I began drifting downriver to Cairo, Illinois, where the Ohio joins the Mississippi.

At the confluence of the two rivers I was going to rendezvous with a lot of memories. I'd been in Cairo (pronounced Kay-row, like the syrup) once before, in the fall of 1969, while traveling with my girlfriend Suzy, and three friends on a raft we'd built out of oil drums. The night before we reached Cairo, the raft ran aground on a sandbar, crumpling the lead fifty-five gallon steel drum like a beer can. Her bow awash, the raft swam like a crippled duck. We tied up a few miles above Cairo, and Suzy and I followed the railroad into town to look for a replacement barrel.

The tracks ran through Pleistocene swamp country into the brick streets of Cairo's ghetto, whose ancient tenements stood soot-black with time. We made it to the business district and found a hardware store run by an old couple. They didn't like me, all dirt and hair, but Suzy told them about the raft and charmed them with her wide, bright smile (her father was a dentist). I asked them where we could find an oil drum.

"Abe Solomon's," said the old man. "But you don't want to go over there."

"How come?"

The old man's face twisted up like he was sucking lemons. "There's been a lot of trouble out there."

"What kind of trouble?" asked Suzy.

"Darkie trouble," the old couple said in chorus.

Indeed. The police and the blacks had shootouts in the Cairo ghetto, not just now and then but pretty much on a nightly basis. The old man in the hardware store had a police radio blaring behind the counter and a shotgun beside it, clearly waiting to resist a Ripple-crazed black tide bent on plundering his nail bins.

Cairo, Illinois. Except for Solomon's junkyard, which turned out to be a junkyard among junkyards, I had no fond memories of the place.

Back in my rowboat that March morning, the riverbank between Olmstead and Cairo proved to be some of the least inspiring scenery in the United States—long, low, treeless banks broken by an occasional grain silo. Still, it was a fine warm morning, lots of blue sky and billowing white clouds. I laid back and let the boat spin along with the current.

Toward noon I could see the river wall of Cairo. Squat concrete walls shelter the low-lying towns along the great heartland rivers, bringing a little bit of the middle ages to the Middle West. As I came down to Cairo's waterfront, a police car drove out a gate and cruised along the road in front of the wall. After it had gone back into the town, I hid my boat in some bushes and walked up to the main gate. Over it hung a large sign reading, CAIRO, GATEWAY TO THE SOUTH.

The street leading away from the gate had been dead for fifty

years. Old and decayed, it was lined with empty two-story buildings the rust color of decaying brick. Weathered boards covered
eyeless windows that looked old enough to have seen Ulysses S.
Grant launch the 1862 offensive from Cairo that would split the
South. The worn, cracked sidewalk was littered with soggy trash.
I turned a corner onto the much-brighter main street, where the
bones of the old buildings were trimmed with neon and plastic. It
was a Saturday afternoon and the street was filled with farmers and
farm wives mixed with teenagers, winos, workers, and assorted
other Americans. I bought a sandwich from a street vendor and
went looking for the post office.

Cairo had its quota of gas stations, burger parlors, supermarkets, churches, and liquor stores, but its police station would have
made Cheops jealous. It was four stories tall, windowless, and so
square that it seemed to be hewn from one massive block of yellow
stone. The wide lawn that surrounded it on three sides was littered
with cannons left over from the last four or five wars. On the
street side stood an enormous flagpole. The building looked large
enough to contain the entire able-bodied population of Cairo with
room left over for any geriatrics who might get out of hand. Behind all this awesome law and order, dwarfed into insignificance,
was the post office. It was closed, but I climbed the steps and
looked out west over row upon row of ancient black row houses,
homely tenements that must have been slums even before they
had sagged beneath the weight of fifty summers and generations
of hard-pressed humanity. In the weak light of the late winter sun,
Cairo sweated ugliness.

Police were everywhere. I was accustomed to living in the
woods where I never saw police, and they made me nervous. Uneasiness hung over Cairo like a cloud of swamp gas, and it felt like
I was breathing it in. I went back to my boat and rowed out onto
the last mile of the Ohio River.

The Army Corps of Engineers' charts for the lower Mississippi began at Cairo and showed a park at the confluence of the rivers. Between the river wall and the park, activity filled the waterfront. Across the river, barges six deep and a mile long were tied to the Kentucky shore. A swarm of tugs crossed and recrossed the river, picking up barges that they hauled out to "make up tows" for the towboats treading water against the current. As I drifted past a highway bridge and down to the park, I came so close to one tug that I could see the grin on the pilot's face.

There were clumps of fishermen, old black men and young white kids, clustered on the Ohio side of the park, so I swung around the point and landed in the gumbo on the Mississippi shore. I hopped around, grinning, excited: I was back on the Mississippi River.

A navigation light, Mile 0.8, marked Cairo Point. (Mile 0.0 was out in the middle of the Mississippi.) A crow bound for New Orleans would fly a little more than 500 miles, but anyone following the meandering river had to travel 950 miles. The marker was a pole with a light and symbol mounted on a pile of rocks that cascaded down to the water, but it marked the southern-most piece of Illinois and the junction of a considerable amount of famous water, so it was easily the most remarkable piece of geography for miles around. There wasn't much to do at the marker, but the view was something to see: two great rivers, the clear blue Ohio and the russet muddy Mississippi, flowed together and swallowed the southern horizon. The point drew tourists like free ice cream.

About a dozen longhairs and blacks were standing on the point, the longhairs in old army jackets, the blacks in leather and berets. They had watched me round the point and do my river dance. I pulled my boat up on to the shore and went over to talk to them.

"Who are you guys? The Cairo Chamber of Commerce?"

Some of them laughed, but not too hard. "Hardly," said one of the longhairs. "We're Vietnam Vets Against the War."

It was 1972. The war was still dragging on—even in Cairo. The vets had come down from St. Louis to support a black boycott of white stores. They were trying to convince the merchants to put pressure on the police to quit shooting up the ghetto. "There's a civil war going on up there," said one of the vets, pointing his thumb across the swamp to the town. In the three years since I'd last visited Cairo, there had been gunfire exchanged 250 nights a year, on average.

The vets asked me what I was doing and I tried to explain. One of them asked about my draft status—a common question at the time. I didn't have any. I'd registered on my eighteenth birthday in Salt Lake City, asked them to transfer the records to San Diego, and never heard from the Selective Service again. Both offices were notoriously inept, but to this day I don't know any male my age who got off so easily. I'd thought about the draft question in theory and had decided—in theory—that if it came down to it, I'd go to jail. Since I never got any greetings from the president, I still don't know what I would have done if I had to face the question that these ex-soldiers had faced. I admired them deeply.

After the veterans left, I wandered around the park, settling in. Behind the point was a three-storied concrete lookout shaped like an impressionistic towboat. A locked-up concession stand took up the ground floor. From the upper decks you could look out over Illinois, Kentucky, and Missouri and see the Ohio and the Mississippi become one as they rolled south, filling up the entire southern prospect. The rest of the park was covered with windblown trees, scattered cement picnic tables, fire rings, and a parking lot. Between Cairo and the park was the primordial swamp, still jungle-like even in the dying winter.

The point had a good feel to it. I sat down on the Mississippi shore and watched the great river roll. It felt like I was back home, and all that rolling water had me transfixed.

❋

The movement of the Mississippi River is a natural phenomenon that is difficult to capture in words. It endlessly changes and is eternally changeless. On a windy day the surface of the river ripples with steady, fluid movement: different currents, boils, sucks, and eddies make the water swirl and slide. You can see, even feel, the massive movement of the river, but it moves so quietly and with so little apparent effort, its motion is so smooth, even, and steady that the river hardly appears to move at all. You can feel the river's power; you can sense its movement, even though they are as invisible as the wind. It seems impossible that so much water could flow so relentlessly without a tremendous roar.

The color of the river is continually in flux. Up close the river is the color of rich, newly turned ground, a deep brown textured with green. It looks so thick that you could almost walk upon it, bringing to mind the old complaint that the Mississippi is too thick to drink and too thin to plow. With distance the river takes on the color of the sky, changing with the weather and the time so that in a single afternoon it can be blue or gray or black or blood red.

No one gets rapturous about the beauty of the Mississippi, as they might about the Grand Canyon or the Great Smokey Mountains, because the river is not physically beautiful, except in rare moments and moods. It *is* powerful, literally awesome. When the river confronts them, most people stare silently or stand and shiver. It is much like looking at the ocean, vast and overpowering, except that the river has an unrelenting, restless, directed movement. It flows.

At Cairo Point I watched the River of the East meet the River of the West. From the sunrise came the Ohio, wider than the Mississippi, swollen with Appalachian spring floods. From the west came the Missouri–Mississippi, a brown and green torrent of thick mud pulled down from the Rockies and the Black Hills and the

Great Plains. Joining at Cairo, these rivers become the Old Man, the great American river.

The River of the West is fed by the Milk and the Marias and the Musselshell and the Moreau, the Bighorn and the Little Bighorn, the Powder and the Yellowstone, the Belle Fourche, the Cheyenne and the Sheyenne, the Arikaree, the Kickapoo, the Chippewa, the Niobrara, the Keya Paha, the Wapsipnicon, the Osage, the Greybull, the Tongue, the Crow, the Sioux, and the Laramie; the Minnesota and the Iowa and the Wisconsin and the Kansas and the Illinois and the Cannonball; the Cedar and the Des Moines, the Frenchman and the Platte, North and South, the St. Croix and the Solomon and the Smokey Hill, the Judith and the Zumbro and the Root, the Turkey, and the Buffalo and the Skunk, the Snake, the Raccoon, the Elkhorn, and the Mackinaw and the Beaverhead, the Bitterroot and the Kettle, the Salamonie and the Sangamon, the Wakarusa, the Wakenda, the Wyaconda, the Calamus and the Pecatonica and the Sugar, the Nishnabotna, the Kaskaskia, the Big Hole, the Big Muddy, the Big Porcupine, the Wood and the Box Elder and the Cottonwood and the Elm and the Maple and the Poplar, the Marais des Cygnes, the Gasconade, the Cache la Poudre or the Poudre, the Loup, the Teton, the Sun, the Meramec, the Chariton, the Sweetwater and the Redwater and the Redstone, the Vermilion and the Green and the Yellow, the James, the Floyd, the Fabius, the Boyer, the Grand, the Mizpah, the Spoon, the Nodaway, the Medicine Bow, the Wild Rice and the Pumpkin, the Dearborn, the Jefferson and the Madison and the Gallatin and the Henderson and the Heart, the Rock and the Red River of the North—all these rivers great and small flow into and become the Missouri and the Upper Mississippi.

The Rivers of the East—the Cumberland, the Tennessee, the Kentucky, the Hiwassee, the Licking, the Kanawha and the Little Kanawha, the Mud, the Tradewater, the Tygarts, the Mad, the Rough, the Lost and the Hocking and the Rattlesnake and the Paint, the Busseron, the Elkhorn, the Embarras, the Miami and the Great Miami and the Muskingum, Big and Little, the Muscatatuck, the Allegheny, the Duck and the Pigeon and the Scioto and the Symmes and the Big Sandy, the Rock Castle, the Pocatalico, the Elk and the Twelve Pole and the Birch, the Reedy and the Pigeon, the Monongahela and the Youghiogheny, the Guyandotte, the Powell and the Clinch, the Salt and the Saline, the Cache, the Whitewater, the French Broad, the Barren, the Wabash and the Little Wabash, and the White and the Green— and their own thousand forks, branches, and creeks feed the Ohio and ultimately unite with the Mississippi.

The names of the creeks that create this great flood capture the poetry, music, and history of the land. They catalog the trees— Locust and Willow and Cherry and Laurel and Flatwillow and Ash and Lodgepole—the animals—Raven, Cow, Dogie, Turtle, Swan, Rabbit, Antelope, Wolf, Sheep, Wild Cat, Wild Horse, Pinto, Spotted Horse, Blacktail, Eagle—and the events—Hanging Woman, Crazy Woman, Bear in the Lodge, Wagonhound, Chugwater, No Water, Arrow, Stockade—that make our history. They in turn are divided into forks, north and south and middle, Dry Forks and Roaring Forks.

All this collected water surges past Cairo to become one silent torrent that nothing can stop or placate or satisfy except the sea, making the spot heavy with history and meaning. The river is a great flood, draining states from Montana to Maryland. Feeding the Old Man River below Cairo are the Homochitto and the Yazoo, the Big Black and the Big Blue and the Little Blue, the Red, the White, the Verdigris, the Coldwater, the Sulpher, the St. Francis and the Boeuf and the Sunflower, the Tensas and the Hatchie, Loosahatchie and Tallahatchie, Yalobusha, the Moro and the Eleven Point and the Ouachita, the Black Bear, Wolf and

Forked Deer, the Obion and Neosha, the Arkansas, the Cimarron, the Purgatoire, the Huerfano, the Sand Arroyo, the Apishapa, the Fountain, the Canadian, the Republican, and a thousand bayous and backwaters.

The moods of the river matched the turmoil of my own. A clear sky could cloud over and break into storm in less than an hour, and a day of relentless rain would break into a sunset as quiet and breathless as a desert. Rivermen say that at Cairo the river changes sex. They call the upper river "she" and the lower river "Old Man," and they have good reason. Below Cairo the river takes on an aura of brute power and an overwhelming, slow-moving majesty. The river sweeps south like time itself, relentless, unstopping, unstoppable.

All my attention was drawn to the south, where the one huge river rolled until it swallowed the horizon. Down that torrent, someplace between the sea and me, whatever it was that I was searching for must lie.

Before my eyes rolled the river that I'd seen so many times in dream and memory, the vision that obsessed and still obsesses me. After some months of River Fever, it was soothing to sit and watch the real river roll on by. There was wholeness to it that I'd never been able to complete in my mind: neither memory nor imagination could retain an accurate notion of the river's power and size. This was the key to the failure of all the writing I'd done about the Mississippi: I couldn't see it, couldn't capture or convey the immensity of the river, the way it moved, or what a deep river it is.

I watched the towboats come and go around the point, black diesel smoke pouring out of their stacks as they pushed impossible loads of practically anything: coal, fuel oil, asphalt, ammonia, gasoline, benzine, kerosene, chlorine and assorted other chemicals, wheat, corn, and soybeans. There are thousands of them on the rivers of the East, far more than there were steamboats in Sam Clemens's days as a river pilot. The modern towboats vary in size from small outfits that push one or two barges, on up to the 10,000-horsepower leviathans of the Federal Line that push as many as fifty-six barges at a time. The steel barges the towboats push are about 150 feet long with a hold nine to fifteen feet deep and a draft of three feet. The lead barges of a fifteen-barge tow are about a thousand feet away from the pilothouse: in tight situations like entering a lock, captains will often use a walkie-talkie to communicate with a mate standing on the front of the tow. The smaller towboats are often not much more than a pilothouse set on stilts above the engine room, while a giant tow like the *America* or the *Mississippi* (the most beautiful of the great towboats) has four decks and four stacks. Petroleum barges are humpbacked like turtles, while coal and grain barges look a lot like a railroad car flattened and stretched out with a slanting bow notched off one end.

Since towboats push and don't tow, the word "towboat" is technically a misnomer. A lot of towboat terminology is confusing. The word "tow" refers to the barges a towboat pushes, not the towboat itself. A standard barge is between 120 and 200 feet long, thirty to forty feet wide, and can haul some 1,500 tons, as much as fifteen boxcars or sixty diesel truck trailers. A single barge can carry 60,000 bushels of grain in its hold. An average fifteen-barge tow is five tows long and three abreast and can haul as much as a train three miles long or a thirty-five-mile line of trucks.

A tow is usually made up in port by lashing a dozen or more barges together using steel cables secured to cleats and tightened with a ratchet bar. At the end of a run, a towboat will tie up one cargo, turn it loose, pick up another load of tows, a freezer full of supplies, a new load of fuel, and start another trip. Sometimes barges would be picked up or let go all along the river: this was the main job of the harbor tows at Cairo.

The towboats themselves, heirs of the sternwheelers *Natchez* and *Robert E. Lee*, have decks that resemble stacks of consecutively smaller cigar boxes pushed flat at the bow. The engine room occupies almost all the lower deck, but here the average modern towboat squeezes in a galley, mess, and recreation room. The upper decks contain living quarters, done up like motel rooms. The reverberation and dull roar of the engines rattle every part of the boat, even the glassed-in pilothouse outfitted in wood and leather and polished metal that sits atop the whole structure. Towboats use radar, radios, and enormous floodlights to navigate at night: even when a dense fog shuts down on the river, the towboats still boom along on instruments.

Towboats—especially large towboats—create tremendous wakes. The most treacherous variety, the prop wake, thrashes out directly behind the boat, rolling whitewater undulating in wicked waves that roll and crest like surf. The bow wake rolls out in a wide "V" and is not nearly as dangerous as a prop wake, but it can become violent enough to capsize a rowboat. Towboats are as dangerous as dinosaurs to small craft. Several hundred thousand tons of steel or soybeans sent hurtling downriver at ten to fifteen miles an hour make right-of-way laws favoring unpowered small craft as ridiculous as they are irrelevant. It literally takes miles to stop a towboat with a full complement of loaded barges.

Most boats are painted white with black or green trim, though sometimes they will be trimmed in blue or red or yellow. Some have fine, deepwater names like *Raja*, *Elizabeth Ann*, or *Badger*, but many are named after politicians, revered robber barons, or somebody's mother-in-law. The best names are those taken from native American tribes or the rivers themselves—the Coast Guard christens its handsome cutters in this fashion. The worst names are derived from the companies that own the boats: the ugliest appellation for anything I met afloat was for the tow *Amoco Missouri*.

Except for a few mavericks, the towboats are kept clean and

tight and holystone seamanlike, swept and hosed down and painted and polished. Ironically, the tows all fly their ensigns behind their smokestacks, so Old Glory is invariably black, not to mention considerably worn and torn up.

Towboats aren't pretty machines, the way a clipper ship or steamboat was a beautiful creation, but a modern riverboat has the beauty of a new diesel truck. Like a gleaming Kenworth or Peterbilt, a towboat projects brute mechanical power. Their design is pure function. Like a diesel truck, a towboat also has a lurking sense of destructive potential. Even more than trains, they convey power in motion, especially when passing close by.

The boats are manned by the same kind of desperadoes you meet on construction sites and oil fields, in jails and at low-rent bars. Working on a towboat is a lot like working in a coal mine: the pay is good, but the work has its dangerous disadvantages. Deck hands and pilots work two six-hour watches every twenty-four hours. The job can get as miserable as the weather, and there are enough grisly stories about deckhands getting maimed, crushed, pureed, drowned, or otherwise destroyed to warn the faint-hearted away from what is truly a mankilling job.

Even piloting, the best job on the river, has drawbacks. Pilots still die on the job, though the boats don't blow up so often or violently as they did in steamboating's heyday. Navigation is much easier thanks to technology and the Army Corps of Engineers, but the river remains treacherous. Threading a mass of steel the size of several football fields through the narrow trestles of an ancient railroad bridge on a bucking, spring-crazed river requires experience and nerve. A pilot once told me, "Don't ever trust the river." The Mississippi is as treacherous as a mule: it will wait ten years just to kill you once. I loved the river, but knew I did not understand it.

The river and my encounter with Fred and the veterans made me appreciate my remarkable freedom. I had no job, responsibilities, duties, debts, or obligations. I had little money but low expenses. Every new day was an adventure, and I was at perfect liberty to do whatever struck my fancy. Like all mortals, I operated within constraints—for example, I had only money enough to handle basic survival—but they imposed few limits on the possible. And not only was I free, I appreciated the astonishing dimensions of that freedom.

As a quick cold March darkness descended on Cairo Point, I made up a bed on the picnic table close to the confluence. All night there was a lot of barge traffic, and it seemed like each towboat turned its light on the point and held it there a long time. I was so fuzzy with sleep that I thought they were trying to figure out what the lump on the table was, but they were probably just lining their lights up with the mileage marker and gauging their distance from the shore. It was like sleeping in a snowstorm of light.

In the morning a harbor tow came down the Mississippi, rounded the point, and tied up on the Ohio shore. It dropped the barge it was pushing, came back around the point, and moved right up next to the beach and my boat. A skinny, tall kid stood on the bow, and I could see a grinning old pilot up in the wheelhouse. "You want a ride?" called the kid. I clambered through the gumbo and up over the low, bluff bow of the tow.

A couple of bunks were squeezed in with the engine, and the small galley and mess were as greasy as the enormous, ancient diesel engine. I climbed up to the pilothouse, which was not much bigger than a telephone booth. The pilot backed the boat out onto the Mississippi and chugged up the Ohio while I got acquainted with the rest of the crew, a deckhand and the engineer. The pilot was in his fifties, a humorous, bear-like man who looked as work hardened as a farmer. "What the hell are you doin' with that little boat?" he asked.

I told him and he laughed—like all river people, he found the idea of challenging the mighty Mississippi in a twelve-foot boat more than a little funny. "You better watch your young ass," he advised. I asked him what the chances were of getting a job on a towboat around Cairo. He said at best Cairo was only a fair place to look for work on the river; the best spots were boat stores and union halls at Memphis and Paducah and on down the river in Baton Rouge and New Orleans. "They're always needin' men," he told me. "Boys'll pick up a check for eight hundred to a thousand dollars and be too drunk two weeks later to remember they ever worked on a towboat. If you really want to, you shouldn't have too much trouble getting a berth."

"What's the work like?" I asked him.

"Not bad. Long hours, but lots of money and no place to spend it. The food's good too, and they pay you half a day off for every day you work."

"Don't sound like I could beat it."

"Hell," he said. "It's the best work there is for a single man, but it'll grow horns on ones that're married."

He plowed up the Ohio to a small dock, guiding the towboat in as if it were a pick-up truck. We talked until his radio began to crackle and the boat got orders from another rig coming downriver. I got off and they went back to work as I walked back to the point, thinking hard about becoming a deckhand.

It was Sunday, mild and fair, and all day people came and went at the park. Carloads of families bound to and from St. Louis and Nashville and Chicago and Louisville would stop, get out, look at the two rivers, load back up, and hit the highway again. I met one old boy from Mississippi, already in the early afternoon deep into some white liquor, who'd come up to trade coon dogs with another old boy from Missouri. I talked with anybody who wanted to pass the time of day. I was interested in people, all kinds of people, and I liked practically everybody.

In the middle of the afternoon a haggard longhair came walking down the Ohio shore, followed by three howling black kids who waved bamboo fishing poles and fishnets as they ran in whooping circles around him. He looked tired but unhassled, like Jesus after a hard day, and he was oblivious—almost—to the three rampaging boys. A full beard beginning to turn gray and patient brown eyes matched his long dark hair. The lines and wrinkles on his face were those of a young man growing old fast.

"Hey Ralph!" yelled one of the kids when he spotted me. "Lookit! Another hippie!"

"Soul brother," said Ralph, without any excitement. The two words were tinged with a New Jersey accent. We stared at each other like the two trappers in the old Remington drawing *I Took You for an Injun*. "What the hell are you doing here?"

Once again, I explained. You might think that as many times as I explained I was rowing a little peanut shell of a boat down the great Father of Waters that I might get tired of it or feel more foolish with each explanation or even begin to doubt my own story, but I didn't. I enjoyed it. Each time there was a different reaction. Ralph merely nodded. I asked him his own question: "What are you doing here?"

"I'm a self-inflicted prisoner of this place. These are my neighbors and fellow inmates. I brought 'em down here to fish." The oldest boy, Thurmond, was almost as tall as I was, though he wasn't more than twelve years old. He and his younger brother, Gabe, flailed at the Ohio with their poles, while their smallest brother looked on in wide-eyed admiration. "Now that I get them down here, they don't seem so interested in fishing." He yelled over to the brothers, "Hey! You bugged me all day to bring you down here to fish, so why don't you fish already?" They paid him no attention, except to lash at the water with renewed frenzy.

Ralph and I got acquainted as the brothers rampaged along

the shore. He'd come down to Cairo from northern Illinois the summer before and now ran a leather goods store called the O & O—the idea being, as Ralph explained, that "Out of nothing shall come something." The bizarre political situation in Cairo had drawn him to the place because he thought it showed a lot of potential for organizing. "Now the place is driving me crazy."

Ralph didn't seem crazy, except for an occasional flash in his eyes. He was one of the calmest people I've ever met, simpatico and placid even, though the entire time I knew him, he was surrounded chaotic, truly extreme craziness. Ralph was instantly likable.

The brothers lived in back of Ralph's store with their mother. They came from a family with eleven children. Their father was in jail. They made their way around the point to my boat and began looking it over. I suggested that we take a ride. Thurmond refused to have anything to do with it, but I coaxed his brothers into the boat and he climbed in, too. I rowed upstream in the quiet water close to shore toward a steel highway bridge spanning the Mississippi. Then I let Thurmond and Gabe take the oars.

"You going to row this boat down to New Orleans?" asked Thurmond.

"No, I'm going down to Natchez or Baton Rouge."

"How far's that?"

"Seven, eight hundred miles."

"Jeesusss ..." Thurmond worked his face up into an expression of profound contempt and disbelief. "What you want to do that for? Why don't you just get a car and drive there?"

"It'd cost more money than I've got and it'd be over too soon. Besides, I want to see the river. Like, look, wouldn't you like to see what's down this river?"

"Shee-it," said Thurmond. "Youah crazy." He dismissed me completely. I tried to explain to him all the advantages of drifting: no gas, no engines, no breakdowns, no noise, very cheap. I laid it on thick, trying to make it sound as romantic as possible. "I get out there in the current and drift along at four or five miles an hour, free and easy and comfortable, the scenery sliding by ..."

"Where do you sleep at night? You sleep in motels?"

"I camp out."

"Don't you get wet when it rains?"

"I get wet when it rains," I admitted.

"Shee-it," sneered Thurmond. "You are crazy. Ain't you even got the sense to be scairt of getting drowned?"

"No," I said. "I'm not scairt of getting drowned."

"You are crazy," said Thurmond. He lurched forward, got close to my face, and spoke with the conviction of an Old Testament prophet. "You gonna be food for fishes is what you gonna be."

Thurmond got to me. Here was a kid who was far smarter and more practical at twelve than I was at twenty-one. But was he so hardboiled that he didn't have any dreams? I glared at him and mumbled, "Maybe so," and took the oars and rowed back to shore. Ralph asked if I wanted to ride up to town. I hadn't taken a shower since I'd left Berkeley and asked Ralph if he had one I could use. He laughed and said, "It isn't much of a shower, but you can use it."

All of us, including Thor, piled into Ralph's battered Lincoln Continental. Ralph was the only longhair I'd ever met who drove a Continental, even one that looked like it had been worked over by John Henry & Hammer. I asked about it.

"Junk," he said. "Pure junk."

We rode over an elevated roadway above the swamp that separated the park from the town. I was amazed at the calm that Ralph maintained while the brothers raged about him. The confines of the car seemed to hype up their manic energies a couple of notches. Hands on the front seat, they bounced on the back, thumped and climbed over each other to give Thor friendly whacks, howling the whole time like coyotes with the Love Sick Blues. Despite the decibel level, Ralph kept up a running conversation with them, talking quietly, reasoning with them as logically as if they had been college professors. Thurmond continually bent his logic.

"Gimme a dollar, Ralph."

"You can't extort any more money out of me," said Ralph. "I'm broke."

"C'mon Ralph, I know you got a dollar."

"Honest, Thurmond, all I got is fifty cents."

"That'll do."

"Why should I give you my last fifty cents?"

Thurmond had obviously reached a familiar impasse. He gave up on Ralph and turned his energies on me. "Gimme a dollar," he said. Then he smiled and did his best to look like Shirley Temple.

"Why should he give you a dollar?" said Ralph. "He doesn't even know you, and he's probably as poor as I am. Just because he's white doesn't mean he's rich."

"Hell," said Thurmond. "Give me a dollar. Fifty cents. A quarter?"

We drove through Cairo's decomposing streets to the O & O Leather Store. It was located in an abandoned café directly across the street from the police station. I'd looked directly at it the day before and had failed to recognize it as a leather goods store: it looked a lot more like an abandoned greasy spoon. We went inside and Ralph chased the brothers out, told them to go home, and locked the door. They beat on the door with remarkable force, threatening to slash the tires on the Continental, and began searching for a window they could force.

The O & O was a strange business establishment. It was dark, and posters hung on the walls, coated in grease in memory of bygone days. Set near the front of the store was a desk covered with papers, pamphlets, and books that might have been organized at one time. As the store ambled toward the back of the building and

Ralph's living quarters, it disintegrated into a chaos of paperbacks, newspapers, magazines, old mimeos, underground comic books, and rolled-up posters that gradually mixed with clothing, kitchenware, and food. There were even two or three rolls of cheap leather, though there weren't any leather goods in evidence.

"Pretty crazy store," I observed. "Do you have any leather goods?"

"Well, it's pretty much a front. I only do leather work when I've got to." He went over to a desk and pulled a leather pouch out of a drawer. "See?" he said. I saw. It looked like a demented Cub Scout had pieced it together.

"What's it all a front for?"

"Me. I came down here to do some organizing. I was hoping to do some organizing."

Organizing. The word alone conjured up images of Joe Hill, Big Bill Haywood, Mother Jones, and Eugene Debs. "What were you trying to organize?"

"Well, I was trying to get some people together so they wouldn't hate each other and spend so much time trying to kill one another. It looked simple at the time."

I looked out at the police station through Ralph's dusty venetian blinds. "This place looks like it could use a little organizing."

"Yeah, but nobody gives a damn. There are eight or nine people who could really do something—maybe—but they don't give a damn either."

"Cairo looks like a hard place to care about."

"Yeah, well, maybe," said Ralph.

"What's with all the shooting?"

"That's what first brought me here, to see what I could do personally about a very violent situation. But most of the violence starts with the police. They get off duty and get drunk and go out to the levee and snipe into the projects. Nobody can prove it's the police, and so far they haven't killed anybody. There's nothing I can do about it; all the power is lodged behind the off-duty cop's right to take pot shots off the levee. Sometimes the blacks shoot back and then everybody loves it. The cops love shooting at the blacks and the blacks like shooting back at the cops. But somebody is going to die. Then all hell is gonna break loose."

We wandered back to where Ralph lived in the old restaurant's kitchen. He showed me how to shower using a contraption of Rube Goldbergian complexity that hooked up to an old commercial sink.

When I was done, Ralph suggested that we catch a minister's open house. We loaded everybody back into the Continental, the brothers included, and drove up through the ghetto. There were rows of ancient shacks and shanties gone gray with age, their stoops and porches covered with tenants sitting in the afternoon sun. The sense of being in a swamp was overpowering; the sagging tenements looked like they were sinking into the ground. Crossing an invisible line into the white neighborhoods, we were suddenly amongst other creatures of the swamp. Paunchy white freeholders cut lawns and washed cars. I kept expecting to see alligators among the Pontiacs.

When we pulled up to the preacher's home, there were so many Buicks and Cadillacs parked around that there was hardly room for the Continental. I began to wonder about the event, pondering whether the preacher would welcome somebody at his open house that the river had literally washed up, not to mention Ralph and his wild horde. I told Ralph I thought I'd sit this one out.

"C'mon," he said. "The preacher'd like to meet you."

Thurmond demurred too. "You know what, Thurmond?" said Ralph. "They've got a table full of cakes and cookies and candy and garbage guaranteed to rot the teeth right out of your head, not to mention punch. It'd probably be better if you sat out here and preserved your dental health."

So we all went into a house filled with nice old white ladies, dressed in pink and white and saffron for Sunday. They looked like aging porcelain dolls. A couple of them got up and left immediately. Thurmond set about looking for the baked goods. The preacher was a young man with a quite pretty wife: they were both open and friendly, though the young lady looked as if she was in some sort of mild but constant pain. The reverend was genuinely concerned about the violence in Cairo. I felt sorry for him. Teaching Christianity to Caironians would be like trying to convert cannibals—hungry cannibals—to vegetarianism.

The brothers finished the sack of the refreshment table looking remarkably refreshed. What they obviously needed was a good dose of sugar to renew their flagging energies. We eased our way out of the house and drove the brothers back home. Ralph gave me a lift back to the point.

"This sure is an American town," I said.

"How do you mean?" asked Ralph.

"When I started traveling around, I had the notion that I was 'looking for America.' I'd lived in California for nine years and I wanted to see the real country, the real heartland—and this is it, Cairo."

"How do you mean?" asked Ralph again.

"Well, look at the landscape—burger palaces and gas stations and supermarkets and liquor stores, lots of asphalt and parking lots. I guess it's really the atmosphere—greed and hate and fear overlaid with boredom and violence."

"You really think so?" said Ralph. "You think that's as far as it goes?"

"Sure. Maybe it goes farther, but it goes at least this far. Look at the police station—how's that for a symbol? Or the ghetto. Cairo. Good God."

"Maybe so," said Ralph. "Maybe so."

That night I built a large driftwood fire and watched the towboats roll by, dark ghosts on a darker river. Their searchlights swept the water like the tentacles of a monstrous insect as the air vibrated with the distant rhythmic pounding of their engines. The two rivers seemed even bigger in the darkness, unbounded, world engulfing. I began to appreciate the power of the place. I smoked a lot, thought deep thoughts, and dreamed strange dreams all night.

I was eating breakfast out of a can the next morning when an immense black-and-white towboat with four stacks pushing a mid-sized load of tows came cannonballing down the Mississippi like a charging elephant. She was opposite the point, banking down her engines to make the turn up the Ohio, when I read the nameplate on her pilothouse and saw that this was *America*, one of the most powerful riverboats ever to navigate the Mississippi. I'd seen her before in 1969 when she was black and yellow but didn't recognize her with her new black-and-white paint job. The huge four-decker looked good in her new paint, and I watched wordlessly as she rounded the point and stopped in the middle of the Ohio to make up a new tow.

The size and power of *America* are legendary all along the Mississippi. She's the stuff out of which true folk tales are made. She and her sister ship, *United States*, were the largest towboats on the river, generating 10,000 horsepower to push their many barges. Everybody who lives along the river knows *America* and can tell horror stories about the power of her wakes. On the raft trip, I heard about her from an old black man in Hannibal, from ex-deckhands in Southern Missouri, and from active rivermen all down the line. Several old-timers looked at our raft and assured us that *America* would reduce her to splinters and drifting oil drums.

I fought my way through the swamp into Cairo where I checked for mail at the post office. There was a letter from my girlfriend in California that lifted my already flying spirits. I crossed the street to the O & O and persuaded Ralph to come and take a boat ride, and we were back at the point straightaway. He volunteered to take a one-way ride and hitchhike back to Cairo if we had to cross the river. The *America* was still treading water out in the Ohio, her engines putting out just enough power to counter the current, while harbor tugs hauled barges from the Kentucky shore to make up her new tow.

I hoped to row out and board the *America* and was excited as hell at the prospect of seeing the King Kong of towboats up close. We loaded up gear and dog and rowed out into the Ohio. Ralph's added weight made the boat ride very low in the water, but the current was weak on the Illinois side, and we headed to the enormous riverboat.

It was perfect river weather. The sky was clean and blue and a mild, warm wind blew out of the south. Ralph was fascinated by the sensation of being in a small boat. It was overpowering: at any distance from shore you felt as insignificant as a coconut on the ocean.

In mid-river the current came alive and swept us away from *America*. It was pointless trying to row against all that concentrated power, and we made for the Kentucky shore. I wanted to tie up to the barges moored there and take some pictures. It was a long row, and Ralph and I got deep into conversation. We'd known each other less than twenty-four hours, but we were already asking each other about the basic mechanics of our lives. Ralph confessed he was an unsuccessful playwright. I told him that I was a failed novelist.

"What makes you do this?" he asked.

"I don't know," I said. "There are a lot of reasons, but I suppose I'm doing it mostly because I enjoy it." It was a stupid answer, and only partly true. "But I really don't know."

"Is this all you do, travel around?"

I thought about it. "Pretty much. I've got a shack out in California where I hole up for the winter."

"What do you do for money?"

"Everything and nothing. I hocked a Volkswagen van to raise the money to do this. I guess I've got about forty dollars left."

"So you take it as it comes, day by day," said Ralph. "That's very existential."

"I'm a good existentialist. I try to keep my dues paid up."

"So you don't worry about security or the future or money?"

"No," I said. By now I was seeing myself in a very romantic light, the penniless wanderer, but it dawned on me that it was bullshit. I didn't know what I was doing on the river. "Wait," I said. "That's not quite true. Here, take the oars."

We switched places, and I dug out my sack of weed and began rolling a joint. It was hard work in the wind, with the boat bobbing up and down like a cork in a hurricane. "See, I do have this get-rich quick scheme. In the bottom of that knapsack is a bag of marijuana seeds. I'm going to start some reefer plantations down below Memphis."

"You're puttin' me on," said Ralph.

"No, Ralph, honest. Think about it: it could work."

Ralph shook his head.

After a long row, we pulled up to a barge tied up to the Kentucky shore. It was an empty grain barge, still littered with kernels of corn. It had a companionway about two feet wide running around the raised bulwarks of the hold so that deckhands could get around. The full force of the Ohio's current rushed in rolling waves alongside, raising a deep sighing sound like an incoming tide. I climbed up onto the ledge of the deck and tied the boat to a cleat. Ralph handed me the camera, and I started looking through the viewer at *America*. She still lay motionless in the middle of the river, black smoke pouring out of one stack, massive as a sleeping whale.

Suddenly Ralph yelled, "An oar's gone!"

I looked down at the boat and sure enough, an oar was gone.

Thor had probably kicked it loose. Immediately I knew we were screwed, and in a flash I could appreciate exactly how screwed; with one oar, the boat was as useless as a duck with one wing. I started running down the line of barges, ripping off clothes and looking for the oar down in the murky, rolling water. My heart jumped and adrenaline pumped. I got down to my Levis and struggled to get out of my clodhopper boots. The laces were badly frayed and knotted, but I managed to kick them off. I ran the length of three or four barges, and finally, in the best cliffhanger fashion, at the very end of the last one, I spotted the oar sweeping along with the current. If I'd hesitated for one second, if I'd considered for a movement, I wouldn't have done it, but I kept running into a dive off the bow of the barge, crashing into the darkness of the river where the sudden bone-gripping cold hit me. Luckily, I came up with the oar in my hand. Then I was overwhelmed by searing amazement and the cold spring flood of the Ohio as it became the Mississippi.

I'd swum in the river before, but always in quiet water behind a wing dam. I'm a pretty fair swimmer and have a lot of endurance, but I was suddenly experiencing something I'd never known before: the full force of the great river in flood that had swallowed me whole. I clutched the oar, tried some uncoordinated strokes, and panicked. Pure physical terror swept over me like a drug rush. The very synapses of my nerves seemed to scream in terror. I fought to clear my head, fighting to get my body side-stroking toward the shore. In a few pulls I was behind the protection of the barges and the water immediately calmed. I cooled down too. I started breast stroking, pushing the oar ahead of me.

The shore was flooded to a depth of about six feet. I grabbed hold of a tree and caught my breath. Then I pulled from tree to tree, back to the barges. I was weak, more spent with fear than exertion, and had a hard time climbing back up the rough steel sides of the barges. When I finally got over the top, I lay down on the warm rust-red metal until I heard Ralph calling.

I walked back to the boat, picking up my clothes and boots. Ralph was still standing in the boat, his eyes wide, head shaking, and he was yelling, "You're crazy! You're crazy!"

"I had to get that oar, Ralph," I said. "I had to have it."

"You're crazy. You've got a lot of nerve, but you're crazy."

I started to say something about how I didn't really have much nerve but knew how much we needed that oar, but then the shock of hitting that blue-cold water and being swallowed and the sudden blow of stomach-twisting panic rushed back and I deflated like a flaming zeppelin. "All right," I said. "I'm crazy."

I climbed back down into the boat. We cast off and drifted down the Kentucky shore. The morning had warmed up considerably and the drifting was as good as drifting gets, which is mighty fine, but we were both shook up and didn't say much. Ralph was already miles from Cairo, so when we came to a landing, I pulled in.

We got out and exchanged addresses. "Thanks for the shower," I told him. "Keep up the good work."

"Thanks for the ride," said Ralph.

I got back in the boat and pulled out into the Mississippi. "So long," I called back. "It's been good to know you."

Ralph cupped his hands and yelled back, "Be careful." Then he started up the road.

III

REVOLUTION IN THE AIR

Was I crazy? The short answer, "You bet," is too easy and only partly true. Looking back, perhaps I wasn't crazy but was young and excitable and naive. I felt crazy and had done a lot of crazy things, but the times themselves were insane. Everyone who grew up ducking and covering from the constant threat of being incinerated by a hydrogen bomb had every right to be deranged. Still, my youth and times doesn't account for my eccentric odyssey. What brought me to rowboat on the Mississippi River? Let us begin at the beginning.

As a child, I lived next to a dense Utah white-oak woods that grew around the East Mill Creek as it tumbled out of the mountains surrounding the Salt Lake Valley. The creek (pronounced "crick" by us country Mormons) took its name from the water-powered gristmill pioneers built to grind corn and wheat on the banks of that rocky trace of swift water. My best friend, Butch, lived on the creek where it pooled up behind an irrigation dam with a wonderful eight-foot waterfall. One of the polio epidemics that raged in the early 1950s had struck Butch; he limped but was a great pal and happy kid who managed to get around pretty well.

In the summertime we'd fish the pond and float logs over the falls. Mormon philosopher and entrepreneur O. C. Tanner's estate and orchards spread out south of the creek for what seemed like a mile east above Butch's house. These woods had an ancient flooded bungalow, immense patches of poison ivy, the ruins of the mill wheel, and another irrigation dam built of great old timbers where the water pooled deeper than the pond in front of Butch's house, creating the finest place to swim in the creek despite the tale that it was full of polio. The creek had cut a deep canyon into the Rocky Mountain granite, and even on the hottest days of summer, its gorge was cool and shady.

I don't remember why, but one thick, lazy summer afternoon in 1958 I resolved to build a raft and float it down the creek. With Butch's help, I nailed some boards together in my backyard and christened the finished product *The Queen of the River*. It couldn't have been very large because we dragged it down to the creek and we were no more than seven or eight. When launched, the raft floated, but it sank directly when we stood on it, my first practical lesson in flotation. We played with the raft for about an hour, renamed it *Tom Dooley*, and floated it down the creek. *Tom Dooley*, AKA *The Queen of the River*, did not survive her maiden voyage and was last seen plunging over the waterfall.

So I caught river fever a long time ago, the way some friends mysteriously contracted polio or rheumatic fever from the whiskey-brown waters of the creek. It may be that I caught it from a book, for the first books I remember are two copies of the adventures of Tom Sawyer and Huckleberry Finn. They were printed in the 1920s and heavy with the dust and mystery of old books. *Tom Sawyer* bored me, even at age seven he seemed like a patent phony, but *Huckleberry Finn* was another story. My father read it aloud to me and my younger brothers Kevin and Pat. Even to a child, the book made the Mississippi a living wonder. We could close our eyes and be on the wide moving waters with its densely forested banks and towheads and the great steamboats blazing upriver.

Huckleberry Finn left me with a dark and vivid image of the river, incredibly exact though I'd never seen more flowing water than I could easily toss a stone across. The clarity of that impression still seems strange and wonderful. It was almost as if I saw the river more clearly then—so young and so high in the Rocky Mountains where the Jordan, the largest river I knew, was a poisoned ditch flowing into a dead sea—than I do now.

The particular copy of *Huckleberry Finn* that my father read to us was mysterious not only because it seemed ancient but because it had belonged to my uncle and namesake, Wilbur Grant Bagley. As a lucky kid obsessed with fast driving during the Great Depression, Bill punched holes in the muffler of his attorney father's V-8 Lincoln to get the sound right. After Pearl Harbor he was a perfect officer candidate for the US Army Air Corps. He served in North Africa and Italy but did not come back. I'd open the flyleaf and see my name written by the original, my lost Uncle Bill. All I knew about my uncle came from a newspaper article and a few comments my parents made. My father loved his lost brother, and I asked him once, when I was old enough to wonder, what Bill was like. He mumbled and hawed, uneasy with the question, and finally said, "It would be hard to describe him with the way things are today." My mother heard this and was much more concise in her opinion: "He was a bum." He was also a great airman.

In my grandfather's basement, I found a newspaper article in a box with his air medals. It was an obituary without a corpse. First Lieutenant Grant Bagley had flown 104 fighter-bomber missions and won a stack of medals. He had been offered a chance to return to the states to train new pilots, but he wanted to stay and see the war end. On April 29, 1945, a week before the war in Europe ended and the day before the Rat, Adolf Hitler, blew out his brains, my uncle banked his P-47 Thunderbolt into a cloud and disappeared. He was twenty-one. Not a trace of the wreckage was ever found, probably because it's at the bottom of the Adriatic Sea. I've often wondered what happened to my vanished uncle. He is surely dead, but I liked to believe he parachuted into a remote, idyllic northern Italian village where he lived happily ever after, drinking lots of vino and making many bambino Bagleys. His name appears on a "Tablet of the Missing" in the American Cemetery at Florence.

My family joined the Mormon diaspora to Southern California when I was eight years old. We moved to Oceanside's suburban frontier below "Mount Ecclessia," the bluff overlooking the San Luis Rey Valley where the Mystic Christians of the Rosicrucian Fellowship had established the international headquarters of the invisible Order of the Rose Cross and built their healing temple in 1911. My dad was assistant city planner and bought a house on Roberta Lane in the valley's first subdivision. Not far away ran the San Luis Rey River, a river that is no more a river than the Sahara Desert is a sea, being a serpentine stretch of sand winding through the black-earth valley. The river had been navigable back in 1798 when Franciscan friars founded the King of the Spanish missions. The river of sand intrigued me; how people could be so river-starved as to call sand a river.

I spent the rest of my childhood in the fattest land ever known to man, where conveniences cover the face of the earth and dark unhappiness dwells at the core of empty lives. Like many members of my generation, I could watch from my tract home as New Frontier suburbs ate up the bordering farm fields and crept up empty hillsides. Before my eyes our burgeoning consumer society literally destroyed San Luis Rey, consuming the natural world that had made it such a magical place. Spiritual desolation hangs over the lower half of California as thick as smog, part of the reason that the spiritual consolation business is so big there. It left me empty, looking for something to fill the holes. Eventually, Desolation Freeway led me to folk music.

My buddy Mario introduced me to Ramblin' Jack Elliot when we were about fourteen. I recall thinking, "There's something here." I couldn't figure out exactly what, but it was real. "I was born on a 45,000-acre ranch in the middle of Flatbush," Ramblin' Jack likes to joke, and at age fifteen, he ran away from Brooklyn to join the rodeo. Elliot led to Okie balladeer Woody Guthrie, and as I grew older, the more Woody's vision came to mean. I longed to see the America he sang about, the back roads and railroad yards, the fields and orchards, the dusty prairies and wide rivers.

As it was, I became obsessed with getting into Leland Stanford Junior University. On that crooked path one year I spent the longest decade of my life in an honors program in Provo, Utah, trying to avoid being brainwashed by Brigham Young University's "best and brightest." My devious scheme worked and the Harvard of the West admitted me, but on a visit to my Oceanside pal Steve Harvey at Palo Alto that spring, I saw the guys behind the sneeze-guard in the dining hall plopping glop. If I went to Stanford, I'd have to join them and wear one of their funny white hair nets and dish to the rich kids, whose favorite word seemed to be "godlike." I had covered my ass and applied to the University of California at Santa Cruz, which was only two years old when I applied in 1967. I got into both, but Santa Cruz promised scholarships, while Stanford only offered a job on the chow line.

I have two fond memories of BYU. One was being the only one of 4,000 freshmen and freshwomen who refused to join the standing ovation for President Ernest L. Wilkinson's triumphal entrance to the frosh convocation in 1967. (Three years earlier, Wilkinson had run for the US Senate and lost. It turned out that he was too conservative even for Utah's notoriously conservative electorate.) The other was witnessing Senator Robert F. Kennedy's impassioned speech to 15,000 students on March 27, 1968. Bobby was on fire; he began his speech with a quip: "I had a very nice conversation with Dr. Wilkinson, and I promised him that all Democrats would be off the campus by sundown." Kennedy said he had "a great deal in common" with Brigham Young: "I too have a large family, I too have settled in many states. And now I too know how it is to take on Johnson's army." He then quoted early Mormon apostle Parley Pratt. When RFK finished, the archconservative crowd went wild. It was the most inspirational moment of my entire life until election night in 2008.

Exactly one week later, I was watching the evening news in the basement of Stover Hall when a bulletin announced Martin Luther King had been shot in Memphis. Half of the male students in the room thought this was great. On June 5 I was back in Oceanside and got in from a night on the town, turned on the TV, and watched as Bobby's celebration of his California primary victory transformed into his assassination. When he died the next day, so did my generation's hope. In March I had heard Kennedy ask, "What is this special mission of this generation of Americans?" It wasn't to elect my psychotic shirttail cousin Richard Milhous Nixon president.

I loved Santa Cruz, but going to college fed my desire to do something real, to experience life instead of study it. I wanted to meet truckers and farmers and miners and builders. I wanted to see the land. I wanted to live the music I'd come to love.

Huck Finn caught up with me in 1969, during my sophomore year at Santa Cruz. I was studying history, music, and drugs, so exactly when it happened I can't say, but it was in the spring and it occurred to me while reading Huck's book under a redwood tree that the river was still there, still flowing and free. One way or another you could build a raft at one end and drift down to New Orleans.

At the same time I was reading Twain, our communal dorm had a Ramblin' Jack Elliot song from his *Young Brigham* album called "912 Greens" on perpetual play. The recording told about Jack's 1953 road trip from New York to New Orleans, busking with the Dusty Road Boys, Guy Carawan, and Frank Hamilton. They found five-string banjo picker Billy Faier at the Café du Monde, and he took them to 912 Toulouse Street over a back fence, up an alley, by some garbage cans, and up and over. A banana tree stood in the middle of the patio and a wooden stair-case led up to a balcony that "connected all the various different musicians" and their different various pads. A three-legged grey cat named Grey "used to lope along and fall down" for he had a stroke and "couldn't run too good on them three legs no how." It was a hot and humid August "with the wind coming off the Mrs. Miller River by the Jack's Brewery." Towards sundown, a tropical rainstorm broke and a "girl there who had once been an ex-ballet dancer" took her clothes off and danced in the rain, "around the banana tree, around and around." Jack followed suit. He stayed about three weeks in New Orleans and never saw the light of day. This masterwork, which Jack has since sung hundreds if not thousands of times, always in different versions, but always ending the with this couplet:

Did you ever stand and shiver,
Just because you were looking at a river?

The raft idea was like a spark and my mind was a tinder-dry prairie; soon there was fire on the horizon. The idea became an obsession and then a fever. Soon I was determined to descend the Mississippi River.

As a college student from suburbia with nothing to hang an identity upon, my motives are easily understood. I sought a vision quest. I knew practically nothing about the real world, let alone the remote backwaters of the rural American South. This journey would push my limits, and I hoped to find myself somewhere beyond the borders of my safe but boring life.

I had evolved a complex and probably drug-inspired theory about fantasy and reality. We created reality out of imagination, at the balancing point of our lives where fantasy intersected reality, at the point of ultimate freedom. With the total certainty of late adolescence, I believed that reality was plastic, fluid, and forged from fantasies. I was young and bold enough to believe anyone could do anything they could dream. To a point, it worked, and it was exhilarating.

The trip appeared to be the answer to many problems. It would cross the American heartland, away from the asphalt and insanity of California, not only to another place but to another time. It would take me back to nature (though I could only imagine how close) and it would go deep into America's mystery of mysteries, the Deep South. In 1969 the South looked to be an uncharted wilderness and the Mississippi appeared as dangerous as the Amazon, the large difference being that the natives were armed with shotguns instead of poison darts. My academic and media-born notions led me to believe I was going into America's heart of darkness where I could find a vanished past. I wrote, "I had just turned nineteen and when a man becomes nineteen he needs something more than slow California beach town days to keep him going, he needs something he can sink his soul into, and the Mississippi looked to be pretty soul-trying ... I had a vague but intense desire to escape from the California scene with its crazy lack of a past and its mad mixing of present and future: if I went far enough back into the heartlands, back to the places that time and progress and money had passed over in the great stampede west, perhaps *there* I might find a place of the past. I figured I'd be more comfortable in such a place than in the smog-strangled paved-over anthill California future/present."

I have known I wanted to be a writer since I started reading. I knew I wanted to write about history from the last Sunday in August 1957 when I read historian David E. Miller's "The Donners Blazed the Mormon Trail" in a *Salt Lake Tribune* magazine supplement. I have been fascinated with history for as long as I can remember and passionate about it too. In a way I was chasing the past, for I thought taking a raft down the Mississippi River would let me experience what life was like in the nineteenth century. The idea inspired me through the spring and summer as I worked to make the fantasy a reality. I was nineteen years old. I was seeing visions. I was hot. In May I managed to win the heart of my childhood sweetheart, Suzy, at long last. It had taken years and years of trying, but that glorious spring I won through.

I had known Suzy for more than half my life and still have vivid memories of her as a child. We met in 1959 in the third grade at Mission Elementary School, when the pepper trees the padres had planted in the San Luis Rey Valley not long after they founded the Mission San Luis Rey de Francia in June 1798 still lined Mission Avenue. After school we'd walk the empty yellow California hills surrounding the valley, then a garden of Japanese truck farms and now a desolation of strip malls, trailer parks, and subdivisions. We found a vast variety of natural and man-made wonders; bugs, birds, caves, cacti, flowers, prickly pears, old wagons and abandoned farm machinery, articles and marvels that lay on the doomed black earth like remnants of another age. She had bright blue eyes, sun-browned skin, a wide, infectious smile, and a glory of golden hair that I best recall done up in braids—a vision of beauty and innocence. I fell very much in love with her at the time (eight years old and in love; wish I could remember the feeling) and stayed that way for fourteen years. Maybe longer.

Students are always the targets and victims of educational fads. Two events—Brown v. Board of Education in 1954 and Sputnik in 1957—redefined our American education. "Tracking" students—dividing them into "gifted" students and something else—had been around for a long time, but belief in pseudo-scientific tests such as the Stanford-Binet Intelligence scales became an article of faith and a trend of the time. Then, as now, tests fed corporate coffers as they measured class and defended white privilege, but such policies always had unintended consequences. I recall being tested in the fourth grade and enjoyed playing the game with the attractive and encouraging psychologist. I aced the test, which led to my advancing from the fourth to the sixth grade in 1960. Suzy skipped a grade too, which created another odd bond between us. Nobody seemed to notice that I was the shortest kid in fourth grade and so by seventh grade had to fight every bully at Jefferson Junior High School, but class privilege cuts both ways. I also learned intelligence tests are bogus: in high school we busted into our English teacher's desk and learned my princely IQ had fallen from exalted heights to barely three digits.

Through the agonies and passions of adolescence, I worshiped Suzy from afar, courted her, endured repeated rejections, hated her, loved her more, and experienced untold anguish trying to get her to love me back. It's easy to look back at all that pain that seemed so intense and unrelenting, but laughter doesn't discount the fact that it was real.

Suzy had an athlete's body, broad shoulders, small perfect breasts, and strong, taut legs, the result of spending a large percentage of her adolescence in swimming pools. When I was fourteen, I'd get up early on summer mornings and go to swimming practice, mostly to watch her swim. She was a champion who set amateur athletic records that endured for decades. I'd swim, too, as artlessly and slowly as a turtle, and leer at her out of the corner of my eye whenever I got a chance: I didn't dare stare at her directly, though at practice she never acknowledged my existence.

The only time I remember speaking to Suzy around a pool was on one sun-washed afternoon. I had mustered the courage to jump off the high dive and mentioned it to her. Suzy told me she could do a back flip, and I insisted she show me. She climbed up to the top of the board and stood perched on the end for a long time. All the eyes in the pool turned to watch her. Just as I supposed she wouldn't do it, she leapt into the air and flashed toward the water, executing a perfect flip and dive. I now figured I had to at least dive off the damn board and gave it my best shot. I remember hanging in the hot bright air, suspended like a flying frog as the flat blue surface came relentlessly closer until I hit the water in a classic belly flop. It hurt like hell, but what really burned was the image of Suzy knifing perfectly through the air.

My Utah relatives credited the move to California with my disillusionment with Mormonism, and that may be so. I tend to credit the basic absurdity of religion married to racism, Mark Twain, and our high school speech teacher Clifford Roche, even though Mr. Roche was a devout Catholic who loved Mormon students for their seemingly natural-born speaking talent. Reading Mark Twain's 1962 bestseller *Letters from the Earth* convinced me all fundamentalist faiths are ridiculous and contributed mightily to my liberation from Mormondom. Mr. Roche taught us critical thinking and demolished my devotion to Barry Goldwater.

Almost all of us can recall a great teacher who changed our lives—made us look at the world in new ways, challenged our thinking, instilled a love of knowledge and drove us to do better than our best: Clifford Arthur Roche was the essence of such a teacher. He had been a successful actor after serving in the Navy and its brigs during World War II. On stage he had been the original Ensign Pulver in *Mr. Roberts* and on TV had a bit part on Eve

Arden's *Our Miss Brooks* before fecund fatherhood drove him to teaching, at age thirty-five, in 1961. He was also a drunk, director, surfer, body builder, welder, coach, rebel, writer, humorist, politician, philosopher, and in 1970 a reformed alcoholic and "minor celebrity in an anonymous fellowship," not to mention an unlikely inspiration to thousands of folks lucky enough to meet him.

Playing a soldier in a summer school production of *The Mouse That Roared* in 1965 introduced me to the dynamic Mr. Roche. That fall I joined the Oceanside High School speech team, where it seemed our main job was spear catching—we were hardly the forensic powerhouse that Oceanside was destined to become under Cliff's leadership. We lost a lot more than we won, and Coach Roche preferred winning to losing. I remember our first tournament: we participated in the preliminary rounds and returned home after they posted the semi-finals.

I never could understand why Cliff turned his back on the drama department. He had great success as Oceanside's Robert Altman with a string of impressive directorial triumphs to his credit. Why he took on the thankless and certainly hopeless task of building a speech team from the dubious raw material Oceanside High offered is a mystery. Even then, it was clear Cliff was crazy, but he did it, and in the process he helped many of us develop talents we never dreamed we had. Especially me. As a Mormon, I had been introduced to public speaking before I could see over the pulpit, but my Anglo heritage rendered my gestures studies in awkwardness. Suzy recalls I gave an impromptu speech with my arms held stiffly in front of my chest. "That's too bad about your broken hands," said Mr. Roche.

Cliff Roche was easily the most demanding and rewarding teacher I ever had. He kept a bell on his desk, and whenever our diction got sloppy with jist, fir, or becuz, he'd clang it. (This technique proved so effective that a student who became a San

Francisco prosecutor recalled how her boss had warned that her excellent diction could alienate jurors. I still cringe when news announcers say fur example "jist becuz.") Emulating his heroes Fiorello La Guardia and Franklin D. Roosevelt, he read newspapers in class, favoring the *San Francisco Chronicle*'s hilarious gentleman satirist, Art Hoppe. It was in his class I first heard about The Summer of Love: he later told Suzy that despite his sarcastic disclaimer that it sounded too good to be true, he could see some of us thinking, "Oh, man, I'm gonna get some of *that*!" When she told him she had moved to a commune, he winced and felt responsible.

Speech class provided a chance to try to revive my romance with Suzy. We unknowingly had a brush with fame when we met Lester Bangs at the National Forensic League (NFL—get it?) qualifying tournament for the NFL California State finals in 1966. I seemed to be making progress at sparking more than a friendship on the bus ride down to San Diego State. That spring day I met Lester Bangs and his sidekick, Roger Anderson, in the bathroom between rounds. Lester was blasting away on his harmonica (which was why he was in the bathroom—acoustics) and proclaiming about the magnificent harp solo on Bob Dylan's masterpiece, "Desolation Row." Bangs addressed the subject with such passion and insight that it's easy to grasp why he became what biographer Jim DeRogatis called him, "America's Greatest Rock Critic," even though drugs killed him in 1982. Back in San Diego, I watched in dismay as Roger charmed my beloved and escaped with Suzy's heart. My clearest memory of the tournament was watching Roger and Suzy stride hand-in-hand up a green hillside as my heart broke.

Suzy became a strong, cynical, and independent young woman. Perhaps this was a response to the temper of our adolescent times. Her surreal "Original Oratory" presentation was about our generation's disillusionment: it began, "The ragman draws circles up and down the block, I'd ask him what the matter is but I know that he don't talk." It made the finals at the NFL state competition but should have won. Skepticism replaced her sun-washed innocence, but her Dylan-Burroughs-Sartre induced sophistication intensified her dazzling sexual power. At eighteen, she'd left me burnt-out and broken-hearted too many times. I'd sworn that I'd never have anything more to do with her, but there I was on my river-crazed nineteenth birthday, courting her in Berkeley to the sounds of "Nashville Skyline." This time, it worked. I swept her off her feet. I was burning so brightly that she could not resist my crazy charm. I lured her to Santa Cruz where we made passionate, inexperienced young love (and there is nothing in creation like passionate young love). I was living a dream.

There was revolution in the Beserkley air. In April 1969, local activists began building a park on a couple of acres of derelict university property between Haste and Bowditch streets and a stone's throw off Telegraph Avenue. Within a month, a thousand volunteers had transformed the abandoned car lot into a garden they named People's Park. At 4:30 a.m. on May 15, Governor Ronnie Reagan dispatched a gross of campus cops and CHIPs to the city and campus. Experts ranked UC Berkeley as America's foremost university, but Reagan denounced it as "a haven for communist sympathizers, protesters, and sex deviants." The state began surrounding the site with a chain-link fence. Four thousand activists spontaneously marched to defend the park, and after county sheriffs swelled the cop crowd to 791 officers, everybody rioted. But the sheriffs had tear gas and shotguns loaded with double-ought buckshot. They fired into the crowd, blinded a carpenter, killed a student watching from a theater roof, and sent at least 128 Berkeley residents to local hospitals. The B-movie governor had unleashed the dogs of war on Bloody Thursday. His excuse for the police riot that followed? "People, being human, will make mistakes on both sides."

(I will never forgive the Great Prevaricator for putting a happy face on racism, destroying a great public university, demolishing the American middle class, while closing mental health services and enhancing the resulting homelessness with endless Republican wars on the poor and mentally troubled.)

On May 30, 30,000 citizens marched to protest the National Guard occupation of People's Park, the gassing of the city with pepper spray, and the mass arrest of peaceful protesters. Along with our Oceanside friends Mario Marioncelli and Diana Harvey, who was also a student at Berkeley, Suzy and I joined what was both a protest and celebration. Impromptu drum and kazoo bands formed to play Lennon and Souza. It was a glorious hot spring day so flowers blossomed everywhere and people donned costumes and shed clothing. Frisbees and kites flew as a small plane trailed a "Let a Thousand Parks Bloom" banner overhead. We marched past the barricaded park, which National Guardsmen troops guarded as street theater troupes danced surreal. Nobody spat on anybody. Women slipped flowers into the Guardsmen's rifle barrels as hippies laid sod outside the razor wire. It was glorious—and entirely peaceful.

Man, was I in love. At nineteen, Suzy parted her long, straight and intensely blonde hair down the middle. She was near-sighted and wore thick wire-framed glasses; behind the glasses, her blue eyes were focused and full of fire, but when she took them off, she looked lost and vulnerable. She had high cheekbones and a roman nose: despite her German surname, she had a lot of Italian blood—what a combination!—and lots of spunk. One evening when we were later living together in Santa Cruz, I made some disparaging remarks about the casserole Suzy had cooked for dinner and she dumped a bowl of the stuff on my head.

My friend Mario was living on macaroni and marijuana and

volunteered to join the river trip. Mario was a tough case. His father had raised him to play professional baseball. He was a fantastic natural athlete, and every one of our female classmates had a crush on him, including Suzy. It looked as if he was on his way to the major leagues until he lost most of the vision in one eye in a parochial school war-ball accident. Though Mario never had much of a jock mentality (a truly gifted musician, he had an artist's soul), he was victimized by sports culture. Young American athletes learn that winning is everything, but life isn't a series of victories and defeats, it's just life. You don't have to win, you just have to persevere. Mario was driven to compete; by the time we graduated from high school, he was academically first in his class, the Rotary Club citizen of the year, high scorer on the basketball team, and senior class president. The object of all this frenzied activity was to be admitted to Stanford University. We both tried and failed. Mario took it hard. In one year he went from being voted "Most Likely to Succeed" to being a drug-crazed junior college dropout and itinerant musician. We used to joke about friends who succumbed to the temper of the times, calling them "Casualties of the Revolution." Little did we know that we'd soon be among the walking wounded.

After high school we worked and traveled around together a lot and started, as they say, experimenting with drugs. By the spring of 1969, we were drug-crazed: we saw our chemical warfare as a way of setting ourselves free of our "conditioning." Soon we were pretty well deconditioned.

About the time I caught river fever, Mario was living with an old friend of ours, Diana. Diana was quiet and intelligent, and she combined a dreamy manner with a wry wit. She was blonde and slightly built: her eyes were gray/blue and somehow distant, like smoke on a sea's horizon. Diana had a lot of charm, and I liked her a lot, but I never understood her at all. She always seemed far away. Like Suzy, she had gone from Southern California blonde blossomhood to hard Berkeley womanhood. Diana was much like Suzy in many ways, so much so that you could have taken them for sisters if you didn't know them well. Both were blonde, blue-eyed, athletic; both came from well-off homes. But if you knew them, the apparent likeness faded. Diana was quiet and passive, an intense observer but often so detached she hardly seemed to be present. Mario and I had planned to do the Mississippi trip alone, but Suzy and Diana would not be left behind. Neither Mario nor I tried very hard to discourage them.

I was surprised when Suzy decided to join the river trip. I still can't explain her motives. I know from later conversations that she wasn't completely sure about our relationship, so the decision was a gamble. I had some reservations about taking her on the trip—I assumed it would be a fairly dangerous undertaking—but down deep I was delighted. I was in love and her presence added another layer of romance to what was already a wildly romantic fantasy.

That summer I worked as Craft Shop director at a Boys' Club camp in the San Bernardino Mountains to raise money for the trip. Mario got a job as a counselor and Suzy found work nearby. They did not pay much but were good jobs that covered food and lodging and delivered one bundle of cash when summer ended. I ran the crafts shop where we made plaster-of-Paris castings and wooden tomahawks for black and Chicano kids from the Watts, El Monte, and Pasadena hoods and boys from the white ghetto at Newport Beach. The job rarely lacked excitement. We watched the moon landing in the mess hall on a television imported for the big event. At the very moment that Neal Armstrong chose to make his great leap for all mankind, a young black cyclone named Jimmy tackled a mess boy and scattered bowls of custard from one end of the lodge to the other.

We even staged the Legend of the Rising Mummy for a camp

of kids from the northwest Pasadena hood. We had awesome acting talent in our pal Wendell Wright, who had been Mario's teammate on Oceanside High's basketball team and, along with Suzy and me, the third person who made it to the 1967 National Forensic League California State finals. Wendell placed in Dramatic Interpretation, and with his formidable talent, charm, good looks, and charisma had a successful career as a stage and screen actor before him. Naturally, I invited Wendell to join the river trip. He so roundly ridiculed the notion of playing Jim in our happy crew that I only asked once. Besides, everybody thought we were crazy to visit the South, and we were all *white*.

We dreamed about the river trip all summer. I designed a raft and built a model out of balsa wood and beer cans in the craft shop. Mississippi fever must have been catching, because the camp maintenance man, a seventeen-year-old named Rick, signed up for the trip. Rick was a tall skinny kid, blonde and rangy. He always dressed in worn Levis and a battered Levi jacket and wore thick, black horn-rimmed glasses that made him look like a teenage Clark Kent.

Rick was two years younger than the rest of us, which at the time seemed like a big deal. Or maybe it was just that Rick acted more like he was fourteen. I had to give him a lot of credit for his technical competence—he knew more about cars, tools, machines and reality than the rest of us put together—but even at the start of the trip, we weren't what you'd call friends. This didn't bother me. I thought that the raw adventure, the simple damn daring of the trip, would submerge any personal differences that might arise. As noted, I was naive.

When our jobs ended, camp director Howard Amend gave us an ancient green Evinrude outboard motor that had probably seen the bottom of Jenks Lake once or twice. He outfitted us with vast quantities of overstocked camp provisions—I especially remember

100 bags of dehydrated scrambled egg mix, a fifty-pound bag of rice, and many mysterious cans of meat. (Diana recalls, "We ate a lot of mystery meat and rice.") We were on our way.

My father offered to help us get back east, so we went back to our hometown, Oceanside, to get some wheels. My old man had taken the problem to a wheeler-dealer pal named Charlie, who had a white 1955 Chevy panel truck that was one of the marvels of the mechanical age.

Mario, Diana, Suzy, and I drove over to Charlie's place in Carlsbad, a great colonial barn of a house rising above Buena Vista Lagoon and its scraggly Eucalyptus forest. Charlie had every conceivable variety of junker. On the ridge above all the other wrecks stood the white Chevy.

"She's been here two years," said Charlie, "but I'll bet she still runs." He climbed in and turned over the engine, or, rather, tried to turn it over; the mighty six cylinders remained silent. "That," said Charlie, "can be fixed."

We got some gas and primed the carburetor. Charlie got into the driver's seat and the rest of us pushed the Chevy toward the road with hopes of jump-starting it. We'd not gone far when I looked down and noticed a long steel shaft lying where the van used to be. I didn't know much about auto mechanics, but the piece of steel looked remarkably like a drive shaft. We stopped pushing and Charlie got out and looked under the van.

"My God!" he said. "Somebody bagged the transmission!"

Dad and Charlie went off to track down a transmission, and we stood in stoned amazement gazing at the van. Underground artistic genius R. Crumb could have designed it. It had an enormous balloon shaped body and a pig-nose front end, but glistening there in the hot summer sun, the Chevy looked mythically beautiful.

Charlie rounded up a transmission that had only one flaw, no reverse gear. "We really need a reverse gear," said Mario.

I contested his point. "Really, Mario, take it for a sign. We can't turn back."

"We need a reverse gear," he insisted, but we set out without one.

After much work we loaded the van with spare tires, sheets of plastic, bags of clothes, sacks of provisions, an old mattress, many sleeping bags, a Coleman stove, tools, cameras, books and notebooks, a guitar, an outboard engine, and all the spare parts we could lay our hands on. We struck out on Highway 101 for northern California and cruised around Santa Cruz and Berkeley. Then we headed east via Interstate 80, bound for the American heartland.

I'll never forget the exhilaration of climbing over the Sierra Nevada in that ragged old van, coming over the top of the stark stone mountains and gliding down to the Nevada desert. When we left California behind, the very atmosphere seemed different, the air thinner and clean. In the open desolate country beyond Reno, the desert drifted by like a dream, unaltered since climate change drained Lake Lahontan at the end of the Ice Age. The road was still a battered two-lane '50s highway, Woody's road and Kerouac's road, a narrow, treacherous asphalt ribbon crowded with diesels that rushed past like tornadoes, a two-lane highway that has about as much in common with an interstate highway (those great bitumen rivers) as a bottle rocket has with a Saturn booster. Time slowed down. We left California and re-entered America. All the romantic road nonsense that we'd imbibed, all our innocent enthusiasm swelled us up with joy; the four of us were on the road.

I've been back and forth across America many times since, but I don't recall a stranger cross-country adventure. We spent our first night at an abandoned radiator shop outside Winnemucca. During the night a tremendous wind came up, blowing off the desert like hell itself, a genuine dust storm. Next morning our clutch burned up twenty miles outside of Battle Mountain. (I had nothing to do with destroying the clutch—it would be years before I learned to drive a standard transmission). We felt more like Okies all the time.

The van—we'd christened it Prometheus after the fire-bringer and Greek god of foresight—was a very slow boat, even when it ran. Topped out, it could barely crack 50/mph. The exhaust fumes that filled the back of the van proved to be real headbenders. We met up with Rick at the bus station in Salt Lake City; he had re-cruited a friend, Ward, to join him. We crammed even more junk into the already top-heavy van. We bought fourteen hotdogs for $2.00 and drove on into Wyoming and the night.

We pooled our money, mostly earned working at camp that summer, and had about $1,800 when we headed east from Utah. That was an enormous sum in 1969, when a first-class stamp cost 6 cents and gas went for 35 cents a gallon. But the road had an enormous appetite for cash and continually threatened to eat more. Plus, the Chevy's rear end was in a bad way. Toward mid-morning we stopped in an empty lot off the dirt streets of Medicine Bow, Wyoming, and let Rick attack it. We were already bleary and travel worn. Next to the field was a gas station, and I think we did a number on the bathroom of the place with grease, because when I eased over to wash up, an old one-eyed cowboy turned gas jockey yelled at me, "You, you!"

"Yeah?"

"You with that goddamn white van?"

I owned up to it.

"Well, now, then, listen, and listen good. If I see any of you get on this side of this fence, I'm gonna get my shotgun and blow you away! And if there are any tools gone from around this place, I'm gonna come find you and blow you away!"

We pushed on as soon as we could, crossing into Nebraska just as the sun was going down. We'd not driven far into the flatness when the twilight began to pulsate red. A state trooper pulled us over.

The trooper wore a Smokey-the-Bear campaign hat pulled tight on his bullethead. His eyes were small and blue, his spotless starched uniform was trimmed with black leather. He hassled us about draft cards and runaways until his partner showed up. The troopers escorted us into Sidney, one car ahead and one car behind our panel truck. They took us to the state police headquarters, a graveled compound with a cinder-block jailhouse surrounded by a tall chain-link fence. They hauled us into a dreary room the color of old newspaper and read us our rights. They called me into the chief's office and read the contents of a state "Permission to Search Form." They pushed it across the table for me to sign.

"Uh," I said. "If I don't sign this, you'll just keep us around until you get a search warrant, right?"

"The paper says I can't make no threats, kid," said the chief.

"Well, how about if I sign it, maybe you'll let us go pretty soon?"

"The paper says I can't make no promises."

We'd eaten what little reefer we had left on the ride in, so I signed the form. The troopers gleefully attacked the van. They were determined to bust us, and even our array of weird junk didn't deter them. They dug through it all. I couldn't understand why total strangers wanted to put a nice guy like me and swell folks like my friends in jail, but they went at it like beavers.

We had even more junk than when we'd left California, including a lawn chair, an ice chest, axes, packs, a car battery, plus Rick and Ward's gear. Despite the abundant evidence, the troopers refused to believe we were going to the Mississippi River.

The first cop saw where I'd spray painted the name Prometheus on the van back in Battle Mountain. The trooper tapped the name and said, "Who's that?"

"The Greek god of foresight," I said, not explaining that it was an appropriate name for a vehicle with no reverse gear. "He gave fire to mankind."

"Uh," said the trooper. "I'm not up on my Greek mythology."

He wasn't up to finding any drugs, either. "Look," I said finally. "Do you think I'd be stupid enough to smuggle drugs in an old wreck like this?"

He grunted. Obviously I was that stupid. I was getting indignant, but at least had sense enough to keep my mouth shut. At last they gave up and let us go.

We ate miserable hamburgers in miserable Sidney and drove on through the miserable Nebraska night. By dawn our heads were bent with blue smoke from the exhaust, our stomachs were knotted with truck-stop coffee, and the constant jolting of the ancient van had twisted our backs. And the rear end was dragging its ass again. We pulled off the highway after we crossed into Iowa and drove on dirt roads back into the harvest-heavy cornfields. Rick went to work while the rest of us tried to regain the use of our legs.

All around us on the gently rolling prairie were September-tall stands of corn, sprawling as far as the eye could reach, growing out of the thick black topsoil. I was amazed, I'd never seen soil so deep and rich. It took a while, but at last I recognized the tall, stringy weed growing in profusion all through the corn. It was hemp. It seemed like just revenge on the Nebraska State Troopers for forcing us to eat our last carefully hoarded joints. We dried some on Rick's canned heat Sterno stove and drove on toward the river.

The last 150 miles from Des Moines seemed endless. We stopped in the late afternoon, burgered out, and pushed on without resting. I was afraid that if the van stopped it would start no more, and so we forged on through the Iowa hills, nerves knotted, stomachs shrunk, eyes red and glazed. It was dark when we crossed Highway 61 and came to the last few miles between the river and us. We climbed one last hill and crossed a high, arching bridge. Below us we could see nothing but black formless water reflecting the lights of the Rock Island shore, but it didn't matter. In the darkness lay the Mississippi River. We'd made it.

IV

BLACK HAWK, JOHN ADAMS, AND THE SUNSET MARINA

Through great good luck, during the summer I'd found the name of a Mr. John Adams, owner of the Sunset Marina in Rock Island, Illinois, the largest sheltered harbor on the upper Mississippi. It was a beautiful piece of water with room for 500 boats. I'd written asking if we could use some of his space to build a raft. He replied by mail, saying maybe. I was eager to find out where we stood, so in the morning, still bone weary and road sore, Suzy drove down to the river and I rode along.

The Sunset Marina was impressive. It lay on Lake Potter, a box of sheltered water that opened onto the river through a small inlet. A hundred or more boats lay in the calm blue water and probably twice that many stood mounted on chocks behind the marina office and workshops. We found Mr. Adams in the marina's showroom.

We must have looked a sight to Mr. Adams. I was growing my first beard and was dressed in Levis and an army surplus shirt. Suzy had her hair swept back and wore a blue cotton smock that showed a lot of thigh. Still, despite our recent journey, we were bright-faced and intensely young and our enthusiasm was probably infectious.

We were nervous, but Mr. Adams put us at ease directly. He was a short, square, blunt spoken man who smoked Camels and told wry, dry jokes. I introduced myself as the letter writer and would-be raft builder. I watched him recollect and grin. We followed Adams through his barn-sized repair shop as he fired questions about the proposed raft at me.

"How big do you plan to build it?"

"Twelve by twenty-four."

"That's too much beam. She'd be hell to steer. Build her narrower, say as narrow as eight feet. What are you going to use for flotation?"

"Fifty-five-gallon oil drums."

"Well, I've got some old pontoons from a houseboat, but if you want used drums, I'll sell them to you for two bucks a piece. What kind of power have you got?"

"An old outboard."

"Good. You'll need it."

We walked out into a graveled field where sixty or seventy cabin cruisers stood mounted on skids. Adams walked to an empty spot between two of them and stopped. "OK," he said. "You can build it here. Keep it clean and don't take anything without asking first. If what you build is river worthy, I'll launch it with that gantry over there." He pointed to an enormous Travelift mechanical boat hoist. "Otherwise ..." He stopped and spoke very quietly. "You don't have any idea how dangerous the river is." He looked squarely in my eyes, seriously, and then relaxed. "But I believe you'll have a good time."

Now all we had to do was build a raft. We had a solid design and attacked the work with a will that compensated for our nonexistent experience. We built a basic frame of 2x10s, from which we hung two rows of nine oil drums secured in place with steel plumber's tape. The deck was pine 1x6s, and we built a box-like cabin 12 feet long using half-inch plywood on a 2x2 frame. The overall length was 28 feet with a beam of 8 feet. Most of the construction was done in four days. The cost of lumber, barrels, and hardware came to about $250.

On our first working day we put the 2x10 frame together with lag bolts. On Friday we lifted the frame up onto braces and began hanging the barrels; to do the job, we bought up all the plumber's tape in Rock Island. It was rough work. Mario or I would lie under the barrel, push it up into the box-like frame, while Rick and Ward nailed the steel tape tight. Saturday we laid the deck planking, and by Sunday we had most of the cabin built. It was the most amazing thing I'd ever done.

Watching Mario, Rick, Ward, and yours truly work, it would be hard to understand how we managed to do it so quickly. Rick and I fought over how something should be done, and Mario and Ward watched us battle it out until somebody won. I'd read everything C. S. Forester had ever written about Horatio Hornblower and threatened to hang Rick for mutiny. He was reading *The Rise and Fall of the Third Reich* and would rant in a German accent and smash stray scraps of wood into splinters. Ward and Mario would lie down. Finally we'd settle the dispute and start talking normally and get back to work, the raft coming alive under our hands.

Sometimes we'd stand back and look at our creation and imagine it out on the river. "Look at it, just look at it," I'd say. "We did it with our own hands." Mario would nod quietly and say, "Yep."

Early on, while Rick and Ward had gone to get supplies, Mario and I got our first look at the river. We walked through the thickest weeds and woods I'd ever seen across the spit of land that separated the marina from the river. Suddenly it opened up before us, the great wide river, shining in the warm autumn sun. The Mississippi, as Sam Clemens wrote, "is not a commonplace river, but on the contrary is in all ways remarkable." Six or seven long patterns of calm and ripple spread out from the surging central current. The day was cool and bright, the sky blue on blue against the moving water. The Illinois bank was choked with green vegetation, jungle-like to a westerner's eyes, but the far Iowa shore looked even greener.

Awed into silence, we were quiet for a long time. This seemed like vindication. "You know, Mario," I said, "if anybody who's said we were crazy could stand right here and look at all this, they'd have to say, 'You're right, you're absolutely right.'"

"No," said Mario. "They'd still say we were crazy."

Our camp at Black Hawk State Park was on the site of Sauke-nuk, the birthplace of Sauk war captain Makataimeshekiakiak, who in 1832 was sixty-five when he led the last major resistance to the whites in Illinois, which ended disastrously at the massacre politely known as the Battle of Bad Axe in August. Black Hawk survived and published a best-selling autobiography, the first by an American Indian leader. The war against the Fox and Sauk was unfairly given his name; it also provided Captain Abraham Lincoln with his only military experience and first elected position. Now Black Hawk had a college, museum, bar, bowling alley, and shopping center named after him. A neon-illuminated aluminum statue, which looked nothing like the old Indian, graced the shopping center. The park was a pleasant place high on a bluff overlooking the Rock River and thick with tall oaks and elms. Many of our fellow Americans vacationed there, but we saw little of them. Mostly they stayed in their elaborate trailers and campers and watched TV.

On the first day the boys worked on the raft, Suzy and Diana kept camp with the first black squirrels any of us had ever seen. We expected them to keep house and provide food when we returned at dark. The boredom didn't sit well with them, and we got back to camp that evening to find them in full revolt.

"Hey," said Suzy. "What's this shit about us staying here all day? What do you think we are, slaves?"

"Yeah," said Diana. "How come we do all the work and you have all the fun?" I didn't have an answer. Being a born and bred male chauvinist pig, I assumed that was the universe's natural order. It's always impossible to justify any form of bigotry, so we backed down and took them along to the marina the next day. The boys, being sexists to the core, set them to running errands. I think this included visiting the Rock Island Engineering District to pick up the Army Corps of Engineers' "Upper Mississippi River Navigation Charts" from Mile 0 at Cairo to Mile 866 in Minneapolis. Diana recalls getting building materials—plywood, plumber's tape to support the oil drums, and clamps—besides working on the raft and watching it take shape. She asked if our pile of lumber would be enough to build a strong raft. Rick held up a piece of plywood and said, "Just try to rip it in half." That settled that.

During our stay at the park, a band of gypsies moved in, forty or fifty of them driving shiny pick-ups and Cadillacs that hauled enormous house trailers. They were Roma, authentic nomads who made their living doing roofing jobs, on their way from Chicago to Los Angeles. They ranged in age from gnarled, proud patriarchs and matrons with long tresses dressed in heavy black dresses down to a horde of jabbering children who could neither stop talking nor borrowing stuff from our camp. At night the park throbbed with their music and passionate disputes in fierce Romanian.

As the raft took shape, people came from all over to look at it; in the days of cheap gas, it was worth the ride. Most everybody who ventured an opinion said it would never work. The guys who worked at the marina thought the whole idea was crazy. Dave, the thin, gap-toothed foreman, ordered us to have the mess completed by Tuesday. Marv, a mechanic fond of guns and stag movies, made jokes. Mike, the marina's carpenter, assured us that the raft would never make it far. Ray, the youngest of the crew, completed a long inspection and said, "Well, you've sure got a lot more balls than I do."

After several technical suggestions and a few outright orders, John Adams finally conceded that the raft would probably do all right and agreed to launch it with his gantry. We hauled out our antique green Evinrude but couldn't get it to turn over. Marv tinkered with it and concluded that it would take considerably more talent than Jesus had demonstrated on Lazarus to get the engine back in running order. Adams insisted we had to have power to dodge sawyers and snags, get out of the way of towboats, and navigate in and out of locks. He sold us a very clean 1959 eighteen-horsepower Johnson Seahorse for $200. It put a big hole in our budget but proved absolutely essential.

On Wednesday, September 24, we were ready to put our creation on the water. Launching the raft was like being present at a birth. Adam's gantry consisted of two U-shaped frames that supported two belts to cradle and lift boats. Like a giant insect, the Travelift crossed the boat yard and moved into position above the raft. We secured the belts, and the gantry began to lift its load. The raft pitched to one side but righted itself and held together. The marvelous machine began its slow pilgrimage to the water. It rolled out to where the raft hung suspended high above the oily waters of the lagoon. The gantry lowered the raft to the water, slowly. One row of barrels touched down and then the other, and at last the *Phillip W. Bell* was waterborne.

(I have often regretted naming the raft after poor Dr. Bell, a scholar and provost of my college in Santa Cruz. He had served as a US Army Air Corps pilot during World War II, worked as a correspondent for the *New York Times,* and was a nice guy who didn't deserve to have some young wiseass mock him. We never called the craft using Bell's name: it was always "the raft." Dr. Bell, a distinguished scholar and economist, later cornered me in a lounge and asked for a picture of the raft. He passed it off as a joke, but as he left the room, he turned and said with real anguish, "Why did you do that?" Frankly, Phil, I don't know. I thought his name had a fine classic riverboat sound to it, but even at the time it seemed plenty dumb. We sprayed the name on both sides of the cabin with "Rock Island to New Orleans" on one side and "New Orleans or Bust" on the other. I've often wished we'd given the raft a true name, like Woody Guthrie or Leadbelly, but that's all history now.)

I fell in love with the raft, so it's hard to give an objective description of our waterborne home. To most folks, she probably looked like more junk floating down the river than a watercraft. Built on its narrow platform of a deck, the main cabin was a plywood box with doors fore and aft and a hinged plywood window up front. We divided the cabin into a kitchen and a bedroom. The kitchen consisted of a couple of tables, kerosene lanterns, and a Coleman stove. We pulled the well-worn mattress out of the van, and Suzy and I slept on it; in the day, we all occasionally used it to lounge upon. She shared the widespread skepticism about whether the raft was river worthy, for Suzy recalled thinking, "If the raft capsized, I would grab my birth control pills."

John Adam's crew towed us to the far side of the harbor where we tied up to a tree. We spent the afternoon getting the last of our gear aboard and talking to reporters; we started to feel like heroes. In the evening we drank wine and got high in the cabin. We laughed until we were giddy—and we were. In six days we'd built twenty-eight feet of raft that was now actually in water only a stone's throw from the Mississippi. Mario brought the van around to the far end of the marina, and he and Diana went off to sleep in it. Rick and Ward slept in the weeds.

Making love on the new raft was very fine. It was like floating on an enormous waterbed. Mario and Diana weren't so lucky. Mario had chosen a local necking hangout as a parking place for Prometheus, and they had just settled down when somebody stuck a flashlight in the window. It was the police.

"All right," said one. "Let's see some identification."

They gave the cops their driver's licenses. "Do you own this van?"

"Uh, yep," said Mario.

"Do you live in this thing?"

"Uh, well, sometimes, yeah. You see ...," and Mario told them about the raft. The cops seemed to loosen up.

"Uh," said one of the cops when Mario was done, "are you two married?"

"No," said Mario.

"Well, you know, that's against the law in Illinois. I believe it's called fornication."

"That's what they call it in California, too," said Diana.

The second cop spoke for the first time. "Y'know, Bud, I used to live out in California, and I think it's legal out there. At least everybody sure did it a hell of a lot."

"You're not kidding about this raft business?" asked the first cop.

"No sir," said Mario.

"Listen, is anybody down on that raft fornicating?"

"Oh, yeah," said Mario.

The second cop persuaded his pal to give up. This was obviously too big. As they walked back to their car, one of them yelled back, "Boy, sometimes you really make it hard on us."

During the summer of 1969, President Richard Milhous Nixon had cracked down on the Tijuana border crossing and created a national reefer shortage. It was the only victory I recall in his "War on Drugs," which he formally declared in June 1971. Like all other wars on nouns (think terrorism), it failed but let crooked politicians build vast bureaucracies to funnel billons to their cronies, imprison their political opponents (think black, brown, and young people), and create free enterprise institutions (think for-profit private prisons and "detention" facilities) that convert taxes into private profits. Wars on nouns never end. Anyway, we had somehow located a lid of grass before the left Oceanside but ate the last of it driving into Sidney.

We had harvested several of the huge hemp plants we found in Iowa. "We thought it was pot," Diana recalls, "but the plants had no THC. I am not clear as to why we brought a bunch of the plants with us to Rock Island." Mario and I smoked it religiously without any detectable buzz, unless it was due to hyperventilation. We smuggled the plants out of Prometheus and onto the raft: Suzy disguised them in yellow raincoats. To Diana, "They looked like huge hemp bouquets." We were young. We were fearless. We were dumb, dumb, dumb.

Early the next morning a reporter from the *Des Moines Register* showed up and got a photograph of us standing in front of the raft's cabin. It was drizzling, and we all appeared half drowned. Suzy and Mario looked happy, Diana looked half asleep, and Rick and Ward looked skeptical. I bore an uncanny resemblance to Buster Brown.

James Ney's article, "Mark Twain Inspiration of Raft Trip," provides an independent snapshot of our venture and its yackety spokesperson. "Bill Bagley, who never had been on a river in his life, started reading Mark Twain last spring in a college course," Ney began. "Now steeped in Twain's river lore, he's sailing down the Mississippi with five friends on a homemade raft," Ney wrote. "I got carried away," I confessed, and wanted "to experience the feel of the mighty river about which Twain wrote so lovingly" and "meet and talk to the people of the river, to see how the river was, and how it has changed since Twain's time." I called Twain an archetypal American personality and said the way he wrote about the river's "majesty and its power, well, I want to experience it and see it like he did," Bagley said. In a week we had "built a 28-foot raft from steel drums, put a plywood shelter on it, and bought a second-hand, 18-horsepower motor" at a cost of almost $300, "more than we had thought," said I. "Some rivermen doubt that the raft will hold up." I used a non-sequitur to argue it would: "we'll stop as many times as we have to to repair it." We had named the raft after my poor provost. "It's a tongue-in-cheek honor," I said. Ney explained the six of us had pooled $1,800 we had earned working that summer and had $600 left. "We'll eat a lot of catfish," I quipped.

The rain stopped not long after the reporter left, and Suzy and I went over to the marina to thank John Adams for all he'd done for us. He took me aside and talked seriously about the river.

"I used to have no respect whatever for the river," he said. "When I was young, I once ran a thirty-five footer onto a stump, holed her, and she started to sink. I ran her onto a sandbar and went to sleep. I wouldn't do it again: I've seen too much of the river's moods to ever trust her that far again. In '65 the river flooded, there was water where we're standing right now, ten feet of water." He paused for a moment and we both looked out to where the Mississippi flowed behind a screen of trees. "The lower river is even worse. I'm really worried about what you're going to run into below Cairo. Around Memphis there are whirlpools that I've seen toss a forty-footer around like it was a child's toy. There are towboats down there that are four times the size of anything you ever see up this way. The worst of them is a big four stacker, the *America*, and she kicks up a ten-foot-high prop wake that bounces off the riverbanks for miles. A boat like that can suck forty feet of water away from the shore and then throw it back again. So be careful, always! That damn river doesn't need more corpses."

His last bit of advice was, "Don't run at night. Do anything else you want to do, but don't run at night. If you do, the river will kill you."

V

BIG RIVER

Mario and Diana volunteered to drive Prometheus to our first downriver rendezvous. Suzy and I stood in the bow with a sapling I'd cut to use as a sounding pole, and Rick cranked up the engine from the short deck behind the cabin that provided a home for a fifty-five-gallon gas barrel, and a plastic trash can containing our water supply, plus a mount for the Seahorse. The tight quarters and obstructed view made steering awkward, but Rick met the challenge. We cast off and he pointed the nose of the raft at the harbor mouth. Slowly, we rounded out of the lagoon and onto the river.

A sharp wind hit us as we reached the open river. Coming up close to the Illinois shore was the *Reliance*, not a huge towboat but big enough. The shining black mounds of coal heaped in her dozen barges rose above the river like mountains. A great sea serpent, the towboat crossed our bow and we rode her wake, rolling up and down in the long swells. It struck me how we knew practically nothing about the Mississippi, but we had survived our first encounter with a river monster. Once through the towboat's wake, we had made it to the river's channel.

High gray clouds were scattered across the sky as a strong south wind churned up the river until it seemed to be flowing northward. The Mississippi suddenly seemed so huge, and I again contemplated our astounding ignorance. Up on her stocks and even riding in the shelter of the marina, the raft had seemed big, but in mid-river the wide waters dwarfed our floating home. When we cut the engine and tried to drift, the wind spun us around like a leaf. We cut away the tires we'd hung around the raft to use as bumpers, trying to improve her sailing qualities. It did some good, but it was clear we had a long, slow trip in front of us.

We quickly acquired an intimate knowledge of our Johnson Seahorse, gaining a profound respect for each of its eighteen horses. It had a pressurized red four-gallon gas tank instead of a fuel pump and a push-button that primed the carburetor and helped get the engine cranking, which it did quite reliably for a long time. I recall using a siphon-hose to fill the four-gallon tank from the fifty-five-gallon barrel about every other day—I can still taste the gasoline. The hand throttle let us generate considerable power when we needed it.

About noon the overcast broke and the wind eased up. The autumn day blossomed, glistening with sunlight and color. We'd left Rock Island behind and there were only a few summer cabins and shacks scattered along the shore. Soon even these disappeared and nothing covered the banks but elms, oaks, cottonwoods, maples, and pines growing tall and majestic with knotted roots that spilled into the gnawing water. We passed a maze of islands with names like Andalusia and Martin and Cisco, some long and spidery, some as misshapen as ink blots.

In the afternoon we tied up to the first named place we came to, Buffalo, a sleepy hamlet on the rocky Iowa shore. Rusted and weed choked railroad tracks ran through town. Sleep seemed to hang over the town like a fog; it was as if Buffalo was waiting for the steamboats and lost trains that never returned. Suzy struck up a conversation with an old man who'd worked on the river for many years. She asked what he thought the raft looked like. "Why child," he said. "She looks like exactly what she is, a shanty."

The first evening on the river added to our appreciation of Midwestern skies. The sun set behind the green and yellow hills of Iowa and turned the cloud-streaked sky red, purple, and orange. The river reflected the sky, on fire. As the last light and color disappeared, the twilight faded like an echo, and from the east an aura of white light shone over the Illinois shore as a great yellow moon began to rise. It was the harvest moon, enormously fat as it transcended the horizon, its reflection a glittering pathway across the water. We sprawled on the foredeck, completely awed by the transformation of day into night. After Mario and Diana retired, Suzy and I sat on the stern, dangling our feet in the cold water, watching the moon-illuminated river. As it mounted the sky, the moon turned white and its reflection formed a column of light on the water. The landscape seemed to be made of beaten silver.

"This is magic, isn't it?" said Suzy.

Next morning I woke up in the dark and watched the sunrise as the full moon rode near the western horizon. During the night a knee-high bank of white fog had shrouded the river. It resembled a snowfield and appeared solid enough to walk across. The first light was pink and orange, transforming the fog into a glowing cloud as the sky went from black to gray to purple to blue. The eastern horizon was a line of black pines and water oaks crowded together on the Illinois riverbank, screening the fire of the rising sun. Birdsong and the soft rush of the river as it swept beneath the raft made the only sounds.

I cast off into the mist and again began navigating the Mississippi. It took a while to develop a working relationship with the river. The Coast Guard maintains a channel between two and three hundred yards wide marked using, I recall, red and black "can" buoys, red to starboard (left) and black to port (right) looking downstream. (Since 2003 the Western Rivers Marking System uses red and green buoys.) The navigation lights and mileage markers begin at mile zero at the Head of Passes in Louisiana and end at mile 950 at Cairo, where the upper river begins at mile zero and continues up to mile 866 at the confluence of the Minnesota and St. Croix rivers. The Army Corps of Engineers published navigation charts for both the upper and lower Mississippi showing nearly every chicken coop and woodpile between Minnesota and the Gulf of Mexico. With the maps and the markers, you pretty much always know where you are. It is difficult to get lost; after all, the river only goes one way.

Our first days on the river are burned into my memory in the bright and fiery colors that began to appear in the autumn woods. Before long we settled into a routine. Mario and Diana built a shelter on the foredeck out of 2x2s and plastic sheeting. Suzy and I slept in the back of cabin, so we had to share our quarters with Rick, who bedded down on the floor of the galley that we built in the front quarter of the shack. In the morning one of the couples or Rick would take off to shuttle Prometheus to a rendezvous, while the rest of the crew sailed the raft downriver. The others didn't mind driving, so Suzy and I managed to spend most of our time on the raft. Rick rigged up a system of wires, pulleys, and a joystick that let us steer from the roof of the cabin, which was much safer and gave us a much better view. It made the little work we had to do even easier. Once or twice a day we'd have to wrestle gasoline out of the fifty-gallon drum and into the outboard tank that we kept on the poop deck, but otherwise we pretty much drifted along, watching for stump fields, sawyers, and towboats.

Towboats made the channel dangerous for small craft—especially *slow* small craft. The channel generally follows the main flow of the current, and since it was autumn, the river was low and the channel was often the only safe water due to stumps and wing dams, so despite the towboat threat we usually stayed between the red and black buoys that marked the channel. Sometimes we'd drop into a chute, a narrow passage between two islands, and leave the larger river behind. In these quiet places we could imagine what the river had been like before the coming of the white man.

The twenty-nine dams above St. Louis made commercial navigation possible on the upper Mississippi. Lucky us had to lock through only thirteen of them. The locks, with their massive gates and crusty lockmasters, were always interesting. We pulled up before a lock and waited until a green signal light gave us the go ahead. The great gates slowly swung open, the towboat locking through lumbered out, and we'd steer the raft into the lock's concrete box. The gate shut behind us and the water would begin to drop. At Keokuk the lock had a drop of thirty-six feet, leaving us at the bottom of a concrete canyon looking up at a small rectangle of sky. The lower gate would then swing open and we'd chug on down the river.

These dams made the upper river more like a series of lakes than a true, living river, especially in low water. They were not truly ugly, but the dams always gave me the feeling that they were strangling the river.

Occasionally a factory or an entire industrial complex dominated the riverbank. Stacks belched smoke into the air and sewage drainpipes poured into the river, but mostly the upper river had a charm and beauty that will not be destroyed until the last tree is hacked down. Iowa's old river towns—Muscatine, Burlington, and Keokuk—all began as fur-trade post and preserved their turn-of-the-century style. Muscatine was especially fine. Perched upon rolling hills, the town could have been a pre-earthquake section of San Francisco. Only one building in the entire town appeared to have been built since 1920. Muscatine looked like a dowager princess dropped in the middle of a cornfield.

It was probably in Muscatine where we learned Jim Nay's article and picture of us had made the front page of the *Des Moines Register* and went out over the wire services.

Our newfound fame had unintended consequences, because Ward had failed to tell his parents he had two female crewmates. He immediately received orders to abandon ship and return to Pasadena, which he did. This was unfortunate, because Ward was a nice guy: he had made some sort of arrangement to provide the *Los Angeles Times* with articles about the voyage, which of course made me insanely jealous. I don't recall he ever wrote a word, but I was too dumb to try to pick up the opportunity. His sudden departure left Rick without an ally and increased his isolation.

Our occasional forays into the countryside when Suzy drove Prometheus to our next rendezvous enhanced our appreciation of the special beauty of flat land. We saw it at its best, autumn ripe and harvest heavy, after the furnace heat of summer had burned away and before the cold hand of winter gripped the land. It was golden. We found corn and tomatoes, apples and pears. As we drifted out of summer and into the fall, the constant green began to change to the scarlet and yellow of October.

On weekdays the sleepy river was quiet, but on weekends pleasure craft appeared as thick as mosquitoes in Arkansas; cabin cruisers, houseboats, and skiffs, usually piloted by drunks, rich and poor. "We know just about everyone out here on the river is drinking," a Kentucky state trooper said about the Ohio that summer, and it was equally true on the Mississippi. The lubricated boaters drove us crazy with their wakes, which could be as bad as a towboat's, but the people were always friendly and curious. We met a young beer-crazed engineer who examined the raft until his face began to twitch. "It can't work," he said, looking at the bluff bow of the *Phillip W. Bell*. "It defies all the laws of physics: it can't possibly work."

One Sunday afternoon below Burlington, we met a rich couple in a Chris Craft who spoke in strange patrician Midwestern accents and invited us aboard for highballs. The lady was very sweet and very drunk. She gushed on and on about how much she liked our raft, but for the sake of beauty, we should certainly consider going back upriver instead of downriver. "It's so much more beautiful up the river. Down there," she said, pointing south, "are places like Mississippi and Alabama. Why would anyone want to go to such places?"

That was a tough question. Without answering it, we returned to the raft with a good buzz on from the highballs. I was pretty thoroughly blasted and the raft staggered down the river under my drunken steering. We'd set a rendezvous point at a state park that was still some distance away, and darkness swallowed us up before we made it. Night transformed the river and John Adams's warning echoed in my head: "Whatever you do, don't run at night. The river will kill you if you do." The moon wouldn't rise for a couple of hours, and after the last light faded away, it was densely dark. We could have been floating in space. Suzy stood on the bow with a lantern and warned me about whatever she could see in the murk, which wasn't much. Finally we could see lights on shore and I began steering straight for them. I heard Suzy call, "Watch out!" and I instinctively cut to port: on my right the broken trunks of trees lopped off just above the water loomed up from the stump field we'd narrowly missed. I cut back the engine and felt my way through the thick night. At last we saw the light of a lantern on a dock and heard Rick and Mario calling to us. When we finally landed, I was stone sober and swore I'd never disregard John Adams's warning again.

VI

FREE AND EASY AND COMFORTABLE

On the Monday morning after our harrowing run into Dallas City, I woke up Mario and Suzy and I drove Prometheus down the river to Nauvoo, the legendary city where Mormon prophet Joseph Smith built his kingdom on the Mississippi in the 1840s. I'd heard tales of Old Nauvoo since my childhood in Utah and was excited at the prospect of visiting the place.

We were soon cruising south through harvest-ready cornfields stretching to the far horizon of the flat, fertile prairie. Before the morning was very old, we pulled into the quiet, shady center of the modern town and walked over to see the site where the Mormon temple once stood. The House of the Lord had been the largest building in Illinois in its day, dominating the view from the town's high bluff overlooking the Mississippi narrows. Now the temple site was only a depression and a few piles of stone, survivors of the ruins that the locals had not hauled away as building materials, scattered across a green lawn next to the hole that had been the temple's basement.

The historic properties in Old Nauvoo are divided along the lines of one of the oldest schisms in Mormonism, with what was then called the Reorganized Church of Jesus Christ of Latter Day Saints (RLDS) holding most of the Joseph Smith family sites, while The Church of Jesus Christ of Latter-day Saints (LDS), the Utah-based corporate branch, owned most everything money could buy. The two branches were traditionally identified as Josephites, the RLDS followers who accepted Joseph Smith III as his father's heir, and the Brighamites, the main LDS Church that followed Brigham Young to Salt Lake and is now known as *the* Mormon church. Polygamy was the main bone of contention between the two: Joseph Smith's family maintained it was the evil invention of Brigham Young, while the LDS Church asserted it came directly from the founding prophet. As an attorney, Joseph Smith III made a valiant legalistic defense of the RLDS position, but historal facts ultimately overwhelmed the argument. Now the Community of Christ, formerly the RLDS, tacitly accepts Smith's involvement in polygamy, while the LDS Church, having renounced the practice reluctantly between 1890 and 1910, would just as soon forget about the whole thing and pretend that neither Smith nor Young ever had more than one wife. Meanwhile, the best expert (Steven Shields) estimates the "Restorationist" movement spawned at least 487 offshoots. Many are polygamous "Joseph Smith Mormon" cults apparently determined to prove what my Great-Aunt Bea (who had life-experience with what "The Principle" was all about) once told me with anger and disgust: "Polygamy was just a way for old men to marry young girls!"

On the corner of the temple lot stood a large stone building with a sign, Nauvoo Restoration, Inc. We watched a movie that made it clear this outfit was closely aligned with the Brighamite church and then took a guided tour of the town in a van along with a couple from Utah. Our guide was a retired insurance salesman who had been a Nauvoo missionary for fifteen years. He drove down to the river and told us how clean the old town had been, how hard the Mormons had worked, and what sons-of-bitches their neighbors had been. Their neighbors *had* gotten fed up with the Saints (as they still like to be called) and ran them out of the state, but I knew it wasn't because the aggravated Illini found the clannish Mormons too neat and industrious. Their neighbors considered the faith's religious practices outrageous (especially the one that involved Joseph Smith and his powerful associates marrying multiple women), their theocratic political doctrines and bloc voting threatening, and their thieving ways aggravating. After the Saints left, the locals may have torched the temple to persuade the Mormons not to come back. It didn't work. Our guide showed us the many historic properties the Utah church owned in 1969. He said they intended to make Nauvoo look just as it did in 1846 and planned to spend $40 million to do so. (They have since spent that money and more, but daguerreotypes reveal that Nauvoo in 1846 looked a lot more like Natchez-under-the-Trace than the Disneyland version Nauvoo Restoration, Inc., and its powerful partners have built.)

Growing up in Utah gave me an appreciation and affection for this odd history, and despite spending half my youth in California, where historical amnesia is state policy, I had an enduring fascination with the human epic, especially in its odder manifestations. I'd long since lost belief in the faith of my childhood, but even in my late teens, I realized that the story of the upstate New York farmboy who translated an ancient golden bible revealed to him by an angel was a great tale. During a year at Brigham Young University, I'd come to accept Smith as charming scoundrel and an exceptionally successful confidence man. Smith's colorful career, during which he founded a uniquely American religion, raised the largest private army in the United States, married upwards of forty women, and got rich speculating in real estate, made the adventures of this Jacksonian prophet both astonishing and entertaining. At the time I considered myself an ex-Mormon, but I've since come to believe that being a Mormon is a lot like being Jewish. Once you are one, you are one. That's how it worked out for me, anyway.

After we escaped from the missionary, we returned to our van to take our own tour. Since I did not know how to drive a standard transmission, it fell to Suzy to smoke the clutch getting Prometheus up the boat launch back at Dallas City that morning, and in Nauvoo the wheezing transmission of our ancient van-god finally locked up for good. We arranged to have it towed to Starr's Garage. Suzy set up a lawn chair and waited for the tow to arrive, while I walked to the lower old town where Joseph Smith had built his brick store on the Mississippi shore and his Mansion House on safer ground.

Nauvoo dominated a bend of the Mississippi at the head of rapids that blocked steamboat traffic most of the year until the river was dammed and channelized. At this bend the south-flowing river turned east. Most of the historic buildings were clustered on the lowlands below the temple and the bluff overlooking the Mississippi. A half-mile down a hill and on the river stood the Smith homestead, an original two-story log home with a later attached frame house not far from the water. Next door stood a reconstruction of the enterprising prophet's 1841 Red Brick Store. The graves of Joseph Smith and his older brother Hyrum lay between the buildings and the river. I'd had any number of fantasies about what I would do at the grave, but the simplicity of the site and the humble devotion of the tourists who came to the final resting place of their beloved prophet relieved me of the desire to do anything rash. Love or hate him, you've got to admire Joseph Smith for his audacity, his enduring legacy, and his astonishing life. Suzy once said I was the most American person she'd ever met, but she never met Joseph Smith Jr.

I toured the Mansion House on Main Street, around the corner but not far from the humble homestead on Water Street. Smith and his family moved into the mansion in 1842. The next year the prophet said he would be happy to feed and house so much company for free, but "the cruel and untiring persecution" of his enemies had reduced him "to the necessity of opening 'The Mansion' as a hotel." It offered travelers "the best table accommodations in the city," and "being large and convenient, renders travelers more comfortable than any other place on the upper Mississippi." The mansion was a two-story frame house built in the Federal style that in its glory could entertain 200 people and stable seventy-five horses. Its guest wings had disappeared, but it was still impressive—and, oh, if its walls could speak.

Just to the south of the Mansion House, the Nauvoo House stood a hundred feet from the river. In Mormon scripture the Lord called it "my boarding house which I have commanded you to build for the boarding of strangers." He even directed that the quorum he assigned to build the hotel "shall not receive less than fifty dollars for a share of stock in that house" and should "not be permitted to receive over fifteen thousand dollars stock from any one man." For some odd reason investors failed to seize the opportunity of an eternal lifetime, and when a mob murdered Smith in 1844, three years after this revelation appeared, only the basement and the brick walls of the first story stood beside the Mississippi. To prevent desecration of his grave, his followers secretly buried Smith in the unfinished basement. Eventually his widow built a modest two-story home on the southwest corner of the foundation. The RLDS church now ran it as a youth hostel: such a building, I knew, must have showers.

Our RLDS guide was a quiet, middle-aged gentleman who knew a lot more about Nauvoo than his LDS counterpart. At the end our tour I explained our situation, and he generously offered

to let Suzy and me use the showers, confirming the Lord's pre-
diction that the Nauvoo House would be "a resting-place for the
weary traveler."

I walked back up to town. We left Prometheus to the kind
care of Starr's Garage. We caught a ride with our gear back to the
Nauvoo House, where we took showers that left us feeling mirac-
ulously clean. We thanked our RLDS host for the favor. I'd never
met a real-live Josephite before, and I couldn't resist asking him
a typically impertinent Brighamite question: "Don't you believe
Joseph Smith had more than one wife?"

Our kind host simply chuckled and smiled.

We were now a couple of miles from the main town and the
grain elevator at the Nauvoo Terminal Wharf where we had agreed
to rendezvous with the raft. We trudged down the unpaved Main
Street through cornfields to the head of the bend dragging our
duffel bags. These fields had once been covered with the log shacks
and shanties of the general Mormon population—I didn't know
it at the time, but David Brinton, my Quaker great-great-grand-
father, had once lived there. Not one of these humble dwellings
survives, leaving only the handful of leadership's substantial brick
homes and buildings of the 1840s standing: most of the old town
had vanished in the cornfields. It was hot, and two-ton farm
trucks loaded with corn kicked up dust as they rumbled past us on
their way to dump their loads at the grain elevator. We were about
beat when a trucker who'd just dumped a load of corn at the silo
pulled up next to us. He waved me over to his side of the cab.

I opened the door, and the longhaired driver drawled, "Got
any money?"

"Uh," I said. "No."

"Here," he said. This young knight of the road handed me a
dollar and blazed on down the road.

We walked down to the riverbank and waited for the raft to show up. It was the only time I ever saw the raft from shore: it appeared in the distance as a speck on the horizon and grew in size until it looked like a big packing crate gone adrift. The raft was boxy and looked as awkward as an amphibious aardvark, but what it lacked in beauty it made up in charm. As it beat across the channel from the Iowa shore, I felt a surge of pride.

The next morning we climbed back up the hill to determine the fate of Prometheus. Starr himself had declared the old Chevy dead as a doornail, and we sold it to him for one hundred bucks.

I left my Latter-day Saint heritage behind when we departed Nauvoo the next morning, but more than once on my rowboat trip, I stopped to ponder how I'd gotten myself to such a strange place and situation. I had to ask, "How did a Mormon boy from Utah wind up here?" I've asked myself that same question many times since and started writing a song about it a couple of years later after the corporation's political operatives helped stop the Equal Rights Amendment to the Constitution inches from being ratified:

I'm just a Mormon boy gone bad,
It's hard to tell about the luck I've had.
It makes my Momma sad,
But in my heart I'm glad,
That I'm just a Mormon boy gone bad.

When I was a deacon, the truth I was a seekin',
But you couldn't be a deacon if your light ain't white.
But in these latter days,
They've come a long long ways,
To pickin' on the ERA.

Over the next few days we drifted past Keokuk and its retired sternwheeler, the *George M. Verity*; La Grange with an ancient population and crumbling brick buildings; and Quincy with its spider-web bridge. As we drifted across the Missouri state line, the country became a degree more wild (in 1998, 11,000 acres of it became the Great River National Wildlife Refuge) and several degrees less prosperous. We stopped in Hannibal and took in the Mark Twain sites—the fence Tom Sawyer didn't paint, the Becky Thatcher Book Store, the Huckleberry Finn Cinema, the Becky Thatcher Candy Store, and the Tom Sawyer Real Estate Office. Only the real estate office had the ring of authentic history: Tom Sawyer was born to sell real estate.

Hannibal was depressing. Development had ravaged the riverfront. A junkyard and a huge white grain elevator now dwarfed Cardiff Hill. Below the mouth of the small craft harbor, a drainpipe dumped raw sewage into the river that gave Hannibal life.

When I walked into town during the afternoon to buy some motor oil for the Seahorse, I passed two old men sitting on a park bench. They were those fixtures of southern society, the town drunks. One was old and surprisingly healthy looking and not that drunk, while the other was lean, red-eyed, and very drunk.

"C'mere," said the lean man. "Are you a hippie?" he asked.

"No," I said. "I'm not a hippie." I didn't feel I had the necessary credentials.

"Where ya from?"

"From California."

"You from Haight–Ashbury or whatever that place is?"

"Worse," I said. "I'm from Santa Cruz." I explained about the raft.

"I'm jealous," said the healthy drunk.

"Now's the time to do it," said his companion.

Hannibal was so depressing that we left the next afternoon and tied up behind Shuck Island opposite town. It wasn't Huck Finn's Jackson Island, which was maybe today's Harris Island, a couple of miles below town, but the island was still wild and empty, a lot more like Huck Finn country than the tourist trap Hannibal had become.

We grew more unwashed, unbrushed, and undressed as we

drifted into the Middle South. It was hard to be harried or hurried on a raft that went twenty miles on a good day. With Prometheus gone, we spent all our time in each other's company; someone once observed that almost any group of people, be they a ship's crew or space voyagers, could get along for three weeks, and we did. We each adopted routines to occupy our time, with all of us sharing duties steering from the top of the cabin. Diana remembered crocheting, "watching the trees and water as we floated along." I worked pretty religiously on a daily journal chronicling our adventures. Memories are shape shifters and our indulgences didn't help: "I think I still have holes in my memory from all the pot I smoked," Suzy recalls, "thinking it was a way to get enlightened." On the side of the cabin I had spray painted a quote from Huck Finn: "Other places do seem cramped up and smothery, but a raft don't. You feel mighty free and easy and comfortable on a raft." That was it: free and easy and comfortable.

Above St. Louis we passed through the Chain of Rocks canal and locked through Lock 27, at the last one on the Mississippi. When the river broke loose of the dam, it suddenly came alive. The current, now swollen by the Missouri River, had been sluggish and slow but suddenly swept us forward, unbound and set free. The constant, powerful, silent, gliding current was as invisible as the wind but just as alive. Its confluence with the River of the West transformed the Mississippi. Enormous sucks and boils now marked the river's surface, and the current bucked like a newborn colt, a true river at last. The current caught the raft and sent us hurtling downstream, and we used the outboard to thread through the railroad and highway bridges and cross the river. We headed for the marina, but the owner wanted to charge us 20¢ a foot to tie up, so we tied up to the old cobblestone waterfront, which still had its steamboat mooring rings in place.

The next day we picked up the Army Corps of Engineers maps

of the river from Cairo to the Gulf of Mexico. We spent the rest
of the morning wandering the big city streets. Near a big hotel we
stopped to listen to a blind black accordion player when suddenly
the Winnepeg Police Pipe and Bugle Corps marched out of a
nearby department store (probably Stix, Baer & Fuller), bagpipes
blaring and kilts flying in the breeze. They seemed to be part of
a salute to Canada, but I doubt the poor accordion player ever
figured out what hit him.

That afternoon we all went to see *Easy Rider,* the hit movie of
the summer of '69. We thought it was the greatest film ever made,
though it did give us pause to think about our destination: The
South. Not long after we got back to the raft, a TV news crew
showed up and interviewed us. The newscaster was Cal Condon,
a somber man in a gray suit who seemed totally devoid of a sense
of humor. He shot questions at us rapid-fire, and we babbled back
incoherent answers about how this was a really BIG river. That
evening Suzy and I found a television in the shabby lobby of the
Baltimore Hotel and watched the news with a morose older gent
who looked like a down-on-his-luck salesman. He seemed aggravated at the company. When we came on the news, he looked
from the set to us and back at the set and then back at us. He
never said anything.

We cast off early into a clear blue morning, riding the wild
current down past the warehouses and factories of St. Louis. I
looked for the Southern Comfort distillery, since its label read that
it was "Distilled on the Banks of the Mississippi in St. Louis," but
if that was true, I saw no evidence of it. We did see the hulk of a
Spanish caravel, a replica of Columbus' *Santa Maria*, which had
followed some improbable course to wind up stranded high and
dry on a wharf in the American heartland. By ten we were out of
the industrial district. In two more hours we had left the riverfront
mansions behind.

Before the van died, Rick had bought a chicken for a buck fifty at a farmhouse. All the scrambled egg mix we were eating probably moved him to visions of fresh eggs. We named the chicken Erica and waited for the eggs to show up. They never did. Erica did not like raft life particularly, if at all. She spent most of her time in a screened box because when she ran loose she defecated indiscriminately. She was a big, old, tough white Leghorn laying hen with an awful personality, but she certainly didn't deserve the knocks that fate delivered in her dotage. Her only consolation must have been that Rick truly loved her. She fell into the river on the way to Nauvoo, and Rick jumped in and rescued her.

We had agreed we'd eat Erica not long after she came aboard, but somehow we never got around to it. That damn chicken went three or four hundred miles down the river with us, but that morning at St. Louis she made a big mistake and shat all over Mario and Diana's bed. Early that afternoon a tremendous wind began to blow up the river, churning the water into whitecaps. Waves broke over the bow and spray washed to the top of the cabin. The barrels and timbers of the raft groaned under the strain, while the cabin acted as a sail, pushing us back upriver. We finally tied up to a rocky beach on the Missouri shore and waited a while for the wind to die down, but it continued unabated and sealed Erica's fate. We were real city kids. None of us had ever killed anything heavier than a fly. We gave the chicken a trial and condemned her to death. Figuring out how to terminate Erica took a lot of thinking. We got some twine and tied up the chicken's feet and slipped a noose around her neck. Mario held the legs and I stretched the neck over a log. Rick hefted the axe, measured off the blow, got ready to swing, and then laid down the axe.

"I can't do it," he said, and walked away shaking his head. Mario later told me he had visions of the raft sailing into New Orleans completely encrusted with chicken shit. He seized the axe and

lopped off Erica's head. I ran down the beach yelling, followed by
the headless chicken. To top it off, we fried Erica: fried laying hen is
like nothing else in this world, except maybe stewed baseballs.

Below St. Louis the liberated river deepened, narrowed, and
picked up speed. As it surged southward, it became poorer and less
populated. The towns were fewer, funkier, and farther apart. We saw
river walls and dying main streets and heard soft rural Missouri accents. At night we sought protection behind towheads or in chutes, a
foot above the rushing water, dreaming about rivers only to wake up
and drift all day down the immense and mysterious river. We drew
closer to the weather and nature and ourselves every day. We saw an
America we hadn't known existed, a nation of vast farm fields that
spread to distant horizons and isolated small towns off lost highways
and dead railroads, and far from the interstate highways that were
becoming the new rivers of commerce.

We began to fight. Cramped together on the raft all day, we got
on each other's nerves. We argued about the purpose of the trip. I
thought it was to go from one end of the river to the other—from
Rock Island to New Orleans. For me it really was "New Orleans
or Bust," like the motto spray-painted on one side of the raft. Rick
and Mario had a different idea. They thought the trip ought to be
fun. Such a notion had never really crossed my mind. I'd expected
it to be hard; it might be fun too, but that was not its purpose. The
journey was much more than merely a pleasure cruise to me. It was
my coming-of-age ritual, my vision quest, my Odyssey—and New
Orleans was the goal. To stop short would leave me an unfinished
man in an age when manhood meant way too much. I wasn't against
having fun, so long as we had fun all the way to New Orleans.

As we approached the Ohio River, I began to suspect that Rick,
Mario, and Diana weren't going to make it all the way, so I pressed
on south hoping to get in as many miles as possible before they
jumped ship. The tension brought me closer to Suzy, who shared

my determination. Her touch and smile offered consolation and relief, for I trusted her more than I trusted myself. I knew that if we had to go the last miles into New Orleans in a rubber dingy, we would do it together.

One afternoon below St. Louis, Rick called up to me while I was steering. "Hey," he said. "Let's pull over and tie up."

"Tie up?" I said. The weather was clear and the afternoon was young. "Why the hell should we tie up?"

"Hey," he said. "What's the purpose of this trip, anyway?"

I wasn't ready for a philosophical discussion, so I said, "Later." After we'd tied up that night, we gathered on the foredeck and had a long talk by the light of a kerosene lantern. "It's pretty damn clear to me what we're doing," I said. "We're going to New Orleans."

"You're serious, huh?" said Mario.

"You bet. New Orleans or bust. I mean it."

"Well what's the rush? You're ruining the trip for the rest of us," said Rick.

"What?" I said.

"Look," said Mario. "You've turned this trip into a big ego trip for yourself. It's not any fun for the rest of us."

He had a point, but I wasn't listening. I was young, I was inexperienced, I was a jerk who insisted he was right. "Did I ever promise anybody it was going to be fun? I sure as hell never expected this to be a pleasure cruise."

"I think you're losing your marbles," said Mario.

"What's the point of fighting over all this?" said Suzy, trying to keep the peace. "We've just got to keep going one day at a time." We didn't settle anything and now divided into two camps. I was sure that the other camp would decamp before long.

In St. Louis we'd heard about an all-you-can-eat restaurant called Ma Hales. Early on a Sunday afternoon, we reached Grand Tower, Illinois, once the lair of river pirates who lurked below *La Tour* until the army in 1803 drove them out from Tower Rock Island. We were about as hungry as piranhas, and we decided to check out Ma's place and her all-you-can-eat $2.50 Sunday dinner. Grand Tower was a small town nestled under colorful bluffs and it didn't take us long to find the restaurant. Ma Hales occupied an old house filled with red gingham-covered tables. The one meal on the menu was served family-style, and that meal contained about everything that's good to eat in America—sweet corn and beans and peas and carrots and mashed potatoes and yams and chicken fried like I'd never tasted before. We ate until we could eat no more.

That evening we took a swim in the river to wash away some of our accumulated mud and all got a dose of dysentery. Dirty weather hit us at about the same time as the trots did. The adversity did none of us any good, but it hit Mario and Diana hardest. Mario seemed to hover near death for several days. We'd come 600 miles and were now sick, cold, dirty, and tired, and Ma Hales reminded us we weren't eating so well besides. Mario laid on the bow in complete misery. Rick and I fought over how the trip should be run. All these bad feelings came to a head a day before we reached Cairo.

Come evening we had tied up to a sandbar in low water. While we were securing the raft, two fishermen—Hal and Dell—walked over and began to talk to us about the trip in a soft southern Missouri drawl. "What kids won't do these days," was Hal's comment on our adventure. Dell had worked on towboats and told us more about *America*. Suzy asked about fishing, and the two men gave her some good pointers.

"You ain't caught nothing yet?" asked Hal.

We hadn't. "Well, I've got two perch I suppose I can let you have," said Hal, and he showed us how to clean and cook the fish over an open fire. It turned out to be the best meal we'd made on the trip.

After the fishermen left, the river began to rise. Rick decided to take the boat around the end of the sandbar and anchor her in quiet water. As he was going full throttle around the point, the raft slammed into a hard-packed submerged sandbank. Rick threw the engine into reverse to pull the raft off and the lead port barrel, bent like a crushed beer can, popped out.

Spitting mad, I jumped in the river and swam after the deformed barrel. By the time I got the barrel back to shore, I was wet besides being mad. I didn't say anything to Rick for the rest of the evening. He crawled off into the weeds to sleep, and Suzy and I used the privacy to talk over our situation.

"Look," said Suzy. "Rick's a jerk. Don't let it bother you. He won't last much longer anyway."

I agreed but didn't feel much better. Thinking about the bent barrel and the crippled raft, I couldn't sleep. I got up and built a fire on the beach. I thought that if I heated the barrel, convection might pop it back into shape. I propped the barrel over the flames and sat thinking in the dark. I thought about all the hassles we were having and I began to worry that the raft would come undone and leave us high and dry. The fire burned under the barrel for a long time and it got plenty hot, but it maintained its crooked shape. At last the fast-rising river drowned the fire and I went back to sleep on the raft.

The next day was one damn cliffhanger after another. The river had risen two or three feet during the night and now the swift, mean current was choked with the tree trunks and uprooted stumps and random junk: flotsam and jetsam always filled the river when it was rising. There wasn't much wind, but the day started out with a dismal drizzle falling from low-hanging clouds. The raft limped along like a crippled duck, water washing up over the bow. I figured that if we could get to Cairo, we could buy a new drum—the old one was clearly beyond repair—and get the raft ship-shape again, but now it was easy to imagine the raft disintegrating into the kind of floating garbage that littered the bank of the rising river.

Mario was too laid up to help with the steering, and about noon Rick came up and told me he planned to leave when we got to Cairo. I almost told him that now that he'd wrecked the raft he might as well leave, but I simply said, "Good."

We tied up a couple of miles above Cairo. Suzy and I walked into town to buy a new barrel. We found one at Abe Solomon's junkyard and still have fond recollections of Mr. Solomon. One of his workers gave us a ride out to the end of the road where we started pushing the barrel down a railroad track to the river. We met Mario, Diana, and Rick going into town, but they wouldn't help us push the barrel back down to the raft. "It hardly seems worth the walk back," said Rick. This got me so pissed off I resolved to remount the barrel by myself.

I had a plan. I figured if I filled the barrel with enough water to cut its buoyancy in half, I could force it under the raft and then siphon the water out. This was a great theory, but it was rough to put into practice. I got the barrel and siphon hose ready, stripped down to a pair of sneakers, and climbed into the river.

It was cold, very cold. I dove under the raft and got a fish-eye view of the underside of *Phillip W. Bell*. I stuck my head up into the air space created by the barrels: I looked down the long dark row and except for the missing barrel everything seemed in pretty good shape. I worked as fast as I could, but before five minutes were up my hands (and other extremities) were blue. The new barrel slipped in pretty easily, and I began siphoning out the water. By the time I was done and had started nailing plumber's tape around the barrel to hold it in place, I could barely move my hands. A human icicle climbed back onto the raft.

I didn't stop shaking for about half an hour. The rest of the crew returned and Rick announced he had decided to stay. My only comment consisted of an obscenity.

Since I couldn't get all the water out of it, my patch job with the barrel didn't work very well. The next morning we swept down past Cairo Point with water still washing over the bow. After the weather cleared up, we found that our gas barrel was nearly empty. We cut the engine and spent the rest of the day drifting slowly down to Hickman, Kentucky. In the early evening we landed and set about refueling and refitting the new barrel.

I was so mad that I stood on the shore and let Rick and Mario get wet. This time it went pretty smoothly. They lifted the bow up onto a cement block, cut loose the barrel, emptied it of water, secured the barrel's plug, and remounted the barrel. The raft was as good as new.

Our relationships were not so easy to patch up. The weather didn't help much, staying gray and cold through the next few days. The countryside grew more southern by the hour, enhancing the paranoia we'd acquired watching *Easy Rider* in St. Louis.

Between New Madrid and Caruthersville, nightfall caught us on an open stretch of channel with no good protected place to tie up. A beautiful afternoon had been capped with a spectacular sunset that painted the long streaks of high clouds fire red while the reflecting river turned to blood. We pulled up hard against the revetment on the Tennessee shore and secured the raft. I tried to make peace with Mario.

We climbed into the plastic house on the foredeck. We got a little high and the barriers that had come up between us since Cairo seemed to fall. I leveled with Mario.

"Look," I said. "I've been convinced for a long time that you weren't going to make it, that you and Diana would leave Suzy and me to finish the trip."

"What about Rick?"

"Screw Rick. I hope he keeps his promise and leaves at Memphis."

"You think we can finish the trip without him?"

"Well, it won't be easy, but it won't be impossible, either."

"I don't know about that. You think you could fix the motor when it breaks down?"

"I think I could find a way. But screw Rick, what about yourself? You got plans to jump ship?"

"Look," he said. "I'll make you a promise: barring some major catastrophe, I'll stick it out."

I felt better about Mario than I had in weeks. We went into the cabin and ate dinner. Suzy and I were tired and we turned in early. We'd just started lovin' when Rick came back into the cabin. I figured he came to get something, but he settled down in the kitchen and started to read.

"Uh, Rick," I said. "Could you give us about twenty minutes alone?"

"God, at least you could have said something before I got my boots off." He didn't move.

I figured what the hell and started kissing Suzy again. She didn't respond, and at last she whispered, "He ruins everything." That tore it for me. I could put up with a lot from Rick, but this was the limit.

"Cut us a break, Rick."

"Look," he said. "I'm gone every other night, can't you abstain for one night?"

"Get the hell out of here, Rick."

"No."

We yelled at each other some more, but I managed to cool down and made one last ditch effort to iron things out.

"You're ruining the trip for me," said Rick.

"Ah, come on. How can I be that big an influence on the trip?"

"I don't know," he said. "You just are."

We haggled on, about steering duties and knot tying. I conceded every point but one: the trip was going on to New Orleans. "If you don't like that, you can leave," I said.

"I just might," he said.

"Promises, promises," said Suzy.

Next morning I got up, started the Seahorse and pulled out from shore, then climbed atop the cabin and began steering. The Mississippi wound and twisted back and forth and a cold wind blew out of the north. It was cold enough to hint that winter was approaching. As the morning warmed up, the overcast broke up, and it promised to become a beautiful day.

I could hear squabbling below decks, and toward mid-morning Suzy came up to give me the news. Despite last night's pow-wow, the rest of the crew had decided to abandon ship in Memphis. I figured it was inevitable.

Rick and Mario came up to take over steering just before we got to Caruthersville. We had to land to pick up supplies and mail, but we ran out of gas as we were running past the town, and we nearly missed the place. We wound up landing at Caruthersville's junkyard.

We left Suzy to guard the raft, and the rest of us made the short hike into town. I hurried ahead of the crew, looking for a john. I found one in a gas station. When I came out, Mario and Rick and Diana were sitting across the road.

"What's up?" I said.

"We're thinking about taking a bus into Memphis," said Diana.

"Good," I said. I went to the post office, picked up our mail, and went back to the raft while the deserters looked for bus station.

That's how I saw it at the time, anyway. Hindsight, a lot of water under the bridge, and more information provide insight into why our comrades decided to pack it in—and help me appreciate what an arrogant piece of work I was at the time.

Long ago and far away, the contented cows of Carnation Corporation produced a perfectly awful concoction that came with flat wooden spoons in cardboard cups holding about six bites of something they sold as vanilla ice cream. Mario, Diana, and Rick bought one at a gas station and "all had two bites," Mario recalled. He "felt the ice cream go in, pause for a moment in my stomach, and proceed down my intestines and out the other end." He did not see how they could get well without medical intervention, and medical services in rural America were almost as awful then as they are now. He told me he was going to take Diana back home, where his mother was a nurse and her father was a doctor, and get her well.

When I got back to the raft, I told Suzy the news. She shared my anger and sense of betrayal. "The sooner the better," she said. "Good riddance." We began loading their stuff onto shore. We'd soon built quite a pile. We must have loaded half a ton of gear off the raft: it rode noticeably higher in the water. We'd pretty much finished when they returned.

I felt relieved that the hassling was over but an immense sadness, too. Mario and I had been friends for years, and now it looked like it was over. I told him, "Tell the people out in California I'm crazy and determined to get to New Orleans."

"I hope you make it," said Mario. "Because if you don't, it'll mean you're dead."

I cast off and clambered up to the top of the cabin, while Suzy started the Seahorse. We pulled out into the current and I turned once and waved goodbye to the vanishing figures standing on the forlorn bank. I didn't look back.

That afternoon we saw our first cotton fields.

VII

NEW ORLEANS OR BUST

The overcast broke up not long after our comrades departed, and the rich warm sun let Suzy and me know that we were South at last. I remember the next weeks like a dream, drifting down all those miles, through the rich autumn southern countryside.

We hit hard water immediately after leaving Caruthersville. Wing dams—projections of rock that slow and deflect the current away from the banks—lined both bends between the Missouri and Tennessee banks. For a while it looked like we too might end our voyage at the Caruthersville junkyard. Whitewater marked the dams, and I cranked the engine from the short stern deck, trying to pull away from the shore and into the current. The trusty motor worked its 5.5-cylinder heart out, and when the current finally dragged us over the end of the dams, there was enough water for the raft to slide over the rocks and make it out to the channel.

We drifted a ways down the river until we spotted a ferry crossing on the Tennessee shore. At New Madrid the wind had carried away our maps so we had no idea of where we were. We put in to see if we could find a place that sold white gas for our Coleman: after we left Caruthersville, Suzy had noticed we were low on fuel for the stove. The crossing was a laid back deep-country place. The ferryboat could only handle two or three cars at a time and apparently had to wait a while on the Missouri side for that many vehicles to show up. We found a few folks waiting for the ferry to return to the Tennessee shore, including an old country doctor. When I walked up, he said, "Well, hello Huck Finn."

"Hello," I said. "Can you tell us where we are?"

"Yessir," he said. "You're near a place called Cottonwood Point."

"Thanks," I said.

"No need for thanks," said the doctor. "You don't meet many adventurers these days."

We followed the road leading from the ferry looking for a store but only found empty cotton fields. The dying weeds along the roadside were littered with balls of cotton left over from the harvest. Frame houses so old and worn they must have been held in place by inertia alone lined the poplar-shaded road. The air was heavy with Indian summer. We didn't find any white gas, but on that lost stretch of backcountry Tennessee road, we found the American South.

Adventurers. Even the locals thought that's what we had become. That night we talked about the trip past and the trip to come. We speculated about New Orleans and how good it would feel to get there, though we were still not half the distance between Rock Island and New Orleans.

"You know, we're going to get there," said Suzy. I believed her.

Alone with each other, Suzy and I were crazy in love. I'd never been in closer harmony with another person. I can no more recall the emotions of those October weeks in Tennessee and Arkansas, now dreamlike and distant, than ashes can recall the green wood. I do remember we were very much in love.

We fell in love with the South, too, the voluptuous green countryside, the fine weather, the slow time, the music of soft southern voices. The region sometimes seemed a parody of itself; soon there really was Spanish moss in the oak trees, there really were magnolias and elegant white-pillared plantation mansion houses and ram-shackle sharecropper shacks hidden behind the levees. We saw wood storks and white whooping cranes and flocks of ducks and geese taking the Mississippi Flyway to the tropics. Spiders floated on the breeze piloting webs that rode the wind like parachutes above the great river. God knows where they got the ability to fly their silky gliders, but we'd see arachnids far out in the middle of the river, half a mile or more from shore. Occasionally these arachnidan aviators landed on the raft, a bad fate because they sometimes landed in her hair, and Suzy squashed them when she found them. The meandering river grew deeper and older and cast its spell over us completely, bewitching us with the feel of the wind in our hair, the sun on our skin and the constant rustle of flowing water all around.

Our fear of the South melted slowly but completely. "So many people helped us," Suzy recalls. Long hair was no big deal—we were, after all, the right color. I had one brush with fear one evening in a jungle-covered part of the state of Mississippi. A skiff came pounding up the river, her aluminum belly beating against the water. Two duck hunters lounged in the skiff, and when they sighted our raft, they slowed down and circled around us twice, coming in closer as they circled. At last they brought the skiff up to the side of the raft and stared up at me with vacant-eyed wonder. They were both drunk and had shotguns in their laps.

"Howdy," I said.

They stared at me wordlessly for a while. Then one of them said, "You want a drink?"

"Sure," I said, and they tossed me a bottle of Jim Beam.

Above Memphis we encountered our first truly big towboats. All the stories we'd heard about the behemoths of the Federal Barge Line, *America* and her sister ship, *United States*, made us wonder if the raft would survive an encounter with either. We'd met fishermen who described the two boats as four-stacked, black-and-yellow creatures pushing more than fifty barges, irresistibly and unstoppably. "What should we do when we see one?" I had asked.

"Hell, son," said the fisherman, "that's easy. Soon as you see one of those boats, you head for shore, git your ass on the high ground, and put as much distance between you and the river as you can."

One afternoon we passed the Third Chickasaw Bluff, which I recall as the loveliest spot on the lower Mississippi. We were relaxing in the sun on top of the cabin when we spotted a large tow far down the river. With binoculars I could see that it was painted black and yellow and was pushing thirty-eight barges.

I put the binoculars down. "It's the *America*," I said to Suzy.

"Quick," she said, "Get off the river!" It would have been a good plan if we'd had someplace to take shelter, but there were no islands or towheads in this narrow stretch, so we rode on down toward what looked like a smoke-belching water-borne dragon. The towboat loomed larger the closer we came to it until we could read her name: *United States*. We rolled slowly past her bows and her long bank of barges. Then the towboat herself, pushing her load like an enslaved steamboat, ran directly by us, huge and mechanical, the deep vibrating bass of her engines pounding across the water. The prop wake writhed behind her like a wounded copperhead, the haystack waves cresting as high as the roof our raft's cabin. Wakes and cross wakes wracked the river for two miles below our encounter with the towboat, as turbulent as a storm, as if sharks and alligators were fighting to the death under the river's surface. The raft lurched through the turbulence like a battleship, knocking the contents of our kitchen around but doing no serious damage. Success inspired us: we chanted, "We made it!" over and over, hugging each other close and closer.

Not far south of Caruthersville we encountered an exquisite white trimaran with its main and mizzen masts stepped down and tied to the decks of its outriggers. A beautiful brunette stood on deck while her handsome young companion steered. "There were two people in sight, a girl and a boy," she wrote in her journal on October 16, "who from a distance looked pretty young." (We did up close, too.) They read the name and slogan scrawled on the side of the cabin, "PHILIP W. BELL—Rock Island to New Orleans," and assumed I was Phil. She gave us a peace sign, and as they came closer, we began shouting back and forth. Hoping to replace the charts the wind had carried off in New Madrid, I asked if they had an extra set of maps, which of course they didn't. They circled us twice, taking pictures.

Memphis, Helena, Greenville, Vicksburg, Natchez—we stopped at all the river towns but usually didn't stay very long. We'd begun to feel uneasy about almost any sort of civilized place. It was all in our heads—we were in the heart of America, not the wilderness—but there was something completely free about being on the river. Even though settled for millennia, "civilized" for two hundred years and bounded by levees thousands of miles long, here the river still had a wild heart. When we were on the water, we felt alone together and untouchable. We got close to the wind and the water and the slow steady rhythms of dawn, dusk, and dark; the music of the river sang in our ears twenty-four hours a day.

In the towns we met kind and friendly people, but we also ran into cops, hostile rednecks, drunks, and the general tension that lies right below the surface of any small southern town. We got to Memphis on a blazing hot October 18, a Saturday afternoon, and bought a new set of maps from an Army Corps of Engineers supply boat. We walked up into town, checked the post office, and stumbled into a black protest march on Main Street. The marchers made a fine parade, but the motorcycle cops looked like they wanted to kill something. We'd planned to spend the night, but we took a short look at Beale Street, walked back to the raft, and fled Memphis, hoping to hide in a bayou.

Thanks to our incredible luck and the bonds of friendship, Suzy and I established a relationship that evening that would last half a century. When we "chugged right up on the beach" of the lee side of Cow Island at mile 715, we found the white trimaran riding at anchor. I had apparently encountered the couple on board, Roger and Martha Goodale Pretzer, earlier that day at the post office but don't seem to have recognized them.

The lushly forested inlet tucked in behind the island lay right above the Mississippi state line, extended about a mile north into Tennessee's Shelby County, and was filled with cranes and egrets. We exchanged greetings, and after finishing dinner, I called over, "Would you like to come over and we could talk?" Roger responded, "Yeah, but how?" Since none of us could walk on water, they invited us to tie up alongside the anchored trimaran, and we did.

"O wad some Power the giftie gie us," Robert Burns wrote about 1785, "To see oursels as ithers see us." Martha's journal did that. "Bill was dressed in blue denim right up to his hat, which looked like a Dutch boy's cap, though I think the intention was riverboat captain. He had a red scarf around his neck. His blond hair hung evenly below his cap and he wore a mustache," she wrote. "Suzy had beautiful, long light brown hair, worn loose and parted in the middle and her clothing was quite conventional, running to sweatshirts, jeans or shorts, and sneakers." After we introduced ourselves, we went below deck and Martha popped some popcorn.

We talked for hours. I claimed we had survived many hardships, including living off our fifty "pound bag of rice, a few canned goods, and dehydrated eggs," and being very low on cash. In most towns, Suzy said, we "were sneered at or just outright laughed at, both for the raft, and for Bill's appearance," but she joked about being put on television in St. Louis. Martha noted I claimed "the trip so far had very much changed them both."

Roger had built the boat in his garage in Ohio; he said he had driven 20,000 screws putting it together. He and Martha had come through Chicago, down the Illinois River to the Mississippi, and now were often making more than 100 miles a day on their way to New Orleans and eventually Florida via the Intercoastal Waterway. We spent the evening swapping tales of the river. I must have appeared jealous of the beautifully crafted trimaran because Roger assured us we'd taken a better approach. "Look at it this way. You run your raft onto a sandbar or snag, all you've got to do is push it off and roll on down the river. You'd have to really stretch your imagination to sink her. If I sink this baby," he said as he lovingly tapped the boat's bulwark, "I'm out $20,000 and two years of my life." As the evening wound down, we gave them a tour of the raft's cabin. "It was dark enough that we couldn't see much detail," Martha noted, "but there were dozens of things hanging from the ceiling, a built-in shelf or two, mattresses in one corner, and mostly bare walls since leaks in the roof caused the walls to become soaking wet," Martha wrote. I told her of my plan to write a novel about our river trip.

We left the raft tied to the trimaran for the rest of the night. At 2:15 a.m., Roger woke me up, for the current had cast both vessels adrift into the far side of the cove. I untied the raft from their craft, and the raft "drifted rapidly into the trees with much crackling and crunching." They anchored, but the trimaran "continued to float around in circles, being sometimes in the trees, and later out in the middle of the cove." They heard what sounded "like medium-sized boulders being dropped into the water." The best explanation Roger could come up with came from Twain's *Life on the Mississippi*, which described huge catfish measuring six feet or more that dwelt in the river depths, along with alligator gar that can reach nine feet and 350 pounds but are still commonly caught at six feet and 160 pounds. (I still recall that one of the details that hooked me on history back in elementary school came from Jacques Marquette's account of exploring the Mississippi with Louis Joliet in 1673, when he described a giant catfish that bumped his canoe as a "monster with the head of a tiger, the nose of a wildcat, and whiskers.")

The next morning our new friends were ready to go at 8:00 a.m. Martha played reveille on her trumpet "to get Suzy and Bill up, or at least let them know we were leaving." We didn't hear it, and the sleek and swift trimaran soon left us behind, but our paths would cross again.

A day or two later below Helena, Arkansas, we camped out in a chute that cut off from the meandering main river. Being out of the main channel, I'd expected we wouldn't have too much barge traffic to disturb our slumber, but the chute cut four or five miles off the channel's route around the meander, and lots of barges passed us during the night. There were no trees growing along the beach where we'd camped, so I tied up to stakes driven in the sandy ground, a lame way to secure the raft. During the night, passing towboats dislodged the stakes, and we wound up untied, caught in an eddy that spun the raft around in circles like flotsam in a whirlpool.

Suzy woke me up. "The raft's adrift," she said, shaking me out of a deep sleep. I stepped out onto the stern and looked out at the spinning, moon-gilded river. I was casual (and sleepy) enough to simply start the engine and drive the raft into shore where I drove deeper stakes and moored the raft again.

Morning came on strong and cold. We pushed out onto a smooth, dark river before the sun came up and watched the sky turn red and the river turn blue. The only trace of the previous day's bad weather was a few clouds scattered across the sky. As the sun rose, it warmed the raft, and we boomed along on a strong, swollen current.

For breakfast, Suzy usually cooked dehydrated scrambled eggs on our last modern convenience, the work-worn Coleman stove. The morning passed quickly, gliding through the southern jungle. About noon we crossed another imaginary line, leaving Arkansas and reaching Louisiana at last. The scenery grew more southern by the mile. Sometimes scrub-like willows covered the banks, growing thick as needles in a pincushion, but usually there was a confusion of cottonwoods, pines, magnolias, and now tall, wide-spreading oaks draped in Spanish moss. Almost once an hour we passed a large towboat, and early one afternoon we passed the beautiful white towboat *Mississippi* pushing a vast load of forty barges. We saw several handsome Army Corps of Engineers vessels, often repairing the endlessly deteriorating revetments that shored up the riverbank, some dredging the channel. Every once in a while cabin cruisers wallowed past us, loaded with retirees bound for Florida. They always left behind the gift of a rocking wake. Sometimes, for hours, we'd have the river all to ourselves.

Suzy and I took turns steering, and even when we weren't on watch, we kept company on the cabin top. We talked and read aloud to each other and sang songs together. Often the long hours were slow and unchanging enough to be boring, but the simple pace of the days—rising with the sun, drifting through the day, and going to bed when it got dark—agreed with both of us.

That afternoon a wake hit us broadside, and we heard a crash from the cabin below. Suzy went down to survey the damage and found our Coleman stove lying in pieces on the deck—so much for modern conveniences. Suzy tried to put it back together and, failing that, decided to see if she could make the contraption work by liberally dousing it with fuel. Soon there was smoke wafting its way topside. I thought, "God, she's set the raft on fire!"

"Don't worry," she called up. "The fire extinguisher works fine!"

By late afternoon we'd had our best run of the trip, seventy-five miles, and we'd made it to the bayou that led up to Greenville, Mississippi. The Corps of Engineers had changed the Mississippi's course forty years earlier and cut off Greenville from the river, so the town now lay six miles up a backwater. We wanted to go to visit the legendary home of the Delta Blues and actual home of planter-poet William Alexander Percy, who described "the great river, the shifting unappeasable god of the country, feared and loved, the Mississippi," which every few years "rises like a monster from its bed and pushes over its banks to vex and sweeten the land it has made." We needed to get supplies and replace our stove parts, but the current was against us. We landed and began walking through the tangled forest that covered the bank. After a couple of miles we came to a compound of trailers that could have been the modern home of the Snopes clan. The residents had decorated the trailers in early hound dog, and they told us it was still three miles to town. We gave up on Greenville and returned to the raft.

We rounded out of the inlet and bought some necessities at a boat store at the mouth of the bayou. We pulled out into the channel and dropped below a sandbar where we made camp. The sun was almost down, and there was no good place to build a fire, so Suzy made up an old reliable, tuna sandwiches, for dinner. We sat in the cabin and read for a while by the light of our kerosene lanterns. Although we usually tumbled into bed exhausted, we made love almost every night.

We caught up with Roger and Martha at Vicksburg about on October 23 after chugging up the Yazoo River and docking above the *Sprague*, the world's largest steam-powered sternwheeler. The city had bought "Big Mama," as she was known, for a dollar and now used her as a tourist attraction and museum. Roger came to greet us, and then Suzy and I set out on an unsuccessful quest for a shower. We met them again outside the Tourist Information Center and walked over to the Old Courthouse Museum but balked at paying the dollar admission. We began hiking to the Vicksburg National Military Park when a cop pulled up to the curb and accosted us for identification. Only Roger had any, so we told him our names and explained we had boats tied up at the Sprague. We toured the visitors' center at the battlefield, which was free, and listened to a recording about the history of the siege. Martha felt she could have been dispensed with it, since young Bagley "had every action, advance, retreat, general, company, date, hour, and battle between his two young ears and was a terrific tour guide." I attribute my later astonishing success as a historian to the infectious enthusiasm that impressed Martha that afternoon. I was "fascinated by the many wars that have taken place since the beginning of time and [was] so familiar with many of them that he could have been there, taking it all down with a movie camera." I claimed to know the "Revolutionary War and the War of 1812 even better than the Civil War," she wrote in her engaging journal.

Martha invited us to dinner again on the trimaran—Vienna sausages, mashed potatoes with sour cream sauce, petits pois, tossed green salad, and cookies, which she termed "real gourmet boat dining." Roger then "gave a two hour monologue of army and YMCA camp stories, and Bill told some of his," she recorded. "Suzy and I just sat there and provided the audience feeling." Oh, what times! Oh, what customs!

The next morning the night watchman came around and collected docking fees. "He probably got his biggest thrills of the day catching big, rich cruisers trying to evade the fee," Martha observed. Roger paid up, but Martha nonchalantly walked to where we'd tied up the raft at the far end of the *Sprague* and woke us up. She warned us "to just untie and quietly drift away," for we had told her of our vanishing cash problem. "The getaway was successful." (The *Sprague* herself was in her twilight years, for on tax-day in

April 1974, she caught fire and burned to the waterline, though her enormous red sternwheel survived.)

Next afternoon we found the trimaran at "a pretty and quiet area that had a perfect spot for beaching." We "ambled in around 4:15 p.m.," landed on the same narrow sandbar opposite the trimaran, and invited them join us for dinner. Suzy collected wood, built a campfire inside our broken Coleman stove, and made spaghetti sauce, while Martha boiled the noodles on her kitchen's built-in white gas stove. Our lively party broke up about 8:00 p.m. under a beautiful full moon.

We actually made it to Natchez before they did the next morning and nestled the raft into the trees near the public doc. We climbed up the bluff from Natchez Under-the-Hill, didn't care much for what we saw, and went back down and hit the river. When the trimaran overtook and passed us, Roger handed over a pan cover we had left behind the previous evening. He and I tried to arrange a rendezvous, but we would not see them again until after almost a week of further adventures.

Within a few days we reached the Old River Control Structure, the complicated confluence where Old Devil River left the state of Mississippi and both shores became Louisiana. It was complicated because it was where the Red River, the Atchafalaya, and the Mississippi's uncomfortable and unconventional union came together. Attempting to manage the unmanageable Old Devil, in 1963 the Army Corps of Engineers had finished pouring more concrete than was then contained in any other structure on Planet Earth.

Engineers have been mucking with Mother Nature at this spot since legendary steamboat captain Henry Shreve dug his mile-long Shreve's Cut in 1831. (In 1814 Shreve's *Enterprise* brought a cargo of munitions from Pittsburg for Andrew Jackson, making her the first steamboat to travel down the Ohio River to New Orleans. Shreve arrived the day after Jackson defeated the British Army on the Glorious Eighth of January in 1815, only to be tossed in jail for violating Robert Fulton's purported patent. He got out in time to make the *Enterprise* the first steamboat to go *up* the Mississippi River against the current.) Near the confluence of the Red, the Atchafalaya, and the Mississippi rivers, Shreve cut through the neck of Turnbull Bend, an aggravating twenty-mile meander. Shreve's cut created a ditch that flowed east to the Mississippi until 1839, when unblocking the Atchafalaya River caused the Father of Waters to flow east when the Mississippi was high and west to the Atchafalaya when the Red River was higher. By 1950 the Atchafalaya River was capturing 30 percent of the Mississippi's flow, so the Corps of Engineers began building the Old River Control Structure to divert the Atchafalaya from its straight shot to the Gulf of Mexico. Otherwise, the Atchafalaya would become the new Mississippi, stranding Baton Rouge and New Orleans high and dry.

The river had been narrowing all day, picking up speed as it slimmed down. The maps showed the Old River Control Structure and the Louisiana State Penitentiary, known as Angola, named after the plantation that once occupied Turnbull Bend. They seemed to occupy the same ground. We could tell it would be a tight place to pass barge traffic of any size, and the passage grew tighter as it flowed downriver. The chart showing the control structure warned, "Tows and other vessels should navigate as far as possible from this area and as close to the left descending bank of the Mississippi River as safety will permit."

We were heading into a bend where both banks of the Mississippi became Louisiana when we sighted the great black-and-yellow towboat coming up to the Angola Ferry. Her bow alone was six barges wide. I sought the protection of a drowned sandbar, but the current was so fast, it swept us downriver before we could reach shelter. I hugged the port side of the channel as closely as I could. *America* rolled past in the narrows the charts called Shreves Cutoff, smoke pouring from each of her four stacks, her wakes rising above us on top of the raft's cabin. We swept around the bend as we passed the towboat and encountered miles of turbulent water looking as if it had been blasted by a hurricane. The raft buckled and pitched through the maelstrom, but we had survived *America*, the worst, we figured, that the river had to offer.

VIII

OLD DEVIL RIVER

Its ending was the craziest time of all the trip. Our idyll on the wild river ended abruptly at Baton Rouge. As we rounded the last point above the city, fifteen miles of straight, narrow river channel opened up before us. It was a desolation. Ocean-going freighters from all over the world jammed the river, many stained rust-red with nitrates, some riding at anchor in mid-river, some nestled up to huge steel docks. The shore was an unbroken landscape of oil refineries and industries that belched fire and smoke from a forest of smokestacks. Rising above this dismal plain was the lone tower of the state capitol building, the legacy of Huey Long. We docked the raft at a boat store and went ashore to look at the city. We walked to the capitol building and rode the elevator to the top, past the marble slab where Huey had died in a hail of gunfire. From the top we could see the flat Louisiana countryside reaching to the horizon, smoky and fungus green, the landscape laced with ominous sinks of black and turquoise water. Up close, around the city, lay the wasted consequences of industrialized civilization: huge square dumping pools bright green with chemicals, steel oil tanks as big as blimps and thick as melons in a patch, and the poisoned river snaking its way through the country like a stainless-steel python. The continental haze lay heavy and brown on the horizon.

When we got back to the raft, we found a Cajun seated on a barrel smoking a pipe. If I had to personify the Mississippi, the Old Man would look a lot like that gray, wrinkled Cajun. "Hey," he said in patois. "How much you want for zee raft?"

"I don't know," I said. "We hadn't thought about selling her."

The old man laughed. "You know this river below Baton Rouge, eh?" he asked.

I shook my head.

"He is a killer who will take your life and not even notice." He paused. "Besides, you get your raft to New Orleans, who will buy it?"

He stopped and let this sink in. Then he offered us $200 for the raft. We were close to flat broke and we'd already seen a couple of derelict oil-drum rafts, so the offer sounded pretty good, but we were determined to take the raft all the way to New Orleans. We turned him down; everything the wise Cajun said about the river turned out to be true.

The stretch of river between Baton Rouge and New Orleans was as rough as it was ugly—and it was plenty ugly. It took us a week to go 115 miles. The poisoned river contracted to a half mile, but the current nearly disappeared as we approached the sea. The narrow river was ditch-like, bare of islands and jammed with all sorts of traffic. The freighters were frightening. They flew up and down the Mississippi at astonishing speed, quiet as hawks on the wing. Coming downriver the damned things would sneak up on us. They always created mother-killing wakes, much deeper and more powerful than towboats. I hated them.

Where it wasn't littered with the marvels of the mechanical age, ferries and docks and gravel piles and garbage the riverbank was covered with stunted shrub growth. It was heartbreaking to see the Great River lose its good looks and lose them so badly; the river seemed to have lost its very soul to progress.

The raft was battered, and our once-pristine Seahorse engine was in worse shape. On the first morning below Baton Rouge, I cast off and tried to start the motor. The spring on the starter coil broke, and we were left on the river with no power. The current carried us across the river, and we tied up to some trees across the levee from Plaquemine, Louisiana. It was early, not yet seven o'clock, when I walked into town. Nobody was around but cops and winos. I waited outside a hardware store until a cop came to direct traffic at the intersection. I told him my story, and he called the sheriff. "Don't worry, son," he said. "The sheriff'll take you where you want to go." But I did worry. I was afraid I was about to get run-in. It was 1969, and I couldn't see why the sheriff of Iberville Parish would want to help a vagrant longhair like me. The sheriff showed up—I believe his name was Lawrence Durrell. He was the perfect picture of a tough southern lawman: knee boots, .38, tight starched uniform, and sunglasses. Riding around with him was a kid on leave from the army named Skeet. As we drove down the highway, Durrell commented on everyone and everything we saw with the proprietary indulgence of a southern lawman inspecting his realm. We stopped at a railroad crossing to let a train pass, and an old blue Ford pulled up next to us. "That's Wally Jons, isn't it?" said Durrell.

"Yep," said Skeet.

"You know what he done, son?" Durrell said to me. "He enlisted in the army and right after basic training at Fort Bragg, he deserted and come back here. The feds came down and got him and shipped him out to California so they could send him to Vietnam. He deserted and hitchhiked back here. They came and got him, he deserted again, and he's been back here for forty days. I ain't gonna bother him, I can't even blame him. Vietnam, shee-it. We don't have no business there."

After we picked up the parts I needed to fix the Seahorse, Durrell drove me back to the levee. "You got a buddy on that raft?" he asked.

"Uh, my girlfriend is back there."

"Well, there ain't nothing wrong with that," he said with a grin. Skeet and the sheriff followed me over the levee and through the weeds to take a look at the raft (or maybe Suzy). They even let us take a picture of them.

I still couldn't get the starter to work right—I'd put the new spring in backwards, so we dropped down the river a ways to a ferry landing. I figured that if you wait around long enough at a ferry on the Mississippi in Louisiana, somebody who knew something about outboard motors would eventually come along, and it worked. We met an old Cajun named Claude Condell who put the starter together correctly and found a broken gas line that he replaced. All he'd take for payment was a dollar for the gas line.

Very slowly we fought our way down the ditched, desolate river. The weather turned absolutely shitty, gray, wet, and cold. The ghostlike freighters played hell with the raft, slipping up the river as quickly and quietly as alligators. We ran out of gas above a nitrate dock and almost ended the trip on the stained bows of a Greek merchantman. The weather bore down hard; two days below Baton Rouge, a great cold wind pounced on us, stirring the narrow, deep river into a rage beneath freezing bitter skies. We crawled around Brilliant Point and out of Rich Bend into thirty miles of straight, east-flowing river that turned us into the teeth of the wind. We'd fight the wind and the pounding river until the raft seemed ready to shake apart. Come nightfall we'd lay up behind a ferry or whatever limited shelter we could find.

Even more than when the days had been green and golden, my love for Suzy burned. She was my warmth and comfort and strength. We'd had as many hassles and insecurities as any young couple, but with all our trials they fell away before the intensity of our shared experience. We were so close we could gage our moods by the other's face. At times it seemed that there were no other people in the

112

world, nor did there need to be. In the cold and wet adversity, Suzy was always there, and our love seemed as strong as the great river itself. At least that's the way I felt: I'm not sure how Suzy did.

At last one evening we'd struggled to within twenty miles of New Orleans. There was no kind of sheltered anchorage, so I moored the raft perpendicular to the bank, so the stern faced the onrushing wakes of passing ships. As we finished our supper, a sleek white freighter came gliding up the river, peeling off waves of wakes behind her. There was nothing we could do but watch the wild water wash toward us. The first wave buried the nose of the raft in the mud of the bank, and then wave after wave broke over the stern and washed into the cabin, soaking everything we owned. As it got darker, the first truly serious mosquito raid we'd encountered on the trip arrived, a whole humming horde come to drink our blood. We smeared ourselves with bug repellant and burned our lantern low and smoky, but these were hungry and determined mosquitoes. When we slipped into our soggy sleeping bag, it seemed New Orleans was as distant as the moon. We clung to each other until we laughed ourselves to sleep.

With first light, I got up and pushed the raft out of the mud and tried to start the engine as we drifted across the river. The mosquitoes went wild after my naked body, and the damned engine did nothing at all. When we came to the far shore, the raft got caught in an eddy. Suzy climbed down into the water and helped me push it off. We tied up to an enormous shell pile and I struggled with the engine until a fisherman came along and helped get it started. So began our last run on the river.

We did not realize we had reached the northern end of the Big Easy. As we rounded Avondale Bend, a small towboat chugged past us. Evidently the pilot read the "New Orleans or Bust" inscription on the side of the raft because he picked up his loudhailer and said,

"Congratulations." It was the proudest moment in my life; an hon-est-to-God river pilot had saluted our accomplishment.

We drifted under the Huey Long Highway Bridge and past the New Orleans Naval Station. The docks that line the New Orleans side of the river began, stretching down the river as far as we could see. New Orleans. We'd done it. The crews of the ships tied at the docks stopped working and stared at us and called out questions. "How far did you go in that thing?" yelled one old seaman. "Four-teen hundred miles!" I called back, proud as a pirate.

We cruised past the excursion boats *President* and *Mark Twain*, riding at their moorings where the old steamboat waterfront had been, and came up to the Algiers Ferry dock at the foot of Canal Street. Suzy killed the motor and I jumped off the cabin and onto the dock. I tied up and Suzy climbed up to the dock and we fell into each other's arms and hugged and danced and kissed.

"We did it, we did it," I said to Suzy. She looked into my eyes and said, "We did it."

New Orleans. N'Orlins. New Awwwleeens. We'd not only managed to reach the elusive port and our long-distant destina-tion, but we'd done it on Halloween afternoon—and on a Friday. We had coffee at the Café du Monde, which brought us down to our last eighty-seven cents. Once night fell, the city lit up like a pinball machine and poured forth music like a hurdy-gurdy—and the show that night was free. By midnight we were dizzy. As far as I knew, I'd never seen a man in drag before, but that All Hallows' Eve every gay and transvestite in the South was either there or wanted to be, painted, gowned, bejeweled, and bombed, along with gangs of prowling party animals, hordes of drunken students from LSU and Ole Miss, stoned conventioneers, the usual cops trying to contain the uncontainable, and lots of unusual crazies. The streets of the French Quarter were alive with maniacs. The night burned like a carnival.

Not long after dark we made our pilgrimage to 912 Toulouse Street in the French Quarter, site of Jack Elliott's "912 Greens" epic. It wasn't any easier for us to get past the walls and locked doors than it had been for Jack in 1953, but we got somehow back to the patio, which still had a banana tree in the middle with no bananas hanging on it, and the wooden staircase leading up to a wooden balcony that connected all the musicians, poets, dancers, and their different various pads. The three-legged cat named Gray and the girl who had once been an ex-ballet dancer were gone, but through an apartment's open door we saw the drag queen who had helped the holocaust survivor poet and dancing girl with green hair find a pad on the wooden balcony after she had hitchhiked in from Chicago in 1950. He was seated at a sewing machine working on his evening outfit and seemed aggravated but not at all surprised when I asked if this was 912 Toulouse. We weren't the first Ramblin' Jack fans, I'd guess, to ask him the question.

I had expected this pilgrimage to result in some sort of epiphany, and maybe it did. In 1969 I was as homophobic as any other young male in that homophobic age, a disease born of the fear of the natural range of desires every human adolescent experiences growing up. What girl or boy would choose to be cast into the closeted, forbidden, and hated world of gay life that had prevailed since the Senate's 1950 "Hoey Report" proclaimed "sex perverts in Government constitute security risks" and the American Psychiatric Association classed homosexuality as a mental disorder in 1952? Seeing the seamstress at 912 Toulouse Street was in a way my personal Stonewall Riot, which had happened five months earlier and marked a turning point in America's sexual and personal liberation. Meeting Randi Ray, who had been there since Jack Elliott's 1953 visit, and whose identity neither broke my leg nor picked my pocket, forced me to confront my own bigotry and fears.

Given our strained finances, we might have taken advantage

of Mother's, where you could get a hearty plate of red beans and rice for fifteen cents. When the free Halloween spectacle that was Bourbon Street finally wore us out, we returned to the raft, where an inebriated ragtime band serenaded us from an excursion boat docked nearby.

Being broke, we needed to sell the raft. We proved the Cajun back in Baton Rouge right: the market for used rafts in New Orleans was awful. Beaten and wake tossed in the water next to the ferry was the wreck of a raft built almost exactly like our own. It seemed like our only chance to sell our rambling wreck would be to take it through the industrial canal that bisects New Orleans to Lake Ponchartrain and then several miles up the lakeshore to the Southern Yacht Club.

So we began our last voyage on the *Phillip W. Bell*, chugging through the locks and under the drawbridges of the industrial canal bisecting the Lower Ninth Ward. Late Sunday morning we prepared to try our luck on the lake. Ponchartrain is forty miles wide but only about eight feet deep, so a wind roaring off the gulf whipped the lake with great choppy waves. Sunday morning was gray with a steady east wind, but it wasn't particularly stormy, and it appeared to be about as good a time as any to attempt our last cruise. We knew the lake would be rougher than the river, but nothing had prepared me for what we saw when the last gate on the last lock swung open. The lake's gray waters were pitching like the open sea, long sweeping combers that smashed onto the steel girders reinforcing the beach, breaking against the shore in explosions of spray. As the raft rolled out onto the lake, it pitched and bucked like a mustang. Waves broke over the bow and washed back into the cabin. Barrels clanked and beams groaned. We wallowed and shook through the crazy water until the cabin began to disintegrate. It seemed our whole beloved contraption must soon dissolve into its various parts.

Steering from the cabin top, sometimes I could look over my shoulder directly down at the water as we rolled and pitched along. The weather cleared enough for hordes of yachts to come streaming out past the breakwater of the marina, and they sailed around us like curious seagulls. A sloop came alongside and the crew tossed us two brews. The Jax beer raised our spirits enough to brave the last miles. It was six miles from the head of the canal to the yacht club: if had been seven miles, the pitching and pounding would have shattered the raft into loose barrels and broken wood. As it was, we eased in behind the breakwater (just in time!) and tied up to the dock of the yacht club restaurant.

We began to clean up and dry out. I drove some nails into the cabin and made the raft at least appear to be in one piece. Structurally our water-borne home had about had it: our floatation barrels were battered, and we rode many inches lower than we had in Rock Island. Still, we loved the raft and wanted to make her look as good as we could.

We'd worked for about an hour when two prosperous young couples came strolling up the dock, clean and dressed as only Southern aristocrats of long standing can dress. The men, a doctor and a lawyer, both had French names and were loaded with alcohol and money. The beautiful belles they had in tow had honey-thick accents. They stopped and looked at the raft and asked about our trip. We told them all about it and charmed them. The doctor said to the lawyer, "You know, Tom, this wouldn't make a bad ski jump."

I didn't have the foggiest notion about how the raft could be made into a ski jump, but I assured them that it would make a swell ski jump, especially since it was available for a low, low price. Before the doctor left, lightened of $20, he was the new owner of the *Phillip W. Bell.* They invited us to go sailing on a friend's sloop, so we spent the afternoon drinking Dixie and Jax beer on a yacht on Lake Ponchartrain. Before we parted, the doctor told me he planned to put an eighty-horsepower outboard on the raft to push it forty miles across the lake to a bayou where the raft would enter its final incarnation as a ski jump. I advised him to pick a calm day and a stout escort and wished him lots of luck.

That night we partied with the local reefer smugglers and got high for the first time in weeks. We traded adventure stories and tall tales of the Mississippi River and the Caribbean Sea. We spent out last night on the raft, and in the morning we sold our outboard for $30. With the help of a Western Union wire transfer, we took cheap flights to California that evening. Suzy flew to San Diego, and I went to San Jose and Santa Cruz.

When at last the jet lifted off into the great dark sky, it hit me that the trip was over; the dream was ending. Tomorrow we would not wake up in our moveable bed only a foot or so above the Mississippi, we would not watch the river and move with it until the sun went down and sleep came again. My friend the fantastic Lloyd Price picked me up at the airport and drove across the Santa Cruz Mountains to the university, introduced me to the latest tunes, and let me sleep on his dorm room floor. During that first night in California, I woke up twice to make sure the raft was safely moored, but the river was 2,300 miles away.

The trip had changed us in ways that took a long time to grasp; our bodies were thinner and harder, and I'd grown my first beard, but the adventure had more profound effects. California seemed like an alien land. It was hard getting used to cars, schools, highways, supermarkets, banks, kitchens, stereos, electricity, showers, roofs, and walls. What I'd grown up with all my life seemed unfamiliar and distant, and when I came to know it again, I saw it in a different way. I no longer looked into the future at becoming something, I just tried to be.

Those autumn weeks on the river became in memory more

dreamlike and perfect. Suzy and I looked back on them as a golden source, but whatever it was that we'd gained on the Mississippi, we'd lost something too. In a way we couldn't even recognize, the river had laid us under a curse. Once you've lived where the mere passage of time is a joy, it's hard to be earthbound again. The glowing memory of how we had lived and loved made everything else seem empty by comparison.

IX

WHEN YOU LEARN TO RAMBLE, YOU LEARN TO LOSE

Through the winter Suzy and I shared various strange living places in and around Santa Cruz with Richard Stockton and Nan Carpenter. Richard and Nan had spent the summer in the Yosemite backcountry and shared some of our scorn for civilization. We spent part of a cold winter in the rented summer home we shared in Boulder Creek. I managed to write the papers I needed to get credit for three field studies and cash my scholarship checks, but the papers were terrible. Writing is nature's way of showing us how poorly we think; for a muddle-headed nineteen-year-old, writing turned out to be a lot harder than anticipated.

As I recall, in December we drove to San Francisco to see Ramblin' Jack and somebody billed as U. Utah Phillips. When we reached the hall, Bruce Phillips, who had abandoned a promising political career in Utah as founder of the Sloth and Indulgence Party and ran as the Peace and Freedom Party's 1968 US Senate candidate before being run out of the state, was standing outside the club, a practice he continued throughout his storied career. We began an acquaintance that lasted thirty-nine years. And I had the chance to tell Jack Elliot how his song inspired a raft trip down the Mississippi and pilgrimage to 912 Toulouse Street.

The four of us moved to a four-plex on the corner of Mission and Green Streets, opposite where Highway 17 debouched into Santa Cruz. Suzy was "safe and secure and BORED! OIAMSOBOEWS! BOREDOUTTAMYGOURD! School is a pile of shit," she wrote Martha and Roger. We decided to get a sailboat and cruise around the world. Even now, that idea doesn't sound too bad. We figured we needed about $20,000 dollars, or about $19,800 more than we had on hand. Richard and I spent long, stoned evenings dreaming up different schemes to get rich quick.

After much dreaming and scheming, including a futile visit to the San Francisco waterfront where we learned you had to join the union to get a seaman's job and to get a job you had to be in the Seaman's Union. The only way we could come up with to make money was hopelessly traditional: work. In the spring Richard and I caught a ride to Colorado and got lousy jobs in construction near Denver. It was more than miserable; we did hard labor for $2.00 an hour, and contractors ripped us off for most of that. We finally hitched back to California and got jobs with a water company in Sacramento. I sanded down the insides and outsides of enormous hot aluminum water tanks, breathing green paint and cursing work.

We were getting nowhere near the $20,000 mark, but by late spring I'd made enough money to buy an old telephone company van at auction and found a fourteen-foot aluminum skiff for $50. I persuaded Suzy to go have another look at the rivers of America. Richard and Nan had accumulated enough cash to finance a move to the Smokey Mountains, so we all left California in June.

Like millions of other longhairs in the days of cheap gas, we went looking for America. We crossed the Mojave Desert to the Grand Canyon, over the Painted Desert, up through the mountains of New

Mexico, and into the panhandle of Texas and Oklahoma. In Arizona we picked up a young Navajo couple. They seemed to be eloping, but they could not speak a word of English, so we couldn't be sure; maybe they were simply escaping from being shipped to a government school.

Hoping to recapture the wonders we'd known the fall before, Suzy and I wanted to take our skiff part of the way down the river between Memphis and Vicksburg. After endless hours of driving through the soggy heat of the central South, we came to the river at Arkansas City, Arkansas. The sun had just set when we rolled into town. The ancient riverfront, dominated by deserted hotels and empty saloons, looked like an abandoned Wild West movie set. The migrating river was now miles away from town, across thick jungle and dismal swamp, having been moved there some years ago by the Army Corps of Engineers. Arkansas City had been deserted by its people and repopulated by mosquitoes that did pretty well by it. We parked in front of a white wood-frame Baptist church and spent a bad night fighting the insects and enduring the heat. The mosquitoes swam through the thick humidity with a high, sickening whine; you could sweep your hand through the air and it would come up black with the bugs. After hours of fighting the airborne hordes, the sheriff showed up. He wanted us to give him some marijuana, but we demurred and he escorted us out of the county.

We drove through the rest of the night south into Louisiana and reached the bridge at Vicksburg shortly after dawn. The steamy Mississippi countryside was already shimmering under the heat. As we crossed the river and looked down, I was once again stunned by its size; from above it was even larger than I remembered. Under the summer sun it took the blows of heat like sheet metal, even in the early morning. Suzy and I decided to pass up boating on the Mississippi and drove up the old Natchez Trace to Tennessee.

Upon leaving California, Richard and Nan had resolved not to return and wanted to look for a farm to rent in the Smokey Mountains. Suzy and I launched our skiff on the Cumberland River on the Fourth of July, and Richard and Nan took the van and went looking for a home.

From the moment the skiff hit the waters of the Cumberland, we fell under the spell of the river. The Cumberland was a completely different river than the Mississippi, swift and narrow, bordered by high, craggy, tree-lined bluffs, its green waters deep and smooth. During the seven days that we drifted between the Kentucky border and the town of Carthage, we hardly saw another soul. Even the weather was cool and light, sweet relief after arid Arizona deserts and steamy Arkansas bayous. We mooed at the cows along the banks (we got so good at it that some of them mooed back) and pulled bug-eyed mud puppies off trotlines. The magic of drifting in a small boat down a fast river made us as playful as groundhogs in the springtime. After so many miles pounding down the highway, it was sweet relief to drift without sound on a peaceful river.

During most of the trip the weather treated us kindly, but on our last night out it began to rain at about two in the morning. So far the rain had sprinkled once or twice, but it had always blown away quickly. Except for a yellow plastic tarp and two cotton sleeping bags, we had little in the way of camping gear, and Suzy tried to wake me up to make some sort of tent out of it all. I was sure the rain wouldn't last long, and I dreamed on for about ten minutes, by which time everything we owned was soaking wet. Torrents fell for another half hour, and then it eased into a steady drizzle. It was a moonless night, pitch dark under the leaking clouds, but we knew we had to get out of our campsite before we sank into the mud. When the rain finally quit, it turned cold. There was nothing much left to do but to get back into the boat.

God, it was cold in the boat. The cold of the river passed directly through the skiff's thin aluminum skin, chilling the water that had soaked us through. Spinning down the river through the deep dark, we could see nothing at all, not even each other. The cold finally roused me out of my stupor and I dug through our gear until I found three wooden matches that appeared to be dry. We landed on the west bank, shapeless and black in the wet dark, and I climbed ashore and dug around until I found kindling that looked dry enough to catch a spark. Then I built a fire; I've built a lot of fires in my time, but I've never done it with such care and patience. I wanted to see a fire—warmth and light! Finished, I pulled out the matches, and one by one I dragged them across a striker: they melted, as wet matches will. It made us heartsick, but all we could do was get back in the boat and row.

It stayed dark and cold for hours. We waited through the false dawn until at last the first true light began to appear. We ceased moaning and slowly started to laugh, quietly at first, swelling until we were hysterical and howling with joy and craziness. We hugged each other's soggy bodies, and I kissed Suzy's blue eyes. Feeling so bad had never left me feeling so good.

Even now, when I think about Suzy, I remember that cold, mad dawn, the light rising up on the Cumberland and Suzy wet and real in my arms. The storm broke with the rising sun, and we spent the last miles drifting down to Carthage drinking in sunlight as sweet as ever shone on Tennessee.

Richard and Nan met us at the bridge in Carthage. They were both exhilarated, having rented a farm on the Tennessee state line in Bloody Madison County, North Carolina, for ten dollars a month. They had bought a red Ford Falcon station wagon. We said goodbye and we loaded our skiff back on top of the Econoline and hit the road again. We drove across the Smokey Mountains, up the Blue Ridge to Appomattox Courthouse and Washington, DC, and

Gettysburg. We stayed with friends in New England for a while, ate clams, and spent an idyllic day drifting down the Kennebec River in Maine. We drove for a week across Canada looking for rivers, but the St. Lawrence overwhelmed and most everything else underwhelmed us. At the end of July we re-entered the USA at Detroit. After the customs service dismantled the van at the border, we went looking for some of Suzy's friends at Ann Arbor. We couldn't find them, but we found an empty parking lot near the university behind an enormous house full of hospitable hippies and camped out there. We were exhausted and hot, and left the doors to the van open while we slept.

During the night I thought I heard someone laughing. When we awoke, we found somebody had stolen Suzy's purse, my wallet, all of our identification and money, my typewriter, even my damn boots, hat, and Levi jacket. We were broke and 2,000 miles from home. Stranded and fed up with driving, we sold the van at a Mitch Ryder concert, bought two ten-speed bicycles, and started peddling west.

We had a lot of good reasons for doing this, none of which is worth remembering. I can blame it, in part, on my romantic attachment to the nineteenth century: I wanted to experience and understand what life was like before machinery gained mastery of the world. I'd always been fascinated by the wagon train migrations across the Great Plains (three-quarters of great grandparents had joined Mormon wagon trains to get to Utah, and great-grandpa Brinton had pushed a handcart from Great Salt Lake City to the Missouri River in 1857). So I thought peddling a bicycle across the prairie would give me a pretty good idea of what the pioneer experience was like. That it was miserable I'd always heard, but I soon learned firsthand exactly how miserable it had truly been.

Considering what we attempted, we actually did pretty well. After the initial soreness wore off, we had a good time traversing

Michigan and crossed Lake Michigan on a ferry. We saw some of the finer sights of rural Wisconsin and spent a couple of wonderful days at a rock and roll band's farm outside Wild Rose. With the help of a brakeman tending a caboose on the Wisconsin River, we caught a ride on a freight train down to the Mississippi and across the river into Minnesota. There we came onto the prairie and our endurance began to wear thin: we found ourselves peddling into a prevailing wind that made our bicycle excursion about as much fun as being a galley slave. We drove through endless August-high acres of corn until we were very tired. We took to hitchhiking, bicycles and all, and we met some strange characters, such as Elizabeth Seaton-Jones, the poetess.

We were hitchhiking in the noonday sun near some godforsaken southwest Minnesota grain town, trying to find a railroad line, when a shark-finned Cadillac convertible pulled over. The young blonde gorilla who was driving got out and tossed our bikes into the trunk without a word, while the older woman in the front seat protested, "No, no! We can't possibly load all that in this car!"

That was Miss Elizabeth Seaton-Jones, an older lady who spoke with an accent so English and so refined that it contrasted with the cornfield countryside the way a thoroughbred racehorse compares with a hog. The driver, a silent Vietnam veteran not much older than I was, ignored her, and Suzy and I climbed into the Cadillac. Once we were rolling again, Miss Seaton-Jones forgot her irritation and gave us Scotch whiskey and ice to drink in large brandy glasses. I welcomed the relief and tanked down.

Seaton-Jones was a bubbling conversationalist, especially when compared to her crewcut boyfriend, who did nothing but grunt, drink, and drive like hell. Between screaming at her boyfriend because of his driving ("You are, after all, nearly thirty years younger than I, and if you can't respect my sex, at least you could respect my age!") and long draughts of Scotch, she asked us what we were doing with bicycles in the middle of Minnesota's cornfields. I tried to explain, and she said, "Why on earth would you want to do something like that?"

"I'm a writer," I said, hoping that would satisfy her. It seemed to work, and she said, "I'm a poet myself." Seaton-Jones told us about the volume of poetry and prose she had published in England.

I was quite taken with Miss Seaton-Jones. She turned to Suzy and told her what a brave young lady she was to embark on such an adventure. "Ooohhh," she cooed. "If I were young again, I'd get myself a bicycle and peddle my ass all over town!"

It took me a while to figure that one out, during which time I drank and watched the prairie miles whiz by. It was a lot more interesting after a couple of drinks. They let us out at a shopping mall (yes, we'd gone looking for America and the farther we plunged into the Midwest flatness, the more it looked as if we'd found it at last; there were 40,000 shopping centers in America, and it started to feel as if we'd seen every one). As we started riding our bikes on down the road again, it felt as though I were bound upon a spoked wheel.

Suzy felt even worse. Sometimes in the flatlands of Minnesota and Iowa, she got so frustrated, tired, and discouraged that she broke down and cried. Sometimes, lost in the vast cornfields, night would come down on us with no better place to sleep than out in the fields: always we slept on the ground. We tried to catch another freight train but couldn't make a connection. Hitchhiking with our load proved slow and hopeless.

Our luck finally changed when we caught a ride with a van that took us through the badlands of South Dakota and well into the Black Hills. At a campground on the Missouri River packed with young crazies on cross-country odysseys much like our own, the aurora borealis crept out of the north, adorning the northern sky with apocalyptic colors. Suzy and I pushed on to the Greasy

Grass where George Armstrong "Hard Ass" Custer and his blus-tering incompetence arranged for the Lakota and Cheyenne to rub out his unfortunate troopers. In Butte, Montana, we picked up an old hitchhiking hobo, and the driver of the van gave us a ride out to the train yards. The hobo showed us which train to catch, and we began railroading on the Great Divide.

We spent three or four days riding the green boxcars of the Great Northern, the railroad that used a mountain goat as its sym-bol. We lurched through Helena and Missoula, on up to the blue majesty of Coeur d'Alene. We slowly climbed up across the Rocky Mountains, over empty stony ranges of peaks, through miles of long smoke-choked tunnels, and down the wide rolling waters of Clarks Fork. We met old hoboes who told us tales of escaped convict cannibals who used these mountains to hide out, and we saw the jungle camps that these hoboes called home. We learned why they called these trains "Old Dirty Face." We experienced riding an uncushioned bound-for-glory boxcar at sixty miles an hour: it was a unique form of motion, akin to riding an avalanche. Sometimes we would be stranded on a siding for a night or half a day. Eventually the long train would jolt into motion, the first heave of the engines relayed down the line of boxcars like a string of firecrackers until at last it hit ours with a jerk that could knock you off your feet. Then, slowly at first, building with a steady rhythm, the hundred cars of the freight train orchestra began to play, the steel wheels groaning, squeaking impossibly high notes and groaning the low ones, the wood and steel boxcars rattling, creaking, and clattering out different percussion lines, the wind adding a flute part as the train picked up speed until finally the wheels sang as the whole mad symphony rolled down the rails.

Crossing the Rockies made us appreciate the timeless nature of freight-train travel. The ride was rough, but it had it all over riding a bicycle. We came out of the mountains one evening near

Spokane, where the train rumbled through the night toward the Columbia River and then turned south. When we awoke in the morning, weary and bone battered, we were surrounded by the most godforsaken stretch of desert I've ever seen—and I come from Utah. We had landed in the Channeled Scabland north of eastern Washington's tri-cities. There was nothing but drifted sand and a single variety of nasty, brutish, and short sagebrush. Off in the distance we could see the control tower of a railroad yard. We unloaded our bikes and made for it.

We spent a long day in Pasco, Washington, waiting for a train to take us to Portland and the sea. I've never been so damn hot in my whole life. The radio said it was 115 degrees in town, and the cinder-and-steel railroad yard beat that by at least ten degrees. Not a breeze stirred, leaving the air as dead as congealing lava. The very rails seemed ready to melt. The yard was home to the most miserable-looking set of hoboes this side of hell. We lay in whatever shade was available like frying lizards. I met the hobo who had helped us out in Butte. He was surprised to see us and broke into a howl of laughter. We must have been a sight, because I couldn't get a straight word out of him.

There was supposed to be a hotshot bound for Portland leaving in the evening, but by two o'clock Suzy and I were crazed by the heat. I yelled at an engineer passing by in a donkey engine, "What's the next train out of here?" He grinned and pointed to a train on a siding, and Suzy and I loaded up our ten speeds and climbed aboard. We waited for half an hour inside the boxcar, roasting like turkeys, when at last the train lurched forward and the air began to stir. We were delirious with joy. The train rolled through Pasco and across the bridge over the Columbia to Kennewick, but instead of picking up speed, the freight pulled onto a siding and stopped. I leaned out of the boxcar door and could see the engine being disconnected. As it backed up past us, I waved at the engineer and yelled, "When will this train get out of here?"

"Two, three days," he called back.

We dragged our bicycles out of the boxcar and across a field to a road. We drove into town and bought two steaks and some beer. We rode down to a swimming lagoon next to the Columbia and immediately dove in. It was sweet relief.

But not for long. We'd been very paranoid about holding on to what little cash we had left, so we kept it tied up in a scarf that Suzy wore tied around her neck. When she dove into the lagoon, she was wearing the scarf, but when she came out again, it was gone.

Broke again.

We exchanged no harsh words; maybe we were too discouraged to speak. We spent the next day diving and dredging the lagoon. We even found a guy with scuba gear who searched the murky bottom. Toward evening, with almost all our hopes drowned, fate smiled upon us, and a little girl found the scarf washed up against a diving raft, complete with its soggy treasure. A true miracle, but the experience left us drained. The next day we tried and failed to get a towboat ride down the Columbia. We began hitchhiking on our last long, slow straggle to Portland and the Oregon Coast Highway, where we began our long ride down the Pacific Coast to Santa Cruz.

Our last day found us pedaling uphill 4,350 feet from San Francisco via Skyline Boulevard to the road's 2,657 feet high summit at Saratoga Gap. It was easily the most beautiful and breathtaking seventy miles of the entire miserable 3,500-mile trek. Even on our overloaded and battered Schwinn Varsities, we powered past clusters of fancy-dressed parties on far finer machines. From Skyline's crest it was all downhill. As if we had grown wings, we flew through Boulder Creek, Ben Lomond, Felton, and at last into Santa Cruz and up High Street, where we knew our friends Pedro and Suzanne and Babette and the McKay brothers, Sandy and Kim, would welcome us to the Big Pink house on Escalona Drive.

The house "was a legend in Santa Cruz for years for more reasons than I can remember," Pedro Castro recalled recently. It was the beating heart of a vibrant community and "served as a connection between UCSC and Cabrillo"—the local community college—"for political activism, a dance hall, a welcoming home to travelers who somehow found us for other travelers, a garden in the back, too many visitors to count and countless beers." Pedro awoke one morning to discover nineteen people sleeping on the living room floor, none of whom had been there when he went to bed. "Magic happened there almost daily."

But, oh, the damn bicycle disaster! This adventure broke something between Suzy and me that we never managed to patch up. Suzy had learned to distrust my nearly lethal combination of naivety and craziness. Almost immediately upon our return to Santa Cruz, we took separate lodgings. My bicycle was soon stolen, but I didn't give a damn. I didn't get on a bicycle again for fifteen years. Later, on the Mississippi, I'd lie cold and lonely in my rowboat in a stiff wind, and find deep consolation in the fact that I was in a boat and not on a bicycle.

X

LONE STAR PEAK

When we returned to California, I was burnt. All I wanted to do was build a shack up in the hills and retire to it and write. I remembered a place Stockton had shown me a few years before, an old hermit's shack atop Lone Star Peak in Bonny Doon, some ten miles north of Santa Cruz. From UC Santa Cruz, I peddled seven miles up Empire Grade, took a right turn onto Ice Cream Grade, and followed it a mile to a meadow on Martin Road.

Lone Star Peak is a white sandstone outcropping jutting up 200 sudden feet from a flat, open meadow. It is covered with odd rocks and manzanita, chinquapin, mixed chaparral, montane hardwood conifer, and a very rare breed of closed-cone pine cypress. Mountain lions, bobcats, coyotes, and gray foxes still preyed on the area's black-tailed deer. Wind, rain, and time had sculpted the mountain's soft sandstone into weird shapes that resembled dinosaurs, mushrooms, and the landscape of the moon. Lone Star looked so wildly western that film companies had made silent movies at the peak. In 1970 you could still see where Tom Mix had carved his name on a sandstone spine at the mountain's eroded crest.

From the ridgetop the view encompassed 200 degrees of the Pacific Ocean, with the vineyards, farms, and orchards of the Bonny Doon district dominating the foreground. Across the bay at night the lights of Monterey decorated the Big Sur Peninsula like a string of pearls. Sometimes in the morning the mountains floated above the bay as distant and delicate as a Japanese watercolor. At night, city lights around the bay shimmered above the sea like a neon railroad. The deep forests and steep fields of Bonny Doon, the most rural of all the districts in the Santa Cruz Mountains, surrounded the peak. Enormous groves of second-growth redwood and Douglas fir filled the canyons, while the level and rising ground was planted in ancient vineyards. The open meadows changed color with the seasons, filled in spring with a glory of wildflowers, in summer with a carpet of green, and in fall with gold. Despite the wide vista, there was hardly a sign of civilization except 1,834 feet below and three miles distant, where by the sea the smokestack of the cement plant in Davenport, once a whaling village, belched white dust over the cliff-walled beaches and fields of Brussels sprouts.

A rich, alcoholic timber and land baron named Dan Staffler, who married Wilma Halsted, daughter of a wealthy San Francisco undertaker, built the shack on the very top of the peak in about 1937. Staffler used the cabin as a hunting lodge—that is, a place where he could get away from Wilma (who was rumored to have been a veritable virago) and get as drunk as he pleased. I only saw the ruin of the original cabin one time; it was a beautiful piece of old-time carpentry, as well crafted as a Swiss music box and stout as a stagecoach. A wide, roofed-over porch surrounded the cabin's one eight-by-fourteen foot room on all sides. The cabin was built out of heart-of-redwood boards and shingles that had been hauled up a narrow trail to the top of the mountain on muleback. The lodge was truly a room with a view.

In the late 1930s a tall, ruddy, razor-thin drifter with bold Indian features and an egg-bald head wandered into Bonny Doon. His unlikely name was Frank H. "Tex" Zoarke. He worked as a gardener and handy man for the Stafflers, and he and old Dan became fast friends. Staffler made Tex caretaker of the Bonny Doon Trap and Sportsman's Club, which occupied the meadow below the peak while Tex lived in the cabin up on top. Tex named the peak Lone Star, carved steps in the sandstone leading up to the cabin, and made the place truly his own, as only a man who owns nothing can. On a jutting rock where the trail reached his shack, he carved the words "Lone Star Peak" and his initials, "FHZ."

I never met Tex, who died in 1956, but I became intimately acquainted with his legend. Although he claimed connection with a phenomenally wealthy Texas oil family, Tex had spent forty years drifting, working and rambling as a cowhand, hobo, gambler, and private detective during his checkered career. He wrote mysteries, westerns, and soft-core porn under the pen name "Astor Royale," though I don't believe he was ever published, and nobody I met who'd ever read any of Tex's stuff had a good word to say about it. He was a vegetarian and a star-gazer; he'd wander Bonny Doon shouldering a towsack filled with the plunder of vineyards, orchards, and gardens, and he'd built a telescope out of tin cans with a hand-ground lens he claimed was a miracle of exactness.

One of Tex's last drinking buddies, M. C. Moquin, lived in a ranch house near the foot of the mountain. He climbed up the peak one evening and introduced himself. Moquin, a retired San Francisco private eye who looked a lot like an aging Peter Sellers, was a man of few words.

"So you knew Tex?" I said.

"Yep," he said.

"What was he like?"

"Tex," he said with a very straight face, "was the original hippie."

A variety of bizarre geological phenomenon surrounded Lone Star Peak, notably an enormous, perfectly round boulder split exactly in two with a narrow passageway between the halves. In the highest and strangest places, Tex had patiently cut his initials into the rock. Every year a San Francisco State geology professor brought his classes to look at the geologic oddities and told me stories about Frank H. Zoarke. "I used to bring Tex whiskey or orange juice," he reminisced. "But as time went on, Tex became much more interested in the whiskey than in the orange juice."

Tex must have been something of a philosopher, because living atop that lonely rock for twenty-odd years would have required considerable philosophizing. Whenever the loneliness of the place made him restless, Tex hitchhiked to Las Vegas or Reno and played Keno. Folk tales related how Tex sometimes returned with a Cadillac full of blondes, but both the cars and the ladies soon went the way of all good things. Tex was supposed to have worked out an elaborate sure-fire Keno system. A legend claimed Tex once went to the casinos in the Bahamas, won $50,000, bought a yacht, wrecked it on the west coast of Mexico, and drifted back to Lone Star as broke as he had started out. He was supposed to have drunk a lot of whiskey, too.

The stories about Tex's gambling and drinking were true, for when I moved in at the peak fourteen years after he died the place was still littered with bundles of heavily annotated Keno cards and empty whiskey bottles. When I first saw the cabin, it was in very poor shape, with the shake roof falling in, most of its windows broken, the entire structure sagging beneath much time and hard service. Many crazies had used and abused the cabin since Tex's demise, and it showed. In the spring before the fall I moved there in 1970, a crowd of drunken young jocks from Felton had pushed the ruined cabin off its foundation, ripped it up, and heaved large sections of the wreck over the sheer cliff on the mountain top's north face. They left nothing standing but the floor and scattered pieces of the porch.

That's how I found the peak, with the broken skeleton of the shack strewn all over Lone Star amidst Tex's old boots, bottles, and booty, with five years of hippie trash piled atop the mess. I was flat broke, but I borrowed a hammer and saw and pulled and straightened nails out of the sound redwood planks until my eyes crossed. I hauled the wood up from the bottom of the cliff, salvaged the shingles, and reassembled the cabin, after a fashion. With the help of the grandsons of Frank "Butch" Hellenthal, the contractor who directed building San Simeon for W. R. Hearst and owned a ranch on Martin Road where it made a sharp turn, I rustled up tin roofing and window sashes. I built a bed with a window facing the ridge where dawn came up over Empire Grade. I crafted a rough desk where I parked an Olympia Monica typewriter. I hustled up an old mattress, an antique rocker, a tin wood stove, and even an oak icebox. By the end of October I was settled in for the winter.

Lone Star mornings seemed eternal with peace and beauty. There is a quality of light and color on the coast of northern California I've only seen elsewhere in October; the sea and the sky have a windy clarity that fairly glistens. The peak was high enough so that in the mornings it rose above the thick white coastal fog that piled up against the rising hills. When the winter rains came, the fields turned from yellow and brown to a brilliant green laced with blue and gold wildflowers. In the lazy long evenings I'd climb a monolithic rock at the west end of the peak and watch the red sun sizzle as it sank into the Pacific. Lone Star was bewitching, slow and quiet as I settled into the movements of the earth and sky. My days moved as slowly as the sun. At night I could see the glare over the mountains from the solidly packed humanity around the San Francisco Bay, but mostly Lone Star Peak felt so remote and isolated that it was hard to believe it was in California.

There I was, Henry David Thoreau with an ocean instead of a pond. Hiding out at Lone Star gave me time to think about everything I'd seen in the last year. During our low-rent travels Suzy and I had met the kinds of people you'd never meet at a university or an airport. We'd met the people on the bottom, hoboes and winos and strung-out road hippies, ancient Indians, and southern dirt farmers. I recall the first time I saw a man working a mule in a steep East Tennessee tobacco patch; I had no idea that people still farmed with animals in these United States. We'd seen hogans in Arizona and share-cropper shanties in Arkansas and the tenements of New York City. Everywhere we'd seen a countryside that was drying up and blowing away, its life and youth sucked away by interstate highways, cities, corporations, and chaos.

We'd peddled through a town in Iowa whose slaughterhouse you could smell from miles away. We'd crossed a river in Detroit that had caught fire and burned down its bridges. We'd seen millions of cars and the Americans in them, affluent but uptight, hopelessly bound to a system that consumed the earth at home as it bombed away our wealth with murderous extravagance abroad. America weighed heavy on my head. I resolved to write a great book to describe all I'd seen and learned in the hope that it might do somebody somewhere some good. I also thought I had a yarn that would make me rich and famous, which sounded all right.

I lifted the title of this masterpiece, "Did You Ever Stand and Shiver?" from Ramblin' Jack Elliot's great 912 Greens talking blues. Like *Huckleberry Finn,* this song had inspired the river trip. I'd made several false starts on it during the previous year and knew what a difficult task lay ahead, but now at Lone Star the book was positively a pleasure to write. In the clear mornings I'd start writing as soon as I'd climbed out of bed and work until it hurt too much to keep typing. I felt sure I was working on a piece of real literature.

Writing a book is a lot like building a house. Both are vast tasks that never really end, though the feeling of accomplishment gets better by the day. Chapters are like posts and beams, words are nails, and pages add up like boards covering framing. There was great satisfaction in watching my creation grow. I built the heart of my story around an encounter with the towboat *America*: in the cliff-hanging finale, the adventurers' raft was destroyed by the great towboat, a piece of symbolism that I figured would have made Melville jealous. At the tender age of twenty years, I was prepared to take western literature by storm.

Strained by our summer adventures, Suzy and I lived apart. In Zayante Canyon, another remote locale in the Santa Cruz Mountains, she converted a redwood water tank into a cabin. We still spent a lot of time together at Lone Star because the water tank was only slightly drier as a cabin than it had been as a water tank, and we were still in love. I was having my first profound encounters with solitude and isolation, and it was always a comfort to see Suzy drive up in the hysterical Volkswagen that she'd traded to Sandy MacKay for her ten-speed. We went through many ups and downs, but Suzy kept me in groceries, a fact I still appreciate even though she made me pay her back.

The feeling that I was living right on the edge, on the sharp-edged precipice of life, fed the feeling I wasn't going to live very long. I was sure I'd die before finishing my masterpiece. Time seemed to be breathing down my neck, though I was healthy as a mule. I don't know where I got these bogus premonitions—it had something to do with the general cult of "Live fast, love hard, die young, and leave a good looking corpse" that was popular at the time. It was also tied into my identification with my Uncle Bill, who vanished so mysteriously. Maybe this foreboding was a reaction to being taught to "duck and cover" in elementary school and surviving the Cuban Missile Crisis in October 1963, when JFK quoted a statement Nikita Khrushchev did not make that after a nuclear war, "The survivors would envy the dead." Studying history showed that empires used the weapons they built, so the

Vietnam War would eventually escalate into an atomic Armageddon, which made long-range planning silly. I lived for the moment, because come tomorrow we could be fallout.

One Saturday afternoon while I was building the shack on Lone Star, some friends brought me the largest pup from a noble litter descended from some of the most notorious mutts in Santa Cruz. He was yellow, charming, devoted, and dumb. I named him Thor for his great size, greater appetite, and fine golden color. He ate prodigious amounts of food and grew quickly. We became fast friends.

It was a timeless season. Perched at Lone Star seemed like sitting on top of the world. I left only when I had to. Lone Star was famous among the freaks of Santa Cruz, and several times a week longhairs would come out to get high and watch the sun go down. There wasn't a grocery in Bonny Doon (it was seven miles to Felton and the nearest loaf of bread), but there was a bar down where Martin Road met Bonny Doon grade, next to the turkey ranch and apple orchard. It sold six packs and I began to acquire a taste for beer. Smoking reefer at Lone Star Peak was far out, but a cold beer on a hot Lone Star afternoon was even closer to paradise.

My love affair with Suzy unraveled. I began to philander, and there's nothing that will destroy love like philandering. Suzy was getting into women's lib. I could not see that white American women were bearing the brunt of the world's evil any more than I could appreciate my own deeply ingrained chauvinism. In theory I believed no human being should dominate, control, or oppress any other human being's individuality and thought I accepted Suzy as my equal. But I walked a different walk. We argued. As our relationship went south, we were both looking for an explanation of something that was hard to accept and impossible for me to explain.

The pleasure I took in writing disappeared as the weather grew colder. The book came to feel like a boulder, while I felt like Sisyphus; I'd roll the rock up the mountain, the boulder would tumble back down, and I'd roll it back up the mountain again. I worked hard, but my masterpiece's glaring faults, like the lack of a single compelling character, and fundamental problems, notably my lack of talent and experience—meant the book did not work. The characters had no depth, the plot was simple-minded, and the narrative voice was an adolescent disaster. The prose sounded like something you'd hear on television. There weren't three good sentences in 80,000 words.

Realizing the true awfulness of my beloved book became clear all at once. After getting a rejection for an early draft of the book from *Rolling Stone*, I got up the next morning and resolved to write like hell. I'd barely started when my hard-rode typewriter began disintegrating. Keys jammed and the roller came unsprung. I was frustrated to the point of outrage, and when I looked back though the work, it was obviously drivel. It was hard to bear. I realized my literary apprenticeship had just begun. I desperately reworked the novel and suppose I'd written half a million words before I finally quit, but by the end of spring, I knew I'd failed. The novel was garbage. I was exhausted and burnt out. I realized that to write a good book, I'd have to throw it away and start from scratch. I was too tired to start pushing the same damn rock up the same damn hill.

Suzy left California in April 1971 to live on the tobacco farm that Richard Stockton had rented in North Carolina. We parted on good terms (for all our ups and downs, we still loved each other), and once she had left, I could see you don't know what you've got 'til it's gone. Depression and loneliness drove me wild. I was broke and ate nothing but potatoes and drugs and ate more drugs than potatoes. The good craziness that had fueled me for so long began to go black. I fell in with bad companions, and for the first time in my life, I drank a lot. I wondered, "How low can you go?" I'd just begun to find out.

Suzy wrote from North Carolina—God's own garden, she called it. She said that land could be found back in the mountains along abandoned farm roads for $50 an acre. Living at Lone Star had convinced me that land was the answer, land in some place forgotten by the twentieth century. From what I'd seen the summer before in the Smokey Mountains, North Carolina seemed like it might be the place to settle down. Suzy even waxed lyrical about the mountain people. "Man," she wrote, "people here are not cynical, slick, false, devious, skeptical, or sophisticated: they are as honest and passionate as you could imagine."

I was stuck in California. Even on the edges of the worst insanity, you could feel the heat. The sea of asphalt that surrounded Bonny Doon was beginning to rise. During that dark springtime, I learned the Staffler heirs and the Hellenthal clan had sold Lone Star and the surrounding five hundred acres to a development corporation that made big bucks turning natural wonders into golf courses and luxury homes. I saw plans showing how they intended to divide it into 315 lots. This upset me. I fantasized about defending Lone Star against bulldozers, highway patrolmen, tanks, sheriffs, and helicopters. Ah, California.

In late May I turned twenty-one. The only way I could have had a worse twenty-first year was if I'd died at twenty. I won't describe the dubious details, but I had strung together enough history courses, independent studies, and creative writing projects to get a bachelor of arts in history. This despite several highly critical evaluations, and a dismal comprehensive exam. I owe much to Santa Cruz's pass-fail grading system and two great mentors, John Dizikies and Page Stegner, plus I owed $1,500 in student debt, which now looks inconsequential. I didn't stick around to attend graduation but in early June packed up clothes and tools and struck out for North Carolina with Thor.

After getting away from the San Francisco Bay, I got a ride with a college girl who picked me up because I was wearing a Stetson. She took me to Reno, and I spent the night drinking copious amounts of wine with students from Calcutta who fed me Indian food that would have scorched the palate of the crustiest pachuco in Salinas. The next morning, on the advice of the local gendarmerie, I walked all the way across Reno and finally started hitching where what was finished of Interstate 80 (which wasn't much at the time) began its long haul across the Nevada badlands. The highway was elevated, and down below somebody had tethered an elephant. After eating all that red-hot Indian food and drinking enough wine to get a swell hangover, the pachyderm hardly seemed out of place. Ah, America.

My first ride took me a few miles out of Reno to a long line of hitchhikers. I took my place at the end of the line. After a short wait a new Chevy pickup stopped and began collecting the hitchhikers ahead of me. When he got to me, the cowboy driver leaned out and said, "You're the last of you sons-of-bitches I'm gonna pick up!" I jumped into the bed of the truck. The driver had a cooler full of Coors beer and an amazing ability to drink beer and keep the speedometer above 95 miles per hour. The Chevy ate up western Nevada, and we were in Winnemucca by twilight. The mosquitoes nearly carried me off, but I bummed a ride out of town. I slept that night on a hill above the highway near Golconda. In the morning I got a ride with a cowboy named Buck who was starting a horse ranch in the Ruby Valley. He offered me a job, which was tempting, but I was lovesick.

Buck let me off near some highway construction. The road narrowed to a single lane in each direction where the tourists and the diesels howled past like so many tornadoes. I stood for several hours beside the road in the Ruby Valley. It was only a few hours' ride to Salt Lake, where I had kin, but it was starting to look like I might never make it. Finally, a beige Corvair blazed by, stopped about a mile down the road, came back, and picked me up. There were three guys in the car, and two of them gave Thor and me the passenger's seat in the front. The driver got the car back up to a cruising speed of about 100 miles per hour.

I've never enjoyed riding in Corvairs, not with the visions they conjured up of death on the highway. I'd seen too many of them split in two to be comfortable in one, especially at speeds over the century mark. I comforted myself that one way or another this trip wasn't going to last very long.

Late in the afternoon, we came out of the salt flats and around the lake and into Salt Lake City, my hometown. The earth felt very good beneath my feet. I walked from the freeway exit to East Millcreek and my grandparent's home. I spent a few days visiting relatives, who all tried to persuade me to stay in Utah. Being allergic to good advice, I hit the road again.

("What a dope," as Bugs Bunny would say. "What a maroon." So far I'd been offered a job as a cowboy with a new outfit in Ruby Valley, and even in 1971 I should have known Utah's Green and Colorado Rivers had America's best white water. It is pointless to wonder about roads not taken, but what about rivers?)

Between Salt Lake and Spring Creek, North Carolina, I took some hard knocks and met people who were getting knocked even harder, particularly truck drivers. Truckers are doing time on the cross. One night at two in the morning, I wound up next to the Chicago city sewer works near the Indiana line. It was on one of the main highways heading south from the city, and a continual parade of diesels streamed past, going so fast that they couldn't have stopped for me if they'd wanted to. I walked for miles in the slipstream of the passing trucks and finally staggered into Gary, Indiana. I climbed off the interstate and went to sleep in some weeds behind a stand of suburban homes. In the morning a siren woke me up; I thought they were after me. I climbed back up to the road where two drunk factory workers gave me a ride to a rest stop that was crowded with trucks. I walked to the on-ramp and started to hitch in the shade of a big diesel. I could see the driver hunched over his steering wheel, motionless as a dead man. After about fifteen minutes he stirred and woke up. Without opening his eyes, he pulled a cigarette out of a pack and lit it. Then he pried open a pill bottle and downed a handful of tablets. He was gone without looking down at me. Another trucker gave me a lift not long after, but the romance of the road had vanished.

After many rides with drunks, preachers, salesmen, and even Tennessee moonshiners, I reached Madison County and Suzy, where I fell in love with the rugged terrain of North Carolina and the tough Scotch-Irish mountaineers who called it home. Madison County borders the main Appalachian Ridge and lies midway between the two highest mountains in the Eastern States. Dick and Nan Stockton had rented a farm in Turkey Cove below Garenflo Gap, which the locals called Devil Slip Gap. The farm's western border marked where the Appalachian Trail began its climb to the 5,000-foot summit of Bluff Mountain.

Twisting roads had isolated the county from development, and the economy was based on Burley tobacco that was raised and harvested exactly as slaves and indentured servants had worked it in 1640. The county had been rapidly depopulating since 1940. Most young people (and some said all the smart people) had moved to the factories of the North, leaving behind one of the last small-farm cultures in America and old folks who spoke a Scots-Irish dialect and played traditional fiddle tunes. Bloody Madison was a place out of time.

Suzy had found a new love, the tomato plant. She was tired of being poor, and so was I, but I wasn't prepared to do anything about it. She was. Richard had taken up farming, and the two of them were going fifty-fifty on 3,600 tomato plants. Suzy and I set up housekeeping in an old log barn above a hog and next to a raccoon named Moon. I reluctantly set about learning how to farm trellised tomatoes.

Raising "maters" was a lot of work, even with the right equipment, such as a tractor with a plow, disc harrow, stake driver, trailer, sprayer, and, if you're really lucky, a machine to ride through the patch when the cursed fruit got ripe. We had a garden hand sprayer and a wheelbarrow, but what Suzy lacked in equipment, she made up for in determination. She hit the field as soon as she got up and lived there while there was light. The blight, a gangrenous black growth, ate through the patch like a cancer. Suzy started spraying for it. Each rain washed the spray off, and since it rained every damn day, we spent a lot of time pumping up that damn sprayer. It was like pissing on a forest fire. I had no love for the mater patch and Suzy took most of the burden upon herself. The chemicals in the spray ate at her skin until she looked like an overripe tomato, though her disposition became more like that of a wounded she-bear.

One evening we sat on the bed in our airy room in the tobacco barn. Suzy seemed distracted, distant as the moon; she seemed to be laying bricks in the wall that had come between us.

"What's the matter?" I said. "What's happening to us, anyway?"

"Everything's the matter," she said. "What's happened to you? You're not the same person I went down the Mississippi with. You used to be ... different."

"What do you mean?"

"You used to have such ... imagination. You knew what you wanted to do, and you did it. Now you seem lost, indifferent."

"I am lost," I said.

"Well, why don't you do something about it? You've got to get a handle on yourself, find a way to make some money, find something to do with your life. If you were a real man ..."

"If I were a real man, I'd what?"

"You'd find a way to make some money."

"I can't believe you're saying this."

"Well, believe it. Look, I've found what I want to do, and it doesn't depend on you. I wish I could help you, but you've got to work this out for yourself."

She was right. I knew I was alone and felt as though I were drowning. After hitchhiking to New York City in August, where the heat and pollution were so bad it turned the sky orange, and visiting New England, I gave up.

How low can you go? Hitching back to California with Thor (we made it in seventy-two hours), I asked myself that question a lot. It was starting to look as though I might find out. I wound up in Southern California working as a laborer for the Appodaca brothers, a pack of wild plumbers and Marine Corps vets whose Colorado and New Mexico ancestors had probably been in America since before Orlando Bagley arrived with the Massachusetts Bay Colony in 1630. We were building subdivisions, after a fashion.

Plumbers are crazy, but these plumbers were a breed apart. They got a charge out of having a white boy with a brand new college degree as a laborer, and they set about rounding out my education.

One long hot afternoon I was lining out a trench with a shovel. My foreman, Foster Appodaca, came up and said, "Give me that," pointing at my shovel. I handed it up to him.

"You know what this is?" he asked.

"Sure," I said.

"It's a Mexican steam shovel, right?"

"Yep," I said. "An idiot stick; a stick on one end and an idiot on the other."

"Good. Do you know what a plumber is?"

"I'm learning."

"A plumber is as low as whaleshit. Do you know what whale-shit is?"

"Nope, Foster, what's whaleshit?"

"Whaleshit is on the bottom of the ocean. Whaleshit is the lowest stuff in the world." He let this sink in. "And do you know what you are?"

I shook my head.

"You're lower than whaleshit."

About this time, I bought a guitar and wrote a song called "When You Learn to Ramble, You Learn to Lose."

Underneath the whaleshit, manual labor saved me. Working with a shovel and swinging a ten-pound jack all day made think-ing not nearly so painful, and after about ten hours of hitting it, thinking was nearly impossible. I lived in an old farmhouse that overlooked 200 acres of doomed oranges with a carpenter friend named Bill Johnson. He had a very steady head and helped pull me through my worst craziness. I'd resolved to make a big pile of money with which to win back Suzy; I was determined to prove myself to her. Bill caught on to this and said, "Look, you don't have to prove yourself to anybody but yourself." I wrote Suzy a very bitter letter that marked the end of our affair. After about three months of scratching the hard earth of the San Luis Rey Valley, I said screw it and I moved back to Lone Star.

I'd resolved to rewrite my novel, but that resolve didn't last very long. Being lonesome, I drank and chased women. It was a long, dissolute winter, what little I remember of it.

Soon I was broke again and crazier than ever. Desperate and de-pressed, I was seized by compulsions to smash bottles and eat beer cans. At twenty-one, I felt like a failure, a burnt-out case, and I hadn't even had a chance to vote yet. The famous Winslow Homer painting *The Gulf Stream* shows a black sailor adrift in a battered open boat, surrounded by sharks, waterspouts, and rolling waves.

He appears to be deciding whether being eaten by the sharks beats dying of thirst in the boat. I was in about the same space.

So there I was, living in a palatial shack on top of what was clearly a holy mountain and all I could think about was sex and money and death. The loneliness of Lone Star Peak preyed on my head, and the end was not in sight. It left me bumfuzzled and suicidal.

One brilliantly clear January morning, I awoke and watched the sun rise over the ridge on Empire Grade. I could have stayed in bed all day; I didn't have anything else to do, but my mind drifted back to the Mississippi River. While a laborer, I'd come up with a scheme to plant marijuana on islands in the Mississippi River (it was just one of many get rich quick schemes I'd come up with while being a laborer). I lay in bed and watched the sun edge its way up over the ridge, and I thought about it for a long time. I thought of all the isolated towheads and islands I'd seen on the river, all that empty country just waiting for an enterprising young farmer. It occurred to me that the river was still there, and the real book I wanted to write about the river was as yet unwritten. I had run into a dead end in California and had a feeling that if I wanted to survive, I'd better hit the road again. Before I got out of bed, I had a raging case of Mississippi River fever. I was committed.

Or should have been. The idea was truly screwy, a good indication of how whacked out I was. Even now I believe that a serious man could grow a lot of reefer on the Mississippi River. I'm sure it's been done. The climate, soil, and water conditions are all ideal. The wild weed farmer's greatest enemy, varmints, might be kept at bay by the river, and finding a spot with the right degree of isolation would pose no problem in the hundreds of virtually uninhabited miles between Memphis and Vicksburg. There are dozens of empty islands and towheads in these miles, not to mention the countless bayous and backwaters that feed into the river. The federal government had a marijuana farm in Oxford, Mississippi, that produced

24-foot plants of legendary quality, and this Mormon boy gone bad was sure he could do better than the federal government. The old dream of going into the jungle broke and coming out rich hypnotized me. So what if the idea sounded screwy; as I said many times about many ideas, it could work.

That of all the places in the world the American South was probably, from a legal standpoint, the worst possible place on the planet to grow marijuana did not cross my mind. Or that it would be hard to come up with a dumber crime, since it must be done outside in the same spot over five to six months. (Even my dear Mormon mother uncharacteristically advised that if I ever decided to commit a crime, I should make sure it was over quickly and paid well.) That I might end up in a state pen—and no ordinary state pen, but let's say a real famous state pen like Parchman or Angola—busting big rocks into little rocks did not occur to me. What I did not appreciate was what a Jamaican Rastafarian later told me: "Weed," Bopo said, "is a seeerious bizniz." I did not appreciate the seriousness of what I was doing; I regarded it as a colossal joke upon myself. A serious weed farmer should have a keen sense of what he's doing. He is, after all, breaking the law and he should be as discreet about his farming as he would be about bank robbery—especially if he's chosen the states of Arkansas, Louisiana, and Mississippi as the scene of his crime. I understood none of this.

Perhaps I wasn't altogether serious about farming reefer, even though I did have visions of sweat streaming off my brow as I hacked my way through a forest of marijuana stalks beneath a sweltering August sun, my machete black with resin, my eyes bloodshot, my hands lacerated from stripping plants and filling towsack after towsack with the herb. But the idea of drifting down the river in an open boat in the springtime flood acquired great power and became very serious.

I soon had another raging case of river fever. It looked to be a way out of the maze in which I'd trapped myself. Not only did it hold the promise of fortune and adventure, it looked like the way out of my artistic box canyon, for the place to write a book about the Mississippi River was on the Mississippi River.

Spring 1972 came early in California with beautiful warm days all through February. River fever revitalized me. I found a carpentry job near Lone Star and began to scrape together money for the trip. It took a lot of time to work out the logistics of the voyage and gave me something to occupy my mind.

The circumlocutions of fate again crossed Richard Stockton's path with my own. He'd returned to work in Sacramento through the winter to raise the money to buy a farm. He was going back south about the first of March and offered me a ride. It did occur to me that I'd be getting back to the river pretty early in the season—I realized that it might still be cold in Kentucky on the first of March, but I figured it would give me a chance to toughen up and get used to the river so I'd be primed and ready when good reefer weather arrived.

I got my gear together for amazingly little money. I sold the guitar I'd bought during my laboring days and found a second-hand boat for $75. It was one of the handsomest boats I've ever laid eyes on, as stout and well-made a piece of woodworking as ever came out of the north country. A Canadian company named something like Pireaux built her. Twelve feet long and four feet wide, she had lines like a duck, a green fiberglass exterior and varnished white cedar fitted and joined like a wooden canoe on the inside. My luck in finding such a fine craft for such a low price was exceptional, and she proved perfect for drifting. She was very handy under oars and was almost impossible to capsize, an advantage over a canoe that cannot be stressed too much on a waterway like the Mississippi. The boat was light enough to drag out of the water without much strain. I was surprised time and again at the great strength those Canadians had built into her. At first I named the boat after Woody Guthrie, but she had such femininity that I rarely used the name. I came to call her *Walk on Water*.

I might have found somebody to join the trip, but I had to do this trip alone. I had the notion that I'd find the Answer out on the river, the Answer to what I wasn't exactly sure, but I knew it was certain to be a very powerful Answer, no matter what the question. I suppose the question was, "How did I get this screwed up and how can I fix it?" I was counting on the challenge and solitude of the trip to get my head straightened out.

On the last weekend in February, I built a rack on the back of Stockton's yellow 1968 GMC pickup truck, and the next week we loaded Thor in the back and hit the road. Three months in the construction fields away from Nan had rendered Stockton pretty demented, and we were both ready for a cross-country rampage. Three days of incessant drinking and driving found us crossing the Mississippi at Memphis. We pulled off into a church parking lot that overlooked the river. I went down to a boat store called Frankie and Jonnie's and bought charts of the river. When I got back, we sat for a while and watched the Mississippi. I'd never seen the river in the spring flood. It was transformed from the languid autumn river: it was the river I remembered gone mad. The current was a living beast, raging as it smashed past the pilings of the railroad and roared under the highway bridges. Again the real Mississippi was many times larger than the river contained in my memory; it cooled my blood by many degrees. We watched a towboat come booming down the flood. "God," said Stockton. "If one of those things ran you down, you'd be dead for certain." I nodded, and we drank Lonestar Beer and watched the river in silence.

We drove all night through Tennessee and into Kentucky. In Ripley the truck's universal joint burned out. It was ten o'clock, but we found a place called Lovelady's Garage with its lights on.

We wandered into the office, but nobody was around. We waited for somebody to show up (mechanics seldom leave a well-stocked garage unlocked and untended for long) until finally Richard phoned Mr. Lovelady's home number. He'd simply forgotten to lock up and turn off the lights. He came back and hustled up a new U-joint and had us on the road again with lightning speed. While he was working, I asked him about the river.

"Yeah," he said, "I fish and hunt ducks out there all the time."

"My buddy here's gonna take that boat we've got strapped on the truck down the river," said Stockton.

"This time of year?" asked Lovelady.

"Yep," I said.

"God, son," he said. "You don't want to go out on the river this time of year."

"How come?" I asked.

"The wind, son," he said, and then he winked at me. "The wind."

Richard was exhausted and climbed into the back of the truck to sleep with Thor, while I drove north into Kentucky through the deserted two-lane darkness. My nerves were raw, and I had achieved that clear, stellar state of mind you reach once you've burnt everything else and are running on the body's pure electricity. It was as if a fog shrouding my mind had lifted to reveal a sky brilliant with stars. I drove deeper into the heart of the night.

Maybe it was seeing the wild river in Memphis, maybe it was just my own madness catching up with me, maybe it was simply that I was thinking clearly for the first time in months, but driving alone through the dark was depressing. It seemed as if for the first time I could see the dimensions of what I was attempting, and it scared me. "What are you doing, what the *hell* are you doing, and what the hell are you doing it for?" The night air was cold, and I could see that the earth was still locked in the grip of winter, dead and frozen. The river journey and the loneliness it entailed was now terrifying. Why did I want to spend the tail end of winter in an open boat? As the truck careened north, I couldn't dredge up a single good answer.

I had a desperate feeling, wishing I was somebody else with a different body and brain and past and an altogether different future: a Japanese autoworker, a Brazilian coffee farmer, an Italian truck driver, anybody but myself. I'd have been glad to trade identities and fates with any of them, simply to acquire a different set of problems. As Scott Fitzgerald wrote, "In a real dark night of the soul it is always three o'clock in the morning." Yeah—and about twenty degrees outside.

I had a failure of courage and an uncharacteristic assault of common sense. While asking myself, "Why?" I got lost, taking a wrong turn toward Cairo. I beat the back roads until I found the highway to Paducah and the Land Between the Lakes. Somehow, as we approached the Ohio, I pulled out of my nosedive. There was no good reason to be doing what I was doing, but now that I was doing it, I was powerless to escape my chosen course. I'd made my bet and was going to have to stand behind it. This trip would kill or cure me, and I accepted my fate. This had a strangely calming effect on my fevered brain, and as we approached the dam, I began to have a manic rush.

I drank a beer and was soon as elevated as I had been depressed. About four o'clock we pulled into Benton and drank coffee at a garishly lit orange truck stop. Richard took the wheel and drove the last ten miles out to the Kentucky Dam.

The smell of water made my blood pound. We pulled off onto the downstream side of the huge dam, looking for a place to launch the boat. The dam was as high and stark as the walls of a prison, and the obstructed Kentucky River seemed to rage with anger and pain. Brilliant floodlights illuminated the huge structure. Its spillways were wide open, and torrents of whitewater cascaded into the Tennessee

River like a watery hell broke loose. The swells surged as high as ocean breakers, louder than any surf or whitewater. Phosphate from half the states in the South was pounded back to foam as it tumbled over the floodgates. The white-lit night crackled with electricity. "You're going down that?" screamed Stockton over the roaring water. "In a rowboat?" I howled in the affirmative like a berserk coyote. My state of mind seemed loosed upon the world.

We drove to the upstream side of the dam and found a marina and calm water. We took the boat off its rack and manhandled it down to the water. Thor ran wild, pissing on every tree he could find, nervous as hell. I loaded my supplies into the boat: two oars and oarlocks; two five-gallon jugs filled with spring water; a lot of pineapple juice, canned peaches, bread, and beans; sleeping gear and pillows (I was traveling for comfort, not for speed); a sack of books, notebooks, and manuscripts; a shovel, an axe, and a machete; maps and charts, a camera, and binoculars; a duffel bag of clothes; and fifty pounds of dog food.

It had been unearthly quiet, but with the earliest hints of dawn first one bird and then another broke into song. The clean cold air was slowly transfused with light.

I'd struck an odd mental balance. "You know what, Stockton," I said. "I'm not crazy. I'm just into something most people aren't into."

When he stopped laughing, Stockton said, "I've got to drive on." I thanked him for the ride. "Take it easy," he said. "And be careful."

Stockton drove away. Thor wanted to have nothing to do with the boat. He jumped around on the dock, crying and pleading with me not to make him do it. I picked him up and dumped him in the boat and got my first rowing lesson crossing the marina. Thor's legs shook, and his first trip on water made him as jumpy as a cat. He didn't know what to make of it, but I could tell he didn't like it much. I felt as calm as a summer's morning.

The fear was gone. I was back home.

Before leaving California, Stockton and I spent the night at his parents' home in Ardin, a suburb of Sacramento, where we had a long conversation with his father, Robert L., who owned and ran the Arvin Water Company.

About the time Richard and I unloaded my gear at the Kentucky Dam, an old friend who worked for the FBI visited Bob Stockton. "Do you know a William Grant Bagley?" his friend asked. Among my pals in Santa Cruz, I had been pretty loose-lipped about my plans to start reefer plantations on the Mississippi River, oblivious to the fact that J. Edgar Hoover still had eyes and ears everywhere, even though his evil heart would kill the old fascist in early May.

"Yes," Bob said. "He spent the night here four days ago. What's he done?"

"He hasn't *done* anything. Somebody just wants to know where he is. Do you know where he is?" his friend asked.

"Yes," said Bob. "He's taking a row boat down the Mississippi River."

XI

THE STRANGE MYSTERIOUSNESS

After putting into the Tennessee River at the Kentucky Dam, the days seemed dreamlike, yet sharp-edged and clear like the late-winter days they were. Once Stockton departed, I rowed across Kentucky Lake. It was a mile and a half from the marina to the dam's lock, a long distance for a novice rower, and I put my back into it. Thor danced uneasily around the boat, getting accustomed to riding on water. He didn't like it, but he gradually got used to it and nestled down next to his fifty-pounds of dog food.

I saw small towboats lock through the dam. Except for a couple of truly dedicated fishermen's boats clustered in its shadow, there were no other small craft out on the water. It felt good to exercise after sitting in Stockton's truck for so long.

It was high noon before I made it to the lock. There was a green light at my end of the structure. I pulled on a rope to signal to the lockmaster to let me through, and soon the wide gates swung open. I rowed into the concrete box and grabbed a rope the lockmaster dropped to me. He was looking down at me from the rail on the lock.

"What the hell are you up to?" he asked.

"Going downriver," I said.

"How far?"

"I dunno," I said. "Baton Rouge, maybe."

"Well, I'll be damned," said he.

The water dropped out of the lock, and my boat dropped with it. Soon the gates at the head of the lock swung open, and I rowed out onto the Tennessee River, now set free of the dam. I caught the current and spun downriver. I didn't get far before night caught up with me. I put into shore and made camp on a sandbar. I suddenly felt lonely as hell, but at least I was lonely in the right place, on a river.

Next morning I approached the Ohio. For as long as it lasted, the Tennessee was a pretty river, full of surprises. I'd round a deserted bend and suddenly be confronted by an industrial behemoth sprawled out along the bank, as ugly as a prison. One such enormous structure was devoid of any sign of human life; I later learned it was a nuclear power plant.

The Tennessee entered the Ohio at Paducah, Kentucky. I walked into town to see if I could buy some tarps. Yes, I'd only noticed my total lack of shelter while setting up camp on my first night on the river. I found a great old-time southern hardware store filled with tools, feed, and seed. The owner, a white-haired Kentucky colonel, talked for a while, shaking his great white mane when I told him what I was doing and where I was bound.

I wandered around Paducah, a classic Southern hamlet whose finest hour looked as if it had come and gone fifty years ago. On a side street, I ran into an old blind black man playing Baptist hymns on a battered Martin guitar. The instrument's cracked top matched the lined face of the old street singer as he thumped his way through "How Firm a Foundation."

Back on the water I drifted along Paducah's riverfront, which was lined with active shipyards welding barges together. I rounded the last point of the Tennessee and got my first look at the blue Ohio River. It was as big as the Mississippi, but this was a very different river. It took the better part of an hour to row across it. At nightfall I landed on the Illinois shore.

I climbed to the top of a low bluff to see what there was to see. I found an abandoned red-shingled farmhouse; in the early spring-time weeds already filled the deserted fields. A rusted International pickup truck stood forlornly by the side of the house, which was falling in on itself as large sections of the roof collapsed under the weight of winter snowstorms. Still, the place was dry, and I even found an old mattress that looked like it would do one more night's work. I went back to the boat and hauled up my gear and watched the sun set from the porch.

I spent the next day fighting bad weather. It went from good to bad to worse, and I sought shelter in a laundromat in a small town called Metropolis. Its name reflected obviously failed hopes but gave the town a connection to Superman, and plyboard cutouts of the hero hung from the metropolitan light posts. By late afternoon the weather had cleared so I hit the river again. Toward evening, I drifted under the highway bridge at Grafton when a scrawny old man with long hair waved me into shore.

"There's a tornado warning out," he yelled. "You'd better get off the river." Dick showed me a shack he'd built in front of the river wall. The shack had no roof to speak of and positively no floor, so it hardly looked like the kind of place in which to pass a tornado, but Dick said I could use it as long as I wanted, gratis. After checking out the shack, I decided I'd be better off out in the open, and I set up my sleeping gear and my new tarp on some high weeds. As it got dark, an eerie calm settled over the Ohio, warm and oppressive, and I sat in the shanty smoking and pondering my fate. Not long after dark, a tremendous wind came shrieking up the river, followed by sheets of rain. Lightning began to fly, and more than one bolt connected with the highway bridge, accompa-nied by rolling blasts of thunder. Rain was soon running in small rivers through the numerous holes in the shanty's roof while I sat mesmerized in the storm. The howling wind played the highway bridge like a lyre, and sheets of lightning randomly illuminated the water-walled dark.

Watching my first tornado left me stunned; I'd never imagined a storm of such ferocity. Running from the shanty to my bedroll left me soaked, but I was exhausted and climbed into the bag and went to sleep. In the morning a freshet ran through the weeds alongside my bedroll, but the morning's splendor made it glorious. Under a bright sky the world glistened in the clean and clear light.

The river ran high and strong all day, a cold wind lashing its reflection of the blue sky. In the afternoon long black bands of clouds marched up the Ohio, while a high wind kicked up white-capped swells that rocked *Walk on Water* like B. B. King rocked the blues. As the bars of cloud swept overhead, I'd pass from rain and shadow back into sunlight and back into the rain. An arrowhead formation of geese followed the river with cries of wilderness on the wing.

As the afternoon wore on, rainbows arched across the river from shore to shore, piercing each new wall of rain and cloud and casting shimmering bands of color in dazzling contrast to the black clouds and blue sky. I stood in my boat as it bucked and pitched, dizzy, shouting, singing, crazy with joy. Inspired by the music in the wind, I wrote a bad song called "Rainbow on the Ohio." At last I saw a vision that would have made old Noah smile, a double rainbow, rainbow arching over rainbow like two golden bridges across the shimmering river. I felt better than I had in months. That evening I made camp on the Illinois shore and watched the sun go down. In the red glow I made peace with the world: the furies that had pursued me for the last year seemed to have lost my trail. I was glad to be alive.

The next morning I met Fred. The day after that I met Ralph. The day after that I met the Mississippi again.

After parting with Ralph, Thor and I drifted south through a warm afternoon, I decided to lie back and enjoy it. This particular stretch of river was good country, high green bluffs on the Kentucky side and thickly forested banks on the Missouri. The joining rivers stayed more than a mile and a half wide—"powerful wide," as Huck Finn said—for some thirty miles as they surged into the South. I lay against the gunwales and drank up the sun. Toward noon, the *America* passed down close to the Missouri side where the channel lay, smoke pouring out of her four stacks as she pushed her forty-two barges downriver. She was almost a mile off but was nonetheless huge and strangely alive, with wakes that rolled past like ocean swells. I settled in close to the Kentucky shore and watched the bluffs spin by through the slow, lazy afternoon.

The natural river was always quiet; its enormous flood moved without even a detectable murmur. Aside from the towboats and the rhythmic throbbing of their engines, steady as a heartbeat (and even this heartbeat was carried away when you were upwind of the beasts), the loudest sounds on the river came from birds and wildlife. Their calls echoed far over the water. Skeins of geese migrating north to Canada and summer, singing in spring with blaring honks as they flew high overhead, made the biggest noise. Their ungainly bodies were graceful in flight, and they sang with the enthusiasm of a high school marching band. Every honk sounded as if it were born of pure ecstasy. Each time I saw a flock of geese was a gift.

The Ohio had been completely barren of islands. The only island I'd seen so far had been in the mouth of the Tennessee River, and somebody was raising pigs on it. Now I drifted past the first true island in the stream, Wolf or Wolfs Head Island. It was typical of the islands on the Mississippi except that it was uncommonly large. At its upper end was a wide beach, many feet of fine yellow sand, the sort of beach that gives these islands the name "towheads." Beyond the beach, cottonwoods covered the island so thickly as to appear impassable.

In the evening I landed on the Kentucky shore just above a ferry dock at a place called Columbus. There was nothing on the riverfront but the dock and mounds of sand and gravel piled below a sharply rising bluff. The mounds spilled down into the hungry river and behind them stood the chutes, conveyers, crushers, and cranes of the gravel company.

The ferry caught my attention. Ferryboats are the funkiest outfits afloat on the Mississippi. Some ran on steam engines built before the First World War. This one was no exception, though it was even funkier than most. It puffed and wheezed into the Columbus landing, looking like a crippled duck too old to fly. A corpulent alkie in the first throes of old age ran the ferry, and his toothless and rail-thin assistant appeared even older and more alcoholic. They looked like a boozy backwoods Laurel and Hardy. I asked the captain how much it would cost to ride across the river, and he growled out an exorbitant price, so I went looking for a place to camp.

The sand and gravel outfit had made that difficult. The ferry came back, and I struck up a conversation with the first mate. He told me that there was a battlefield park at the top of the bluff. He showed me where a path to the park started just in back of the old school bus he called home. I asked him if there was anyplace nearby where I could buy some beer. He said it was a dry county, but if I'd meet him later on the porch of the mansion house up in the park, he'd call on a bootlegger and bring up some beer.

The path wound up the bluff through woods littered with all sorts of Americana, empty cans and bottles, lost paper plates, and wind-blown newspapers, but up on top it was like being back on the plantation. Acres of close-cropped grass and clusters of oaks and elms surrounded a white wooden mansion house that had served as a Confederate hospital in the Battle of Belmont, which was actually fought across the river from Columbus in Missouri on November 7, 1861. The manse now served as the battlefield museum. The fight was a chaotic and soon forgotten mess but managed to kill and wound 1,464 men. The WPA built today's Columbus–Belmont State Park and filled it with great depression-era stonework. On its heights Confederate General Leonidas Polk built what he called the "Gibraltar of the West," packed it with 143 cannons, and anchored a mile-long chain to Belmont, Missouri. The park displayed the anchor and the only surviving sixty feet of chain found after a two-acre landslide in 1925. Polk hoped to block Union gunboats and stop Winfield Scott's Anaconda Plan to seize the Mississippi River, split the Confederacy in two, and strangle it with a naval blockade. From the park's highest bluff, a round WPA stone kiosk overlooked forty miles of the Mississippi, while to the west the plains of Missouri rolled to the horizon.

I set up camp on the museum's covered porch. In the near dark on my last trip up the hill, I met the old boy from the ferry landing. His name was Ernest and he'd procured a six-pack and a pint of Old Crow bourbon from the bootlegger. We went up to the museum and sat on the porch and set to drinking. He wouldn't let me pay him for the beer, even though he didn't drink any of it. I suppose he just wanted somebody to talk to.

We talked for hours, starting with Ernest's life story. He'd been born on the Missouri side sixty years ago, and he'd never ventured more than ten miles away. Ernest was especially fond of the place because he could get into trouble on one side of the river and simply cross to the other side to get out of it. Having kin in both states, he could always count on time and blood relationship to cool off his Missouri troubles while he laid low in Kentucky, or vice versa, although he told one convoluted story about the time that a Kentucky sheriff (his cousin) arrested him, put him on the ferry, and deported him (so to speak) into the waiting arms of a Missouri sheriff (his brother-in-law) who re-arrested and put him back on the ferry bound for Kentucky.

Ernest's life story only took about a half-pint of liquor to tell, and then the talk changed to bootlegging and sex. He told tales about some mighty strange women all living, evidently, right here within a ten-mile radius of Columbus, Kentucky. Ernest offered to set me up—"An' she's goood lookin', son," he assured me—but I declined. He gave a verbal walking tour of the bootlegging establishments of western Kentucky. After he finished his pint, the old man got sick, his thin body shook and gagged until I thought he was about to die, but he finally settled down, his head in his hands, exhausted. I felt stupid as hell and asked if there was anything I could do for him. He mumbled, "Nothin'," and sat motionless for several minutes more.

After a while he began to move again. He pulled another pint out of his pocket, took a drink, and came back to life. Ernest told me his troubles. As the night got darker, he talked about dying, how he was ready to welcome it. I didn't know what to say. When he started to leave, I asked if he wanted me to go down the bluff with him. He didn't and went off into the dark alone. I felt bad about drinking all his beer and then leaving him to stagger off into the woods, but there wasn't much else I could have done. The next day I saw him riding the ferry back and forth across the river, a regular American Siddhartha. Altogether he didn't look much worse for the wear.

Since the sky was threatening, I spent the day at the Columbus Park. I liked the place. The overlook was as fine a view of the Mississippi as I'd seen in my travels. You could see all the way back up to Cairo and dozens of miles to the south where the river took a bend to the west. I sat there most of the day, writing and working on a song. I went up to town to get some crackers and sardines, but downtown Columbus wasn't much to see, just a post office and a couple of gas-station groceries. I found a plaque in the park that said that in the 1830s Columbus had been considered as a site for a new capital of the United States; there are worse fates than being a small country crossroads.

I wandered about the battlefield and wondered about the fight. The battle was one of the first steps U. S. Grant took toward Vicksburg and glory. As something of a Civil War buff, I'd come to appreciate what a horror show it was. The soldiers said it was a rich man's war and a poor man's fight. As usual, the poor man lost.

In the quiet of the evening, I cooked up quite a meal on one of the WPA barbecues. After dark I paced the porch of the old mansion, smoking and thinking. The strange mysteriousness settled in, but it didn't make me uncomfortable. I felt alive and ready; wherever I was bound, I was surely going to get there.

The Strange Mysteriousness usually came over me at night, beside the dark river. It was almost a physical feeling, though I suppose it was more a state of mind. It had something to do with my quest, though it wasn't really a quest since I didn't have a clear idea what I was looking for, and most quests are seeking something specific, be it God, gold, or grail. Stranger still, though I couldn't name what it was that I was searching for, I felt certain I would find it. This seemed especially strange, because though I'm wildly romantic, I'm only mildly superstitious. I couldn't escape the feeling that something important would happen, that the cosmos was about to let me in on some strange and mysterious secret. Maybe I'd find riches on the river or some sweet southern belle who'd show me that the answer was love. Mostly the Strange Mysteriousness made me certain that some event would change the way I perceived the world. I didn't have any notion what it might be. Partly I wanted to come to terms with the fear of some dark nights of isolation and loss, a feeling that I was becoming nothing more than a part of the darkness. What was I afraid of? I was afraid of myself.

I ultimately resolved the Strange Mysteriousness this way: somewhere down the river I was going to find what I needed to live.

❀

I may not be the world's worst fisherman, but if you listed the ten worst, I'd be on it. If I had to depend on fishing to eat, I'd starve straightaway. It's not that I don't try, either. I'd bought a cheap rod and reel at the Kentucky Dam, and I'd bait it up with cheese or bacon and hang it off the stern of my boat. The damn line would sit there for hours, scorned by countless fish below. In the evening you could see fish jumping everywhere and eventually I came to believe that I had a better chance of a fish jumping into *Walk on Water* than I did of catching one on a hook. I'm somewhat short in the skill department, but sometimes I have to blame it on a lack of faith. Either that, or the damn fish really were smarter than I was.

This was unfortunate because I love to eat fish. In the early morning when I left Columbus, I had a stroke of luck. As the sun was breaking through the mist and clouds, an old fisherman, bald and red and smiling, brought his skiff up next to mine.

"Do you eat fish?" he called to me.

"You bet," I said.

He heaved an enormous spoonbill paddlefish into my boat and was gone up the river without another word, his skiff slamming into the swells and the mosquito-like sound of his outboard fading in the distance. Our new passenger intrigued Thor, and he sniffed, snapped, and poked at it for hours. The damn thing was nearly three feet long.

I camped that evening in the harbor at Hickman, Kentucky, next to a Coast Guard dock surrounded with a chain-link fence. I landed about mid-afternoon and walked around town. Toward sunset many single females in cars and trucks began to show up at the river wall. I thought my luck had changed, but then the Coast Guard cutter came in and docked. It was a large, very clean, three-decked boat named *Chickasaw*, built like a towboat though not designed to push barges. The crew of about twenty-five spent the better part of an hour getting everything ship shape. Then they walked through the gate in the fence and up to their cars, wives, and girlfriends. Not one of them came over to talk, none of them even looked at me or Thor or the fish. It was as if we were invisible. I couldn't figure it out.

I cooked the catfish, after a fashion, and wandered around the waterfront. As it got dark, I met two young children, a brother and sister, who had come down to meet their father. He ran a towboat, and after the trim and friendly Irishman landed, I talked to him and even asked him about a job. He ran the boat with a cook and a young kid and didn't need any help, but he assured me I could find work farther down the river.

In the morning I got up and rowed out of Hickman before any of the Coast Guard crew showed up. It was clear, windy, and cold as hell. I hadn't drifted very far before I was frozen to the bone, so I landed and built a fire. Even the rising sun was too weak to overpower the knife-edged cold of the wind, so eventually I put on all my clothes and launched *Walk on Water* again. Out on the river I huddled under my sleeping gear next to Thor. Then I could drift along pretty comfortably, reading *The Lord of the Rings*, doing a spell of rowing whenever I needed to warm up or get back in the current or avoid the path of an oncoming towboat.

The river was wide and meandering, twisting in bizarre contortions through the scruffy, swamp-like country that made up the last stretch of Kentucky. It took all day to round a fifteen-mile horseshoe bend and get to New Madrid, and even then I didn't make it until after dark. And it got very dark; as I came up toward town there were a few lights on the river wall, but in the murky dark there was no way to distinguish between water and land. Swallowed by night, the river was a different creature, formless and menacing, and I got more than a little edgy as I worked the oars in the deep blackness. I was much relieved to grind into the shore and haul my boat up on a stone-littered beach. I decided to find some fried chicken to ease my hunger and calm my frazzled nerves. I tied Thor up to the boat and walked into town.

On the raft trip we'd stopped at New Madrid so Mario and Diana could see a doctor about their dysentery affliction. It was a windy day, and we unwisely left our charts on the top of the cabin, and a big gust carried them away while Suzy and I crossed the river wall to see what was left of the one-time capital of Spanish Louisiana. The Spanish influence was not nearly as evident as the impact of plain old all-American poverty. The place was mostly made up of shacks and shanties baking in the noon-day sun, though far away we could hear music that came closer until at last we turned a corner and there was the high school marching band, flashing us peace signs and thumping away at "Gentle on My Mind" for all it was worth.

The town, in 1812 the site of an earthquake that rocked Dolly Madison's White House and rang church bells in Boston, now lay deserted in the darkness. I wondered if I'd find any fried chicken, but on a back street I came across a small home-cooking-looking café. I walked up to the front door and peered through the glass at its warmth and light. Even out on the street I could smell the rich, warm aroma of southern cooking. The place was empty except for an old white waitress and a round black cook who was laughing and smiling as she told the waitress a story. She glanced at the door, spotted me peering in, and her wide, friendly face suddenly contorted in absolute terror. She did a convulsive jig and screamed, loudly.

For a moment I was too stunned to move. I didn't know what to do. Granted, my short, hairy, gnome-like figure had been known to scare children, but my looks had never yet drawn an actual blood-curdling scream from an adult. My reflexes woke up, and I pushed the door open and walked inside, whereupon both women broke into prolonged laughter. This left me at a loss for something to say, and every time I opened my mouth to try and get something out, both women burst into renewed hilarity. The beautiful old black woman thumped the counter and held her head in her hands and went from wild laughter to broken sobs, only to raise her head and look at me again, go crazy, and start laughing all over. Finally she pulled herself together, shook her head, and said, "Oh, chile!"

"Ummm, ladies, could I get some fried chicken here?"

"Oh sure, honey, you can get some chicken here, but, son, you like to scare me to death when I looked over at that window and saw you! I didn't know what to think!"

"I like to die myself," said the waitress. "We don't see too much of anything that looks like you come round these parts."

The cook disappeared into the kitchen but was soon back to join the waitress in being warm and friendly and motherly. They both got very concerned when I told them about my rowboat, though the cook was flat-out incredulous. "That river don't scare you, honey? That great, big, wide, deep river don't scare you?"

"No," I said. I couldn't tell if I was lying.

"Well, I'll tell you what, chile. I lived next to that river all my life, and if you got any sense, you gonna get scared."

By the time the waitress brought the food, my appetite was as sharp as the wind I'd lain under all day. It was perfect: light and golden chicken, thick and real creamed potatoes, southern gravy, light-as-morning biscuits and cornbread cooked in a frying pan. It was the first real food I'd seen in a while, and I attacked all of it with enthusiasm. When finished, I felt like a new man. The ladies were closing up and wished me luck. They both had the same parting words: "Be careful."

The town was now stone dead and dark, and I walked back to the levee without seeing a soul. Maybe it was the contrast of the dark, cold, rock-strewn beach with the light and warmth of the café, but whatever it was, I started feeling awfully lonesome and blue. The black and shapeless river rolled on, its limits lost beyond the reflection of the few lights on the shore. Clouds crept in, high, thin, and star-obscuring, and it got even colder. I felt too full and lazy to build a fire, so I sat in the sand and scratched Thor's ears. I thought about all the people I'd met in the last few days, which made the loneliness seem not quite so hard. It was always possible to touch lives with somebody, no matter who or where they were. Somewhere down the great dark river, I felt I'd come to terms with loneliness and conquer its bitterness and power. The strange mysteriousness came upon me again.

Yes, I thought, after years and years of asking, "Why?" I might find an answer.

XII

TORNADOES

Between New Madrid and Caruthersville, nightfall caught me on a barren stretch of shore with no good place to camp and bad weather blowing in. I was drifting in the channel, close to the Missouri shore, where revetment, a devilish invention of the Army Corps of Engineers consisting of broken rocks and boulders, covered the bank. Now and then I saw asphalt revetments, but these were clearly inferior to the standard rip-rap revetments. The river ate up the asphalt as though it were ice cream. There's a lesson here: even the army can't pave the Mississippi. It was a hell of a place to try to land a small boat, especially a wooden boat, but the Kentucky shore was low and flooded, and my maps revealed there was no better landing place for miles downriver. Dark was coming on fast, and quite suddenly the air became still and warm, with a thick, heavy feeling of menace, a sure sign a tornado was brewing.

I remembered the tornado I'd slept in up on the Ohio, recalling its bodacious rain and twisting wind. I wasn't thrilled at the prospect of camping out in another such storm. The hot, calm prelude to this new storm made Thor nervous, and I pulled up on to the rocks of the revetment with a lot of work left to do before the storm hit. I unloaded the boat, put most of my gear under tarps, and hauled the empty shell up onto the rocks, cursing the

Army Corps of Engineers, wishing great evil upon their arrogance. A towboat was plowing upriver, and I barely managed to get *Walk on Water* out of the reach of her wake. The riverboat was a fully loaded petroleum barge, low and heavy in the water, and it passed not thirty yards from shore. Even in the dimming twilight, I could see the expressions of her pilot and crew: their tanned faces were twisted and nervous with the weather. Her wake slammed against the rocks on the shore as rolling thunder.

This miserable stretch of riverbank made a wretched camp, but I didn't have many choices. A wooden pallet had washed up amidst the weeds and saplings, and I used it to make a bed; it would at least keep me off the soggy ground. I built a fire in the shelter of a log and managed to warm up some beans before the rain came. When the sheets of water began to fall, I crawled under my tarp and listened to the wind and the rain and watched the fireworks for a while, falling asleep in the heart of the storm.

I awoke in the morning having managed to stay dry through wind and rain and finally hail. I was getting better at the business of survival. The rest of the world had taken a real bath, and there was no dry wood to build a fire for breakfast. I poured the water out of *Walk on Water*, floated her, loaded my gear, and set out on the cold, gray river.

There are many warmer places than an open boat, especially in a stiff March wind. I spent a lot of time rowing just to keep the blood circulating. When that got old, I'd climb under my gear and drift and freeze. This was the coldest day of the trip—flurries of snow fell now and again—and under the influence of the cold, I pondered the dimensions of my stupidity. I was learning firsthand that only someone feeble minded or mad would attempt taking a rowboat down the Mississippi in the butt-end of winter, and most of the time I felt like a feeble-minded madman.

Hunkered down out of the cool, wet breeze, Thor stared at me with undisguised contempt, his gaze steady and unrelenting.

"C'mon, Thor," I said. "Give me a break."

Thor wouldn't give. "How could any creature on God's green earth," his brown eyes seemed to say, "get himself into such a cold, hopeless place? I've got more sense than you do, and I'm a dog." He'd act as though he didn't know me sometimes, and there we were, the only creatures for miles around (excepting the bugs and the fishes) and both of us in the same twelve-foot boat. Sometimes his contempt would be edged with despair. Today he looked so frozen, forlorn, and certain of his own doom that I climbed over and petted and scratched him in a vain effort to cheer him up.

"Listen, Thor," I said. "I swear you'll chase the deer around Lone Star Peak again." His eyes remained frozen with despair. He wasn't buying it. Thor had more common sense than I did. Sometimes I think he had a better handle on the cosmos and knew his fate. Maybe he just knew me.

We drifted through two or three days of miserable weather. Time seemed to stop, and the days became indistinguishable. I spent the good part of one afternoon in the rusted wreck of an old Packard, waiting out the rain. In the evening in camp, I'd root around in the underbrush or driftwood or pull dead branches off of trees until I had enough kindling to build a fire. I appreciated the spiritual consolation to be found in fire. On white foggy mornings after a night on the ground, I'd feel as if I'd been bone-cold for days, and the only thing that would renew life was a fire's friendly crackle.

Memories of the raft trip haunted this part of the voyage as Kentucky slipped into Tennessee. The sights were strangely familiar, like a dreamscape, and the place names brought back a flood of memories of Suzy and the raft. Being cold and lonely didn't help.

The gray sky was oppressive, and after a time it seemed as though the blank steel clouds had locked onto the river permanently. Each morning seemed a little bleaker, and it definitely was getting colder; the wind knifed through my cotton clothing. One morning, feeling particularly cold and hopeless, I looked at the map and realized I'd be in Caruthersville by mid-afternoon.

Caruthersville! After what seemed like a long stretch on the river, the name conjured up visions of civilization. There were actually warm buildings in Caruthersville, restaurants that sold hot food, hotels that rented showers and beds. All the fruits of the ascent of western man (at least those available to poor folks) could be had there for a few lousy dollars. I had about twenty dollars left and resolved to spend them on getting warm. I calculated it was Saturday and further resolved to spend some of my dwindling resources on a good time. I was as excited as hell. The prospect of sleeping in a real bed fascinated me; it was not even outside the realm of possibility that I might find a Caruthersville woman to sleep with. Anything could happen.

Caruthersville sits at the lower end of a horseshoe bend, so I could see its radio antenna and water tower long before I rounded the point and saw the place itself. A fine southern town opened up with several tall Victorian houses complete with widow's walks towering above its river wall. There were a few commercial docks, but I dropped down to a grassy landing that faced onto a square dominated by a large white church. I landed and pulled my boat ashore.

I wandered up through the farmer-crowded town and found a place to buy some hamburgers. Then I went to a liquor store and bought a pint of Wild Turkey. The afternoon had already warmed up some, and the firewater took the rest of the chill out of my bones. I went back to the landing and sat around watching Saturday afternoon happen. The square was evidently on the main cruising drag because every high school kid in Caruthersville cruised by. A carload of musicians drove up, and we rapped about my boat. They were working on a pint of vodka and were already pretty well soused. They invited me to come and play with them that night at the Climax Bar and Grill.

Shortly thereafter I met Morrell. She was cruising through town in her father's car, and she parked at the park to look out over the river. She was one of those strikingly beautiful young women that dumpy southern towns spawn prolifically, with long blonde hair, deep brown eyes, and gentle curves, round and soft. She'd been born to break hearts. She stopped to look at the boat, and we got acquainted. Morrell was as smart and charming as she was pretty. Her accent was a river of honey—I'm a sucker for accents—and she seemed as unselfconscious as a young wild animal. She offered to show me Caruthersville, so I left Thor to guard the boat and got in her car.

We drove out a street littered with the flotsam of American civilization—fast-food joints, car washes, beer palaces, used car lots—out to a large rococo cemetery nearly covered up with gravestones, statues, and monuments. Morrell showed me a statue of the Virgin Mary that late at night would cry or wink or wave. We drove past the girls' high school, which like most American high schools looked like a combination prison and workhouse. But I didn't pay much attention to Caruthersville; I couldn't take my eyes off Morrell.

Beside the river she pointed out the largest of the Victorian houses, now vacant and boarded up except for the upper-story windows. Long ago a river pilot had built the house for his young bride, complete with a widow's walk so that she could watch the river and see his boat coming; at night she kept a candle burning in the window for him. Anticipating Faulkner, the pilot died in a gory blood-and-fire disaster. The widow naturally never accepted her husband's death and kept the candle burning in the window for years, speaking through accumulating decades about her husband's imminent return.

"She died a few years ago," said Morrell, "but sometimes, even now, late at night, you can see a candle burning in the window."

Back at the landing we sat in the car and looked out across the river to a large sandbar on the Tennessee shore. Morrell told me that she spent a lot of time in the summer out on the sandbar, sunning and swimming on the beach. "When I get to feeling blue, I'll come down and look at the river. It always makes me feel better. I love that old river," she said. My heart melted. Morrell was the only person I'd ever met who lived next to the river and actually liked it—no, loved it. I was gone.

"Maybe I'll come back tonight," she said when she dropped me off at the landing, "and we can go out to the cemetery and see if the Virgin Mary will move."

Yes. I felt very good. It looked like I'd better get cleaned up, so I walked up the river wall to the Climax Bar and Grill. A small sign outside said "Rooms," and I walked inside.

The Climax was in an old brick building that had been a tavern long before Prohibition. It was divided into three sections, a grill, a bar, and a long, narrow dance hall that was lined with tables. A low stage stood at one end of the dance hall. I went into the bar and told the bartender I wanted to rent a room.

He looked me in the eye and said, "No, you don't."

"Sure, I do," I said.

"Listen," he said. "There's a motel up the street. They got good, clean rooms. Go rent one of them."

"But I want a room here."

"Kid," said the bartender, "nobody lives up there but winos and degenerates. You don't want a room here."

I explained to him my situation and how I couldn't afford a motel room. He finally relented and rented me a room for $2.50. He even showed me a fenced-in lot out back of the bar where I could park Thor. To me, the room didn't look bad at all. It had an overstuffed chair and a matching bed. The bed was inviting. The shower, which served the whole floor, was something else again. It looked like a wino had died hard in the shower and been left there until he decomposed down the drain, but it did the job and washed away layers of smoke, sweat, and Mississippi mud. I came out warm and refreshed, ready to party.

I went down to the grill, which was run by a quiet and smiling lady. I ordered a hamburger. While I was waiting for my order, a burly truck driver dropped a platter of fried chicken in front of me. "You look like you need it," he said.

I talked with all kinds of people, including a tiny alcoholic old man in overalls and a railroad cap who told me of his great fame on riverboats back in his prime. I met a drummer, and we went back into the bar and started tossing down Budweisers. The jukebox thumped out good and gritty country music. The barmaid looked exactly like Elizabeth Taylor, or more precisely what Elizabeth Taylor would have looked like if she'd spent forty-odd years in Caruthersville instead of Hollywood. Anyway, she was beautiful and gave us free beers.

Within the hour I was feeling all right and had acquired about twenty new firm friends. The drummer and I slipped down to my boat and smoked a reefer. By now it was dark, and Caruthersville was gearing up for a small-town Saturday night. It was a Saturday night the likes of which I'd never seen in San Francisco or New Orleans or New York, places which had nothing on Caruthersville, where people were *serious* about their Saturday nights. I waited around the landing for a while, hoping Morrell would return (and I would have waited a lot longer if I'd known more about what goes on in graveyards the length and breadth of the South late in the night on Saturday), but it seemed hopeless and it was getting cold. I went back to the Climax Bar and Grill.

There was now serious honky tonkin' going down. People

jammed the bar and the dance hall. Beer can tops popped like firecrackers on the Fourth of July. I guzzled a few more beers and watched the place start to cook. By nine o'clock everybody in the building was plastered. The band started playing and the crowd commenced boogieing.

I wound up at a table with two quiet countrymen and a very high-powered older woman, still very much a fox. We hit it off right away and started tossing lascivious remarks and plain old obscene propositions back and forth. We got looser and looser as the beer went down. She went off to powder her nose, and I resolved to get her to a dark place as soon as she returned.

"Man," I said to one of the guys at the table. "That's a lot of woman."

"Yeah," he said. "That's my wife."

I decided to take a walk and see how the rest of the town was doing. Down the river wall was a large, barn-like building that was exploding with dynamite soul music. I went into the liquor store next door to see what was going on. Behind the counter was the most uptight white man I've ever met. He looked like he momentarily expected somebody with a large caliber weapon to walk in the door and turn his chest into mush. He appeared certain he had about five more minutes to live and wasn't happy about it. Behind him, placid and calm as a rock, a veritable bridge over troubled waters, stood two-hundred-and-sixty-odd pounds of young jock who looked like he could cripple you with a handshake.

"What's going on in there?" I said, pointing at the bar.

"Boogies. Jigs. Coloreds," said the old man. "Every coon within twenty miles of Caruthersville is in there drunk on his ass."

"I've got to see this," I said and I spun around on my heel. Before I could get out the door I felt his hand on my shoulder.

"You stay out of there. Ain't no place for a white man." He got back behind the counter.

I spun around to talk to him. "Jesus, this place looks dangerous. Don't it make you nervous?"

He looked like he was going to turn blue. "I've got this," he said and pulled a silver-plated .45 automatic out from beneath the counter.

"Yeah, well, be prepared," I said and walked out of the store. I slipped around to the entrance to the bar and walked inside.

The cavernous, dark hall, packed with humanity, momentarily overwhelmed me. About a hundred heads turned and looked at me, and a hush fell over the whole place. The crowd appeared about as surprised as I was. Some started hooting and whistling, and others burst into howls of laughter at the astonished white boy. It occurred to me that I might have been the first white person to ever enter this particular establishment, and for a moment I stood not knowing what to do. Then I recollected I was in a bar, and I stepped up to the counter to order a beer. I only got about one step toward the bar when a pair of hands grabbed my shoulders and yanked me out the door and into the parking lot.

It was the guy from the liquor store and his boy, who did the yanking. The man was purple with anger.

"What the hell are you doing?" I yelled at him.

"I told you not to go in there, goddammit, and I meant it," he said.

I was pissed off at being handled like a duffel bag. "Whaddya mean I can't go in there? What is this, Russia or something? This is still a goddamn free country and I'll go where I goddamn well please!"

"You won't go in there," said the old man. He looked like he was verging on a coronary. He turned to the kid. "Get the gun," he said.

I left.

By now I was good and drunk. Back at the Climax I had a lot of company. The place was wall to wall with party-mad Missourians, the band was pounding out fevered country rock, and couples clinched in lustful embraces across the smoky, crowded dance floor. Women danced on tables. Casualties already littered the floor. It got crazier.

At this point my memory fades. The last thing I remember is singing "Proud Mary" with the band, the first public performance in what became a checkered musical career. I actually don't remember singing the song, what I remember is yelling "Rollin', rollin', rollin' on a river," into a microphone. The song has surely been sung much better, but seldom with such feeling.

God knows what happened the rest of the night, and she's probably trying to forget. I woke up in pain next morning, stiff and sprawled in the easy chair across the hall from my room, having evidently been unable to fit the key into the lock. I'd blown my big chance to sleep in a bed. Damn. It felt like somebody had tried to beat me to death with a club and nearly succeeded. I could hardly see. It was the fiercest hangover I'd ever known. Even the light filtering into the dusty hallway was painful.

I recollected my lack of recollection. I felt to see if I still had my wallet. I did, and still had about six dollars. I got paranoid not knowing what had happened in the dark drunken hours of the early morning and decided I'd better get my ass or whatever was left of it out of town, quickly. I went into my room, gazed ruefully at the undisturbed bed, got my gear together, and staggered down the stairs to the grill.

If I looked half as bad as I felt, I looked three days dead. The waitress who had served me a hamburger the night before was behind the counter and looked at me and my load.

"You going now?" she said.

"Yes'm," I mumbled.

She broke into a gentle grin as puzzling as the Mona Lisa's.

"Be careful," she said.

XIII

PAPOOSE

"Be careful." Two words that were starting to give me the willies, everybody telling me to be careful instead of saying a plain old "Goodbye." I was obviously not a careful person, and it was swell advice, but it was getting to me; after all, if you spend your time drifting down one of the world's great rivers in an open boat, you could worry yourself to death trying to be careful. I was already worried enough and every day became more aware of exactly how powerful and dangerous the river could be. I'd long resolved to be as careful as I could, for all the good it would do.

Fortunately, Thor was still behind the Climax Bar and Grill. Eager for breakfast, he followed me to our boat. Sunday morning was coming down sunny and warm as I rowed my hangover out into the current and slipped away from Caruthersville, but the brightness of the day did nothing to ease my physical torment. The sun mercifully clouded over in late morning, dampening the head-splitting glare on the water. I drank water and pineapple juice until I swelled up like a pumpkin, fearful Saturday night had caused permanent brain damage. I lay in the bottom of the boat, suffering. Thor's silent canine stare still seemed laced with contempt.

I'd scared myself with my drunken craziness. I could have ended up in jail, not to mention some low-rent formaldehyde-scented mortuary with pictures of Jesus and lambs on the walls. I felt lucky to escape Caruthersville even half alive. It was time to clean up my act.

As the afternoon wore on, a gray bank of fog settled onto the river. I drifted past a construction site where a four-lane interstate highway bridge was being built out in the middle of nowhere. About half the huge concrete pilings had been raised, and the river pounded and surged around them, making a muffled roar. Being Sunday, the work site was deserted, and in the wind-blown fog, the pilings looked more like a ruin than something that was being built.

In the gray afternoon I spotted *Delta Queen* coming up the river. The last passenger sternwheeler still plying the Mississippi, she added to the dreamlike quality of the fog-haunted afternoon. I'd never seen *Delta Queen* on the river before, and she looked like an old-time steamboat, delicate and proud. Above the black line of her hull, her startling white paint and stacked, progressively shorter decks—lower deck, cabin deck, Texas deck, and sun deck— made her look like an ornate wedding cake gone adrift. The cabins on the lower deck appeared to extend all the way to the side of the ship, their walls notched with tall, rectangular, heavily curtained, double-sash windows. Above the lower deck, the cabins were set back by promenade decks with square white railings that gave the appearance of gingerbread to what was a surprisingly spare design. A single small lifeboat dangled at the center of the Texas deck. A crane jutted from the *Delta Queen's* bow to support a gangway that projected over the river like a bowsprit.

Due to the weather (or maybe it was meal time), the decks were bare of passengers. A box-like pilothouse stood above the head of the sun deck. Two gangways extended at right angles from the pilothouse, reaching out over the water. A single squat black smokestack—not throwing any visible smoke from the boat's diesel engines—stood directly behind the pilothouse.

As she churned past, *Delta Queen's* magnificent sternwheel came into view, cascading a waterfall of white water into the gray-green river. The enormous wheel, centered on the black line of the hull, rose up to the base of the Texas deck. The sound of the wheel's falling water drowned out the submerged rumble of her engines. If I hadn't felt so miserable, I'd probably have been moved to song. I watched her until she rounded a bend and disappeared from sight, vanished like a dream, a steamboat hallucination.

By evening the cloud of fog was thick and wet. I still felt terrible and needed to find some kind of shelter. An oppressiveness in the air forecast days of bad weather ahead. I knew there was a ferry at a place called Cottonwood Point just above the Arkansas line, and I hoped to find some kind of shelter at the landing. When I rounded the bend, hugging the Missouri shore, I found the *Papoose*.

She was a derelict riverboat tied up to a flooded stand of cottonwoods, so ancient and weatherworn that it was hard to guess how old she was, though I'd seen damn few active towboats that looked like *Papoose*. She must have been more than fifty years old, but she clearly wasn't going to get much older. Her peeling paint showed that she had once been a trim green and white, but her exposed metalwork was now oxide red. Long and narrow, sixty or so feet long and maybe twenty feet wide, she had one long single-storied cabin topped by a pilothouse. The cabin was broken up into many small sleeping cabins filled with built-in bunks, a galley, and a cavernous hole filled with the ruins of her engine. Nearly all her glass was broken, and rats and teenagers had gutted the cabins. In the settling fog, *Papoose* looked most ghostly. I landed next to her and tied up to a cleat.

Through the fog I could hear the ferry several hundred yards downriver chugging back and forth across the Mississippi, the sound carrying clearly over the open water, but being aboard *Papoose* made me feel isolated and invisible. For all its dirt and dampness, the old towboat was a regular godsend, the best shelter

I could hope to find. I chose to room in the old captain's cabin, and I dug up the driest mattress I could find.

As bad as the old riverboat looked (as bad as everything looked), I was glad to have found sanctuary. Night slipped in through the fog, gray turned to black. I was asleep as soon as it got dark.

There was an aluminum boat house floating on oil drums in the sheltered water next to *Papoose*. In the first light of morning I heard the fisherman who owned it take his skiff out on the river. I got up and could see the river was going to stay fogbound all day. The temperature was dropping. The fog lingered on the river for three days, and I spent them on my fellow derelict, watching the thick haze swirl up the river. I read and got lost in daydreams up in the pilothouse. The disembodied movement of the fog sometimes made it seem as though we were adrift. Since the sun had been my only clock, the eerie atmosphere suspended time.

The second evening when the fisherman came back in he brought me over a kerosene heater from his boathouse. It was the second time we'd seen each other. On our first encounter early in the morning, I'd said hello, and he'd stared at me and then gone on without another word. When he brought the heater over, he asked, "You know how to work one of these things?" I did. "Good," he said. "Leave it in the boathouse when you go." He finished tying up his skiff and got in his black Ford pickup and drove off.

The fog clung to the river like cotton to a boll. It varied in quality and color, going from an impenetrable dark soup to a cloud-like white, sometimes lifting in patches to reveal the colorless river. The sounds of passing tows, muffled like a distant heartbeat, seemed to come out of nowhere. At night their futile searchlights shimmered like a circle round the moon.

I spent the timeless daylight hours up in the pilothouse reading *The Lord of the Rings*. The book's bright images and simple lyricism—"In every spring, in every glen, there is a different shade of green"—were heady stuff in the fog. When it got too dark to read, I'd pace up and down on the top of the cabin, my mind afire.

Once I was walking round the boat to warm up, thinking and looking out over the river, when far across the water I caught site of what seemed to be an illusion. Out in the sweeping current, I saw what looked to be an invasion; it was real, a double kayak, low and close to the water. I could see the flash of paddles and the movement of wet-suit clad arms. Another kayak appeared close behind it. I called out across the river, "Hello!"

Four heads turned my way, and somebody waved a paddle.

"Where you going?" I couldn't think of anything better to say.

"New Orleans," the answer came back. Then the kayaks vanished, sweeping downriver into the fog and the distance. I thought about this for a long time.

One cold day toward evening, I went over to ride across the river on the ferry, partly to take advantage of the coal stove the ferrymen kept burning and partly just to talk to somebody. The crew consisted of good old boys who told me the *Papoose* had been tied up behind the point since last summer. They thought somebody would eventually buy her for scrap and tow her away. This saddened me because I'd grown attached to the old wreck. I had long fantasies about making a showboat out of her. What a fine life it would be, going up and down the river playing "Dixie" for the folks.

I thought a lot about the farming I planned to do down the river. Even now I oftentimes wonder how a nice Mormon boy, born in the LDS hospital and raised in the very mountain heart of Zion, wound up wasting his youth as an itinerant marijuana farmer. I don't know how reefer farming got into my blood, but once it did, it seemed to have found a home and got hotter and crazier every springtime. It became an obsession. I wanted to raise acres of grass, I dreamed about endless green rows of the lovely plant gently swaying in the late summer heat, taller than corn and prettier than posies. I wanted to see lots of the living illicit weed soaking up God's good sun, drinking life from the ground. I wanted weed to roll in. I wanted to eat a reefer salad. Like many people who don't know the business end of a hoe, farming fascinated me. To turn a single seed into an enormous living plant with merely soil and sun and sweat and rain was powerful magic.

I only knew enough about farming to know that I knew nothing about farming. My time in Suzy's tomato field and experiments in the sand at Lone Star gave me a place to start. I knew that randomly sowing the seeds wouldn't cut it—no matter how perfect the climate and conditions, I knew the young plants would have to be tended through at least their first critical month of growth. It also appeared, from all the tree-covered islands I saw, that I'd have to clear some ground and plant amidst the stumps. I poured over my maps looking for suitable sites.

On the afternoon of the third day, the fog began to break up, but I stayed aboard *Papoose* and finished reading Tolkien. It was April Fool's Day, and I had a personal observance. I felt good again, young and able and strong. Even if I were a fool (was there any doubt?), even if I were crazy, I still had a chance at making good. The Bible had something to say about the fool who persists in his folly. After seeing the loony Canucks in the kayaks, I did not feel so all alone.

The next morning the sun burned away the last of the white morning fog and spring broke winter's hold upon the land and the river. The Mississippi, gray and formless the day before, became a shining horizon of blue. The river ran high and fast, and all along its shore life blossomed into green spring. As evening came, instead of turning cold, an amazing warm richness came into the air: trees were beginning to leaf and flower, and the rich scent drifted across the water. I entered the bayou below Osceola, Arkansas and rowed up toward town. I decided to invest some of my last resources in some more southern fried chicken. I landed my boat under a stand of tall oaks and climbed over the levee.

The folks who built it, the Army Corps of Engineers, proclaim the Mississippi levee and flood control system a miracle of modern engineering. It is one of the marvels of the mechanical age—wider, higher, and many times longer than the Great Wall of China. It does about as well at keeping the river contained as the Great Wall did at keeping the Mongols in Mongolia. The natural basin of the Mississippi River flowed through a flood plain some twenty miles wide. The course of the river wandered, and through the years the swamps and backwaters its rising and falling levels created acted as natural holding ponds and absorbed the basin's excess runoff. The river was continually changing and renewing itself. The river that DeSoto discovered had ceased to exist by the time LaSalle descended the Mississippi, along with the great civilizations and cities that lined the river. Today nothing remains of the river LaSalle explored.

In *Life on the Mississippi*, Mark Twain described the changes in the course of the river he observed in his lifetime. The shifting river naturally shortened when the Mississippi cut through the bottom of a meandering loop; Twain joked that, if the river continued the process, it would soon be a short walk from St. Louis to New Orleans. The human-engineered river channel accelerated the process. During the siege of Vicksburg, U. S. Grant set his troops to digging a cut through the base of the meander that took the river past the city. The new channel would have allowed him to take his gunboats down the river without coming under the guns of Vicksburg. Grant was unsuccessful, but after the war the river took his hint and changed course: the old Vicksburg waterfront is now a backwater fed by the Yazoo.

Early in the twentieth century, the Army Corps of Engineers took control of the Mississippi River Valley with full authority to tinker with the river, and tinker it did. Flood control and defining and maintaining a navigable channel became the prime purpose of the corps' new battle with the Old Man. It built the great levee system, forcing the bed of the river into a narrow, mile-wide ditch, eliminating the swamps and backwaters that naturally regulated the annual runoff. The corps built twenty-seven locks and dams above St. Louis, and the engineers controlled the flow of the lower river with wing dams and revetments. At the confluence of the Red and the Atchafalaya, it spent millions of dollars to build a series of dams and waterways now known poetically as the Old River Control Structure. The consequences of these improvements were unforeseeable. Some of them proved disastrous.

Today's river is compressed into a narrow channel that flows relentlessly toward the sea, unable to distribute the load of sediment it carries from half the continent. It blasts this sediment into the Gulf of Mexico, and the coast of Louisiana (built of these sediments) is swiftly deteriorating. The millions of dollars spent on the Old River Control Structure tamed the Old Devil temporarily, but the river threatens to wash all the concrete away, find its fated shorter outlet to the Gulf, and leave Baton Rouge and New Orleans high and dry. The levees themselves are able to protect some communities, but all that water has to go someplace, so in flood years the excess water inundates lower Mississippi and Louisiana.

The Corps of Engineers' attempt to domesticate the Old Man are wildly presumptuous. The river has been flowing through the Mississippi Valley since the last ice age, through flood and drought, bound only by the laws of hydrodynamics. Any attempt to contradict these laws is doomed. If the river decides to obey the laws of nature and cut through to the Atchafalaya Basin, all the engineers in the army and all the money in America will not stop it.

In some places the levee system is built miles back of the riverbed, but sometimes (as in Osceola) it stands right next to the riverbank. The levee looks like a moderately steep hill running up to a flat, drivable ridge. The land is usually leased to cattlemen who keep it covered up with cows, and this was true of the levee at Osceola. As I came up over the levee's crest, the broad Arkansas landscape of flat farm fields opened to the west. Grazing cattle filled the green levee running down to the town. I admired the pastoral scene, but Thor went nuts.

I can't really blame him. He'd spent a long day crouched in the boat after being penned in on the *Papoose,* so the sight of all those cows proved to be too much. Thor lit out after them. I yelled and followed my cow-crazed dog, swearing and mad, but he was gone like a shot, howling in pure canine ecstasy. Some thirty cows, calves, and steers turned and fled, lumbering along with that loping bovine gait that looks so ridiculous but moves so fast. They all ran toward a low corner of the pasture, where they turned and stood behind a large black bull. I stopped and waited for the inevitable. As the cows formed up behind the bull, Thor practically ran into him before he realized that the thirty large, unhappy animals he had pursued so blithely had now turned to make a stand. He stopped in his tracks and stood barking, but the timbre of his voice changed, and his bark lost all conviction.

The bull made a tentative advance, and Thor decided discretion was the better part of valor. He slipped his tail between his legs and turned to run back up the hill, toward me, with the enraged bull and his entire harem in full pursuit. I ran down the levee, angling away from Thor and his newfound friends. Inspired to swiftness surprising in one so short-legged, I wasn't going to let a bunch of cows turn me into hamburger. Thor and I made it to a fence at about the same time, shortly before the cows. He came running up to me with a stupid smile of doggie joy on his face, almost proud. It was as though he expected me to congratulate him. He grinned and slobbered. He looked so damn happy.

"You stupid son of a bitch," I panted. Thor continued to grin and slobber as we slipped under the barbed wire.

We followed a dirt road up to town, past shacks and trailers. I walked a good ways down the main street looking for a place that had the prospects of good eats. A large new red and white restaurant named Ye Olde Colonial House had put the greasiest spoons out of business, but I found another place with the right atmosphere and prices, not to mention a pool table. I sat at a back table and drank beer while I waited for my chicken.

Soon an old man walked in, fat, bald, loud, and drunk. He looked as though he might sell cars or work in a feed store when sober. He was a big man, drunk enough to be belligerent. He looked the place over, saw me, and said, "Uuunaahh, whazat?" He wandered back to where I was punishing my beer. He stood next to my table and stared at me for a while. I'd been through this movie so many times before that I could guess his first question.

He pointed at my beard and said, "How long did it take you to grow that thing?"

"Six months," I said.

"Six months! Jesus, all that hair in just six months!" He thought about this for a while. "Don't it itch?"

"Nope," I said. He eased his massive weight down onto the Naugahyde opposite me.

"You from California?" he asked.

"Yep," I said.

"What the hell are you doin' in this backwater?"

I told him. "I've got this rowboat, see ..."

"Goddamn," he said when I was finished. "Just like Huck Finn."

"I am Huck Finn," I said. He thought this was great. He laughed and slapped his ham-sized palm on the tabletop and ordered me another Pabst.

"You know what?" he said. "I always wanted to do that, take

a boat and go down the river. Just say to hell with everything and go, all the way down to New Orleans. Hell, all the way to the goddamn Gulf of Mexico!"

"You ought to do it," I said.

"Hell," he said, and stared off into space. When he refocused, he looked at me with a sort of wonderment. "You know what?" he said.

"Yeah. I'll bet that if you were my age," I said, "you'd let your hair grow long."

"Damn right," he said. "Down to my goddamn knees."

The food was pretty terrible, but I wolfed it down and walked back to the levee in the moonlight. I got back to the boat exhausted. I searched out a place where the cows couldn't find us and fell asleep immediately.

Drifting. When I remember drifting, it's easy to forget the long, cold, gray days in the wet wind. I mostly remember days like the one that dawned in Osceola, when drifting south on the flood was like falling into the arms of spring. Budding cottonwoods glowed with such a fresh green that they glistened in the sun; the quality of light was still sharp and clear with the last traces of winter. There was not a breath of wind, and the surface of the river was glasslike, not rippled by the slightest breeze or current. I'd never seen the river so smooth and quiet. The sun climbed over the ridge and into the brilliant blue sky as a bright orange ball, its direct light warm and rich. Borne along by the swift and invisible current, I spun down to the Chickasaw Bluffs as the river narrowed and flew past the finest scenery on the southern river. The great bluffs rose up from the Mississippi like towers so ancient they'd overgrown with trees. A towboat came upriver but failed to break the sheen of the surface or the magic spell in the air. *Walk on Water* swept along like a leaf.

So close to the water, I could lean out over the gunwales and see the agitated motion of particles of sand in the cloudy flow or touch the great clots of phosphate foam wandering with the current. Even the swirling rainbow colors of the occasional oil slick radiated a deadly beauty. I was so close to the hulking tree stumps that filled the rising river, rolling along leisurely like basking whales, that I felt a kinship with them. The pace of the current and the debris moving with it flowed no faster than a man could walk. The world moved slowly; from mid-river in a wide place, it hardly seemed to be moving at all, the river was so vast and my boat so small.

It took hours to round a bend, where one vista opened up as another disappeared. The motion was remarkable. The spring flood had swept away the snags and sawyers that littered the river during low water, and now the wild river's motion was one continuous flow, unbroken, unopposed, constant. *Walk on Water* moved as the river moved, as slowly as if she had all the time in the world. It was a perfect metaphor of time, floating and whole but never the same from moment to moment. As Heraclitus said, you can't put your foot in the same river twice, assuming it's possible to put your foot in the same river once. The river, like time, existed only in its fluidity.

Days lasted long. Mornings alone seemed to be forever. Below the Chickasaw Bluffs the country became gently swelling hills. The river widened and slowed down. I lazed in the bottom of the boat, on top of the gear now instead of underneath it, drinking long draughts of sunshine. I felt as a groundhog must feel on his first day out of the hole. After the endless fog, when everything had been gray shades of light and shadow, the world exploded with color. The cottonwoods and willows were green and everywhere. Poplars, sugarberries, sweet and redgums, sycamores, and persimmons began leafing out, while here and there scattered dogwood trees flowered white like enormous carnations. The oaks—water oaks and swamp chestnut oaks and willow oaks and white and red oaks, along with elms and maples and river birch and pumpkin ash—began to bud as isolated stands of black locust and hickory still stood winter-naked. The earliest wildflowers appeared, soft yellows and blues that glowed in the intense clarity of the spring light.

Along about noon I was appreciating the view when I noticed a brown cloud clinging to the southern horizon. It had to be Memphis, and as I looked closer, I was surprised to see the city's skyline poking above the horizon, blue and sharply defined though it was still almost ten miles away. Through the long afternoon I watched the city grow larger and it filled me with a strange excitement: mighty mythical Memphis on the muddy Mississippi.

I drifted down the garden-like river until I reached the industrial desolation marking the city's northern limit, where civilization had demolished nature and stacks of oil refineries shot blue flames into the sky. The buildings dominating the blue skyline took shape and color until the sprawling city with its web-like bridges filled the southern horizon. In the early evening I dropped below the unfinished highway bridge arching halfway across the river, rounded the point, and rowed into Memphis harbor.

XIV

SOUTHBOUND

I had first seen Memphis from the raft and remembered the day clearly, especially the view of the city as we came into the harbor. The business district loomed above the sloping cobblestones of the old waterfront where steamboats once had moored. Atop one of the tallest buildings—a massive concrete remnant of the Babylonian Revival—a huge neon sign proclaimed in large block letters, "MEMPHIS, HOME OF MUZAK."

On my second approach to the city, the sign was still there. Boat stores that serviced the towboat trade dominated the shore of the harbor, some of them quite imposing. A marina sheltered a few big motor yachts and a host of smaller craft. I hoped to get up to the post office before it closed, so I tied up to the marina's dock and walked up to town. Both Thor and I had been in the boat since sunrise, and it felt good to stretch our legs, even though the stone and asphalt swayed beneath our sea legs. The post office was closed, so I made my way up Main Street, looking for some food.

Suzy and I spent a Saturday afternoon in Memphis. The streets had been crowded with about every kind of person that can be found in the South—matrons and hookers, businessmen in sagging seersucker suits that never seemed to fit, old bleary winos of all races, farmers in overalls and farmwives in hats, ancient black

men, fifties-style greasers, sweet southern belles, and knots of
young black men strutting more stuff than I'd seen on either coast.
This swirling mass of humanity crowded the wide sidewalks and
gave the street the feel of a carnival.

We had walked down to Beale Street with its the nightclubs and
pawn shops and beaneries. At the corner of Main Street, a horde of
motorcycle cops came roaring up on screaming Harleys. They were
a nasty looking clutch of cops as they turned and formed up on the
Beale Street corner after clearing Main of traffic. Behind them we
could see why the cops were clearing the street. An enormous protest march was coming down the road, thousands of black people
chanting, "Don't shop, boycott!" The police sat motionless on their
rumbling Harleys, machinelike themselves in round black helmets
and combat leathers, eyeing the marchers like hungry wolves. They
fondled their billy clubs and tossed racist catcalls among themselves. They didn't like this duty, and some looked as if they were
aching to break their clubs on some black heads. The procession
marched past us, the pumped-up marchers in high spirits, all kinds
of black people proud and happy, plus a scattering of college radi-
cals and a few high-minded brave white ladies. The march turned
down Beale Street, and the cops followed in a hurricane of noise.
After they had all gone, a fire truck came screaming down Main
Street, sirens blaring and bells clanging.

The evening of my second visit was much quieter, though
the street was crowded with workers and secretaries catching
buses and sailors on leave from the naval station out looking
for a good time on Friday night. Thor was baffled by the noise
and the crowd and ran circles around me. He was upset about
something, and nothing I could do would make him heel. He
actually appeared to be looking for something. I lost sight of him
for a moment, and when he returned, Thor seemed to have found
whatever it was he was looking for. He trotted up to my side,

happy and contented. A group of sailors, high and loose, came up with him, howling with laughter.

"Hey," said one of them, red faced with beer, his eyes nearly streaming from laughter. "Is that your dog?"

"Yeah," I said.

He laughed some more and then said in a broad Texas accent, "He just took the biggest dump I've ever seen right back in the middle of Main Street." He bent over and scratched Thor's ears. "That's a good dog," he said.

On a side street I found a cheap diner that sold good hamburgers and ate about three of them. I bought another and fed it to Thor. Then we wandered down Main Street again looking for Beale. I didn't recognize it when I got there, mostly because it was gone. The whole west end of Beale Street had been torn down, and now plywood walls and wooden sidewalks surrounded the empty blocks. Red, white, and blue signs with Richard Nixon's name at the bottom proclaimed that this was urban renewal. I started back to my boat.

I was coming down the hill from the post office when I met a young couple, not more than sixteen or seventeen, sitting on the hood of a beat-up Ford. They had driven down from some Illinois backwater to get married. Now their car had broken down. They were a strange mix of joy and despair. I saw them again the next day, still sitting on the hood of the Ford. They were living in it, waiting for somebody to wire them money through Western Union so they could drive back to Illinois. It must have been a pretty bittersweet honeymoon, but they were both happy in a child-like way.

My own financial situation was looking bleak. I had some change left, and not a lot of it. I had food in the boat and the owner of the marina was letting me sleep on the dock, so I wasn't desperate, and my brother had promised to forward my tax refund check to Memphis from California. It was a suspenseful trip to the post office the next morning, but I was in luck. I got the check along with letters from friends. I sat out on the stone steps and read my mail and looked at the check. It was for almost $275. I was rich again and decided to use some of my newfound wealth and buy a guitar.

I went back to what was left of Beale Street, the unregenerate part that defied urban renewal. There were half a dozen pawn shops in two blocks, all filled with guitars. I found only one instrument that was really worth playing, a fine old Gibson, and if the pawnbroker would have come down below $300 I probably would have spent all my money on it. I shuffled through the shops until I located the darkest and sleaziest pawnshop on the street. It had an entire back wall covered with acoustic guitars. While I looked them over a salesman oozed up out of the murk.

"Want a guitar, huh?" he said. He was lank and pallid, looking as if he'd never seen the sun. He had thinning red hair and wore a plaid sports coat. His accent was straight out of Chicago and he seemed to be a graduate of the Richard Nixon School of Used Car Sales.

"Yeah," I said. "I might buy a guitar."

He pulled down an ancient Stella and began pointing out its finer qualities, though it didn't have any. I looked at a Japanese imitation of a Gibson Hummingbird and a pretty serviceable Harmony.

The salesman started lying about the fake Hummingbird. "This guitar's made by Gibson, y'know, only it's got some tiny defect so they don't put the Gibson name on it and they sell it real cheap. Yessir, that's a real guitar, you can't go wrong for the money, I guarantee."

"This guitar is made in Japan," I said.

"Sure," he said. "All guitars are made in Japan these days."

"How about that," I said. The folks in Kalamazoo would be disappointed to hear that.

"Yeah," said the salesman. "Pretty soon everything is going to be made in Japan."

Despite the salesman, I liked the guitar. It was flashy and didn't play or sound too bad, either. We haggled over the price. The salesman was itching to part this particular fool from his money, and he gave me some advice that hit me where I lived.

"Listen," he said. "What's the good of having money in this life if you can't buy the things you want?" His wisdom pushed me over the edge. We settled on a price of eighty dollars with a set of strings and a case thrown in. When I got back on the street, I was as happy as a pig in clover. I had a guitar! Maybe you can't buy happiness, but you can buy guitars.

I arranged to leave *Walk on Water* at the marina for a few days and walked with Thor out to the freeway and started hitchhiking to the Smokey Mountains. I had vague reasons for doing this, but mostly I wanted to see some familiar faces before I disappeared down the river, and though I wouldn't but half admit it to myself, I wanted to see Suzy again. She'd sworn to shoot me dead with her pearl-handled .22 caliber Saturday Night Special if she saw me again, but that didn't stop me. On the river my thoughts constantly turned to her. I did not expect to sweep her off her feet and charm her back to the river, but I did want to talk to her again.

Nothing much happened beyond staying in Nashville for a while with a family whose kids had picked me up near Shiloh. I spent some days hitching across Tennessee and one day in Madison County with Richard and Nan. They assured me Suzy didn't want to see me. I gave up and accepted that we were finished.

It was a strange interlude. Hitchhiking, like life, is one-third joy and two-thirds sorrow. I remember one sunny afternoon carrying my guitar through Nashville toward the highway. The owner of a gas station called me over.

"I'll give you fifty cents if you play me a song," he said.

I pulled out the guitar and plugged through all seven verses of "When You Learn to Ramble, You Learn to Lose."

When I was done, the gas station owner gave me fifty cents. "I just wanted to see what kind of guitar you had," he said.

Another tornado had blown up the river while I was gone, so I hadn't missed much in the way of good weather. I was glad to get back to Memphis and the river. I cleaned out the boat and reorganized my gear. Wherever I was going, I could tell I was getting close.

I walked around Memphis again that night. It was a weekday, and the streets were deserted and lonely. The empty glass and steel buildings stood unyielding and cold. In the whole forest of stone, I hardly saw another soul.

I got up early in the morning and rowed out to the river. I drifted under the old highway bridge and the railroad trestle and down around the bend. Memphis, the last big city for four hundred miles, slowly disappeared. I soon drifted into the wilds of the state of Mississippi.

The weather was dirty during the days it took to go seventy river miles to Helena, gray and windy days, but now the south wind was warm and no rain fell. That was all right by me. It felt good to have survived to see this season. Several times I had been sure it was my fate to freeze, but now the signs of spring were everywhere. Thick green foliage covered the river's banks and levees. I could almost taste the salt and warmth of the Gulf of Mexico in the wind. The backwoods of Arkansas and Mississippi, so forsaken by humanity that they are still the province of black bear, bobcat, deer, and possum, looked beautiful. I was falling in love again with the South.

I'd resolved to get a job as a deckhand on a towboat. Working on the river would give me a true understanding of it, a familiarity that a casual tourist like me could never hope to gain. I knew practically nothing about the river, and it seemed it would take years to understand the Old Man well enough to capture the river's great unceasing motion, its terrible beauty, its thousand changes, its moods, its timelessness. Working with men and women who had known the river for years, living next to it every day for weeks and months, seeing it through all its seasons, then perhaps I could truly write about the Mississippi.

Despite the number of towboats we met on the river, I couldn't take my eyes off one when it rolled by. The largest and newest boats were all spit and polish with glistening paint and gold-lettered nameplates, while the older boats were as unpretentious as hobos. At times I'd carry on pantomimed conversations with the crews; one deckhand would see me, and he'd call his buddies out of the cabin, and we'd sign back and forth across the water while they laughed at the fool in the rowboat.

Towboats occasionally blasted their horns at me, and one pilot used his loudhailer to order me out of the channel. It was in a particularly wide part of the river where the only place the current was worth a damn was in the channel. I figured it wasn't his business, and besides, I kept my eyes open. When he saw that I was ignoring him, he hailed me again, "Get out of the channel." His disembodied voice was so mechanical it sounded like the towboat was talking. I got pissed off. I may have been the entire crew and cook besides of my boat, but I was also captain. Just because his craft was larger than mine did not give him the right to give me orders. I'd read *Rules of the Road for Western Waterways* and knew who had the right of way—I did. He gave his order a third time, and I stood up and waved my fist at him and told him to put his orders where the sun don't shine.

Fool that I was, I never did lose my awe of the towboat's tremendous power and size. When they steamed past, it was like standing by a four-lane highway while a convoy of tandem-trailer diesels howled by at eighty miles an hour, sucking away the very air. Watching a towboat sweep past was awesome; the slanted bow of a towboat pushing empty barges loomed fifteen to eighteen feet above of the river, a slanted wall of steel hundreds of feet wide pushing ponderously through the river, hissing like a boiling teakettle. Looking down the relentless line of a barge's bows as it lumbered past in a show of brute force and naked power was like peering down the throat of leviathan. I tried to give the big boats lots of room.

I drifted past one especially new and clean towboat, with white paint so smooth and fittings so bright she could have left the shipyard yesterday. She was big, probably the flagship of her line, and though her design was strictly utilitarian, she rode the Mississippi like river royalty. I hoped she had some fine Indian name, but as I came close her nameplate bore the humble words *Wilbur D. Mills*. She was named after an Arkansas congressman, said to be "the most powerful man in Washington." What a homely name for such a beautiful boat. And this was before Wilbur ended his career and acquired a nautical reputation for frolicking with a hooker in the Washington Tidal Basin.

I was in love with the big ditch. The river had restored my mental balance and renewed the joy of being alive. It had brought me back in touch with the gentle rhythms of nature, the endless roll of the wide waters, the rising and setting of the sun and moon, and the cycles of the seasons. I no longer felt suicidal or self-destructive and was embarrassed that I'd sunk so low into misery and self-pity. The idea that I was gambling my life while seeking salvation on the river lost its appeal. I had no desire to be dead by drowning. I'd come to terms with being alone. It was the price of freedom, and I was certainly free.

I was thinking about this one afternoon when it crossed my mind that I knew nothing about dying. I'd never even come close. I'd never been in a car wreck or even done so much as break a bone. Still, I'd always been afraid of dying, and like many of my generation was certain I'd die young. "Live fast, love hard, die young," should have been tattooed on my chest. I once heard that death is always with us, standing six feet to the left, and it seemed especially true in my small floating shell, but death had never reached out to grab me. There was something profound and important in this small revelation, but I couldn't figure out what it might be.

Every day grew longer. Drifting was a fine pastime, but it got boring. Long stretches of the river are remarkably the same, and when the scenery does change, it does so slowly. I'd read or write or play guitar. Toward noon, I'd tie up to an island or beach and stretch my legs and let Thor run wild. I'd cook something or climb up the levees and survey the wide stretches of farmland, the young fields covered with new corn and soybeans as far as the eye could reach. Or I might bait a hook and let the hopeless line trail along behind my boat, while I contemplated the dark and strange waters; deep in the murk there were bizarre prehistoric creatures like the alligator gar, a beast with the head and jaws of an alligator and the body of a fish. The alligator gar lived in the mud on the river bottom and grew to lengths of sixteen feet. Locals trolled for them with great hooks baited with whole rabbits and chickens.

The river and the woods and the very air teemed with life. Once I rounded a point and startled a flock of whooping cranes plucking fish out of the shallows. Snow white and big as turkeys, they were a strange combination of grace and grotesque. The cranes took wing and filled the sky with beauty. It felt far removed from the twentieth century, but it was impossible to escape modern America. Even in darkest Mississippi, where the river was its wildest, plastic milk jugs floated everywhere.

Thor had adjusted to life in the boat. Mostly he'd lounge in the bottom, resigned but apparently comfortable. He'd even gotten in the habit of drinking out of the river though he fell in twice while perfecting his technique. He'd dog paddle beside the boat, closed-jawed and looking worried, until I'd reach over and haul sixty pounds of cold, wet dog back on board where he'd shake loose a cloud of dog-scented water. Now that the weather had warmed up, he didn't seem to hold a grudge against me.

I camped one night at the head of an island. It was about a hundred yards long and a hundred feet wide and as sandy as an ocean beach. The island was covered with young cottonwoods, their trunks about as thick as a man's leg, and it was littered with driftwood and the assorted junk the falling river had left behind. The sand got in my bedding and in everything I cooked, but it was soft and warm to sleep on. I got up in the morning and began rowing toward Helena, Arkansas.

Late in the afternoon I had a close encounter with a towboat and almost capsized. A small tow pushing about six barges sounded its horn several hundred yards upriver, and I rowed out of its way. The barges were heavily loaded and had scarcely more than a foot or two of freeboard above the water. I passed close to the boat, so close that I could see a deckhand's belt buckle. Riding so low in the water, this tow threw out a particularly rough wake that hit *Walk on Water* exactly wrong, broadsides, pitching my rowboat up to an almost ninety-degree angle before it crested the wave and righted itself. In the trough of the wake, I grabbed the oars and turned the bow into the next wave. The close call left me rattled because I wasn't ready for a swim, but I buried my uneasiness and made a mental note to be more careful.

Night settled in while I was still several miles from Helena, but the town had a good anchorage, and I decided to run on through the dark. Some miles downriver I could see the light at the head of the bayou below the town, but except for the lights and the quiet rushing of the water, I could have been drifting through space. It made me nervous as hell, and I cursed myself for taking a chance that I shouldn't take at all, but the lights drew me on irresistibly. The current was strong and close to shore, but it seemed to take an eternity to reach the light. There was a quiet menace in the thick night air, and weird forms and shapes lurked in the shadows of the bank. It was hard to gauge when I was opposite the harbor mouth even though the boat was running very close to shore: I made a false turn before I finally slipped into the quiet waters of the bayou. It felt as if I'd escaped a pack of voiceless, ghostly hounds. The lights of the marina glimmered across the water. I rowed to a dock and tied up.

An old Arkansan told me an old story explaining how old Arkansas was settled. A sign at the main river crossing into Arkansas pointed west and said "Texas." Everybody who could read went to Texas. Everybody who couldn't stayed in Arkansas. This story is especially poignant if you've ever been to Arkansas and wondered what could persuade anyone to live in such a flat, hot, swampy, mosquito-infested, godforsaken place, but it is hardly fair to illiterates. A man doesn't have to know how to read just to have a little common sense. There are some beautiful mountains in the state, they raise fantastic watermelons, and the weather is great at least two weeks out of every year. Experience suggests you can discount about 10 percent of all the bad things you hear about Arkansas as being at least partially untrue.

Helena stands on the last hills on the western side of the Mississippi. Below the town, all the way south to the Gulf of Mexico, the river has created every acre of the delta's black, rich, wet, and flat land. From the tallest hills west of town, vast tracts of farmland stretched to the horizon, as immense as an ocean. Helena claimed 20,000 people, though it hardly seemed that large. It was a sleepy place, an agricultural center, caught in the time lag that has ensnared much of the rural South.

The natives of Arkansas and Mississippi initially scared me "like to death," but after meeting a few of them, I came to see that they believed religiously in minding their own business. They definitely were not going to go to all the time-consuming trouble of shooting a stranger unless that stranger had done something singular enough to warrant shooting.

Suzy and I had reached Helena after a beautiful autumn morning that was clear with the special color and intensity of October. The leaves were in high color, and clouds of butterflies filled the gentle wind.

We had tied up the raft immediately inside the bayou early in the afternoon. There wasn't much of a marina, only a few battered docks, but the shore was littered with the blackened hulks of several ancient wrecks. There were more wrecks on the shore than there were boats in the water, even counting our raft. People lounged in the Sunday afternoon sun. The loungers didn't even go through the motions of fishing; mostly they sat and watched the river roll. We started walking up to town when a guy in a red Ford coupe pulled up next to us.

"Where y'all goin'?" he asked. When we explained we were going after groceries, he insisted that he'd take us up to town in his car. "C'mon," he said. "I'm just loaferin' and ain't got nothin' better to do."

We got into his car. He shook my hand and said, "My name is Sam Stewart Jr." Sam was short but stocky, built stout as a bull, with jet-black hair as thick and bushy as his eyebrows, which ran in one dense ridge below his forehead. His accent was pure Arkansas. He was thirty-five, and except for a hitch in the army had lived in Helena all his days.

"Where y'all from?"

"California," I said.

"The coloreds still raisin' hell out there?"

"Uh," I swallowed. "I suppose you could say that."

"Heh, heh, I bet I could," said Sam. I was always surprised that southerners, despite our appearance, always assumed we shared their prejudices. This was my first close encounter with a certifiable southern redneck, and I was paranoid to the point of active fear. I didn't want to discuss civil rights with him, so I asked, "You come down to the river often?"

"Yep," he said. "I come down every Sunday and watch it. I used to own that boat"—he pointed at one of the burned-out wrecks—"but a barge blew up in the bayou here and set her afire."

Sam learned I was a Civil War buff and gave us the grand tour of Helena. We drove far back into the hills to where the Battle of Helena was fought along the deep-cut backcountry roads on the Fourth of July in 1863, as Lee retreated from Gettysburg and Grant won the siege at Vicksburg. The battle was another disaster for the South, which outnumbered the Union forces but lost anyway. We stopped at the Confederate cemetery, which sat on the highest ridge of Maple Hill. We could see the hills fade into the South and miles of flatland farms and forest now orange and yellow and red with the colors of high autumn. Far below, reflecting the sky, the river meandered in and out of our line of vision, huge and twisting as a blue anaconda. The cemetery was old and crumbled by time. Besides a monument to Confederate Major General Patrick Cleburne, who died leading a charge at Franklin, Tennessee, but had been a druggist and lawyer in Helena and is now buried there, only a few of the stones were marked with names. Some listed only dates and some bore only the names of haunted places—Chickamauga, Chattanooga, Pittsburgh Landing, and Vicksburg.

We drove down to the flatlands by the river and passed the fertilizer plant where Sam worked. He showed us the biggest damn soybean silo on God's green earth. Sam rambled from telling us all the wonders of the soybean plant to an insider's view of the levee system. "The levee's a foot higher on the other side of the river," he said. "But if the river ever gits up that high, me and some boys got some dynamite tucked away, and we'll make damn sure that Mississippi goes under before Arkansas. Just coloreds over there anyway."

Sam included a racial jab in about every line he spoke. "Y'know," he said at the cemetery. "I got to admit that the folks up north won the last war—otherwise this country wouldn't be in the shape it's in—but we've got it all figured out how to win the next one. We're gonna let the coloreds burn down Detroit, Chicago, Washington, DC, then we'll pick up our guns and march right through 'em." He howled with laughter and pounded on the steering wheel, probably as amused by our discomfort as by his joke.

Sam drove through the black section of Helena. Generations of families relaxing in the warm Sunday afternoon covered the porches of the sagging gray frame shacks. They'd be smiling and laughing, taking it easy, but as soon as they saw us their faces froze into blank stares as they silently watched us drive by.

We passed two young blacks carrying dismantled shotguns. "See that," said Sam. "They know better than to come out of the woods with those guns in one piece. It'd be the last mistake they'd ever make." He told us that whenever any of the blacks got together or threatened to make trouble, the white men would run all the black men out of town. Sam warmed up and starting expounding on the race war that he saw as imminent and inevitable. I sat and listened to all this crap without saying a word. I was scared. When he picked us up, I figured he had some crazy friends out in the woods that'd love to use us for target practice, so I shut up and sat and listened.

Sam took us to a grocery store and offered to pay for the food we bought. He invited us over to his place to eat and spend the night, but we begged off, and he took us back to the waterfront. He left us puzzled; aside from his irrational obsession with racism, he was a nice guy. My silence and cowardice left me feeling sick. We got on the raft and left Helena behind.

Three years later I came around the point that dark night in the rowboat, I could see that progress had come to the marina at Helena. They'd hauled away most of the burnt-out wrecks, and half a dozen cabin cruisers were now tied to a new covered dock. A small office sat out over the water. Opposite the marina was a house trailer, and I walked over to ask if it was okay to sleep on the dock. A friendly, easy-going guy named Bill lived in the trailer and acted as caretaker. He said I could sleep anyplace I wanted, except on the cabin cruisers. He invited me inside, gave me a beer, and we watched some TV.

The next day was pretty unremarkable. I bought forty dollars worth of groceries (which in those days would last a long time), cleaned up *Walk on Water*, reorganized my gear, wrote letters, and wandered around town. That night I called my brother and told him not to worry if he didn't hear from me for a while.

During the evening some of the local high society came down to the docks, including Porter C. Young, who owned part of the marina and the newspaper besides. They were very friendly and a little tipsy, and without much persuasion, they got me to sing some songs for them. I'm still a lousy guitar player, but back then I was truly rotten. I sang old cowboy songs like "Jesse James" and "Blue Mountain," and they actually appeared to enjoy it. After a while I sang some of the new songs I'd written about the river. It was the first time that I was able to entertain people with my music.

I suppose Porter must have liked my songs because he wrote me up in his column, "Taming the Mississippi," right next to an article by his brother, General C. M. Young Jr., USAF, Retired, called, "The Tragedy of the Titanic." I don't like being called "boy" any more than the next guy, but I'm not going to criticize the prose style of anybody generous enough to let me take a shower. Here's the story as it appeared in the *Helena-West Helena Arkansas World and East Arkansas Record*:

> A boy... his dog ... and a guitar! Wednesday night well after dark a boy in a 12 foot rowboat came to the docks from upriver. He was

tired, saying he had rowed 40 miles that day against a strong South wind. With him was a large dog, part golden lab and German shepherd. The boy said he was from California. He put his boat in at the Kentucky Dam and was headed for Natchez. Asked why not continue to New Orleans, he said that two years ago he and a girlfriend made the trip down the Mississippi on a raft. He said the river offered no excitement below Natchez as the big ocean liners crowded the river. He is right.

He entertains himself with his guitar. His small boat is crowded with provisions, a sleeping bag, dog food, etc. He said he has yet to fall in the river but his dog has fallen in twice. Thursday morning he took a hot shower then headed for a laundromat to clean his clothes. That afternoon he spent his time writing letters, his diary, and reading. Friday morning he got some more provisions and set out for down river. He sported a full head of hair and a full grown beard. He was 21 years old; wants to get a job on a towboat. ... Rains in the eastern part of the country have caused the river to rise again. For the next several days the Mississippi will continue to climb, then should start to fall again. However, I am not predicting what the river will do. It gets mighty contrary at times.

As this very clean longhair was getting ready to leave on the morning of April 14, Bill came out of the trailer and snapped some pictures. I told him to give my thanks to everybody for their hospitality. As I rowed away, he waved and said, "So long." He walked across the gangway toward shore and I thought I had made good my escape, but he stopped and turned and called out, "Be careful."

XV

MONTEZUMA BEND

It was a gray morning, blustery enough to raise white caps on the river, but the warm and heavy wind blowing out of the south carried no threat of a storm. I rounded out of the harbor at Helena, rowed into the channel, and caught the main current. The river was high, so despite the south wind and rough water, we swept along at four or five miles an hour. *Walk on Water* spun downriver and under the high arching Helena Highway Bridge where the echoing engines and tires on the wind-played steel of Highway 49 sounded like amplified music. Watching the river buckle and howl against the bridge's massive concrete pilings, I slipped past the big soybean silo below town and into the empty, open river country.

Despite the overcast, it was springtime and the air tasted sweet. I pored over the Army Corps charts and plotted the next stage of our trip. I carefully examined the bayous and backwaters and towheads, mudbanks, and islands scattered along the next hundred miles of river. There was an excellent situation thirty or forty miles downstream near the mouth of the White River where several islands clustered around a long, navigable bayou, with as bright prospects for reefer as Sutpen's Hundred had for cotton in 1833. It was an easy day's drifting away, so with luck I could begin planting tomorrow. I considered rowing and riding the current closely so as to get to the projected site early, but I had a bad case of spring fever, and laziness persuaded me to relax and take it easy.

Thor was anxious at being on the water again. He circled around the bow of the boat until he finally made himself comfortable and settled down for the long haul.

I lay in the bottom of the boat and watched the world glide by. It felt so good—I was young and ready and alive and seemed to be in exactly the right place at the right time. It was warm, with the wind full of the kind of promise that makes animals shed their winter coats. The boat rolled along like a natural part of the river, see-sawing with the swells, inevitably southbound. There was nothing to do but watch for towboats, keep in the current, and lie around as our slow passage carried us to wherever it was that we were bound.

One or two towboats ran past, and then I had the river all to myself. I settled back and started reading a book. It was about Edgar Cayce, a work of pseudo-cosmology about yet another American religious quack, but it got me thinking. The river was a perfect metaphor of life: born of diverse threads and sources, constantly changing and renewed, bound for the inevitable sea, it was almost more likelife than life itself. Drifting into Montezuma Bend, I put the book down and contemplated the Arkansas shore about seven miles south of Helena.

Over my shoulder, upriver, I suddenly heard a high, loud hissing, the sound a cobra might make. I looked around to see what it was. It was a vision horrifying enough to raise hair on a rock; one glance was enough to yank the rest of my body around to face it in an instinctive, terrified crouch. Not fifty yards distant, the exact center of the bows of three empty petroleum barges loomed over the river, a solid wall of slanted steel rising fifteen feet above the water and spreading out some 200 feet. It was sweeping down the river, already so close it swallowed up the horizon. Towboats fly a flag in the middle of their barges' bows to be visible when they come around a bend in rough water. I was exactly in line with the pennant, in the precise center of that dark, onrushing steel wall. It slid toward me, hissing, relentless, mechanical, and huge.

In one frozen moment, I had three profound reactions. I could not believe what I was seeing; my eyes must have conjured this up with no help from reality. I laughed, then laughed at its undeniable reality, for it seemed enormously funny, hysterical, until finally the truth hit, and terror engulfed me.

The shock provoked a fierce adrenaline jolt, jerking me onto the rowing bench where I pulled for a stroke or two before realizing that rowing was absolutely pointless. The bows had already eaten up half the original distance between *Walk on Water* and the wall of steel. The bows rolled downriver at twice the speed of the current, their subtle hissing grown intolerably loud. My every nerve screamed—"You're a dead man!"—but I managed to devise a plan. Maybe I could wedge an oar between my boat and the barges and so manage to keep from being sucked under. It was utterly impossible, and I instinctively knew it, but under the circumstances it was all I could come up with. Within a few racing heartbeats, I braced the oar against the stern and waited for the onrushing steel bow. Thor too was now alert, his mouth hanging open in wonder.

Time slowed to a crawl. My head pounded with a single thought, "You're a dead man." The fear grew as the bows swept closer, and I yelled, screamed, howled, "Help!" hoping that someone on the barges would hear me, but it was like yelling into the teeth of a hurricane. The bows, rust red and streaked with black, came steadily on, looming up larger until they engulfed my vision and finally were on top of me. I jammed the oar against the river-blackened steel and watched the steel slip over the stern of my boat as easily and naturally as a rattlesnake swallows a mouse. I caught one last look at Thor as my hands went up against the cold, corroded, slimy metal.

Suddenly I was lost in wet, cold, and noisy blackness. The subaquatic world was completely dark. As the barges rushed over, I breast-stroked like a bullfrog. At first, my buoyancy pulled me up against the moving barges, a sickening feeling like the fingers of death scrapping along my back, but I pushed off against the steel with my legs as my boots filled with water and went deeper into the dark river. Horrendous submarine noises throbbed through the dark water like a steel drum band playing intensely on the bottom of the river in time to the weird music of the towboat's twin propellers. Now, for all the terror and adrenaline, I thought about Huck Finn and how he had wound up under a steamboat in much the same situation. Huck dove to the bottom of the river and hung on to a root until the man-eating sternwheel had passed overhead, but I was not about to try that number, being now as close to the bottom of the river as I ever hoped to get, pulling with strength born of fear through the black water toward, I hoped, the Arkansas side of the barges and not a spinning set of matched bronze screws.

My lungs emptied of air, and I kept expecting to feel the suction of two twisting steel blades. I swam and I swam, thinking about the props and the growing fire in my chest. At last I let go of some of the used up air. My lungs now emptied, but I had no idea how much farther I'd have to swim under that sheet of moving steel, which even fish must have found unnatural. I swam and swam.

Suddenly, an amazingly bright golden light filtered through the hair hanging down over my eyes. It meant I was nearing the edge of the barges, and I felt an exhilarating rush as the light grew brighter. Pulling out from under the hellish darkness, kicking desperately toward the light, my head at last broke the surface. I gasped greedily for air and came up with a mouthful of water. I choked and tried again and this time reached oxygen.

Realizing how cold the water was and the tremendous force of the current tempered my joy. My hulking workboots, bound to my feet with frayed laces, pulled down like a ball and chain. I fought to stay afloat because I knew that, unless I could catch the attention of somebody on the towboat, I was going to be in a very hard place. I ripped off my shirt and got ready to wave. The towboat came up very quickly. I had one short glimpse of her approach: I rolled under a wave and got a second quick look at her—a big three-decked towboat with two black stacks and white sides, clean and trimmed with red, but not a soul in sight or so much as a hint that men controlled this machine, and it was not some great, omniscient river monster. On a third glance, she was exactly opposite me. I waved at no one I could see and yelled, knowing exactly how puny the water-choked cry would be against the tow's pounding engines. I went under again and came up to catch a glimpse of the tow vanishing downstream. She disappeared with incredible speed, paying me no more mind than an elephant does the ant crushed in his track. Then the towboat was gone, and I was alone in the river.

I had to get the boots off: I knew they'd drown me if I didn't. It was hard work getting them off on dry land, but now, holding my breath and fumbling with the frayed laces in the bitter water while the current tossed me around like a scrap of driftwood, getting the damn boots off was nearly impossible. I tried to slip my knife out of my pocket, but my pants were too tight. The current was sweeping me around the bend and away from the Arkansas shore. I couldn't see it; I knew it was probably only a hundred yards away or so, but now the current had me, and maybe I'd have to go with it across the river to the Mississippi shore. This involved a lot of swimming. I was already worn out, and the dead weight of my boots filled me with dread. The fear-crazed part of my mind kept reminding me I was going to die.

I began to tread water and do a dead man's float to rest and regain my breath. I was drained and weak and cold. The boots drained my flagging strength. The river was so choppy that I could only manage about two breaths of air to every lungful of water. It began to look a lot like the end. Dread washed over me again. I experienced a sudden rush of images that brought my life into incredible focus. They filled me with an abysmal sense of failure. When balanced against a feather on Osiris's scale, my life had come to meaningless ruination. Having done nothing in all my days to justify displacing air, now it was all over and there never would be any such justification. I'd betrayed everyone I'd ever loved and accumulated a debt I could never repay. To die as I felt like I was dying was like hell itself. I remembered the awful stories about what the river did to those who died in its grasp. I'd not simply and honorably failed, I'd blown it completely. I thought about my mother. I figured I'd vanish like Uncle Bill had vanished and leave behind not even a corpse but instead a constant uncertainty. It was beyond terrible. I thought, "This is dying, and I hate it, and I never had any idea it would be like this."

But I was not dead yet. A comforting thought came to me: all I had to do was stay alive as long as I could, fight with death until there was no more breath to fight with, resist it to the end of resistance, and then it would be easy. There was comfort in this. The dread disappeared, and a sense of peace and composure flowed through my weary sinews. Everything seemed all right. Revelations rushed through my head like dawn coming up over a mountain. "Twenty more minutes and I'll probably know what it's like to be dead," I thought. Dying held no more terror, I was placid and curious. It felt as if I'd come to an edge or a gate or a wall, and with time I'd cross or merge or melt into something that felt like warmth; when I closed my eyes, I could see light. All that was important now was to resist, fight to stay alive as long as I could.

I set to work again at getting my boots off, and it occurred to me that I was either going to wind up naked and alive on the

Mississippi shore or clothed and dead in the Mississippi River, but it no longer seemed to matter. Not only was I detached and serene, I was getting positively euphoric. I floated for a while, trying to get more air. After resting, I tried to catch sight of the shore but saw only waterscape. I could have been in the middle of the Atlantic for all the land I could see, but a great dark object suddenly came into my line of vision. The towboat was backing water and launching a skiff. I was saved.

The tow had launched its lifeboat, a skiff that was now rocking with the swells next to the gangway. In the stern of the launch, a deckhand pulled the starter cord of an outboard. It seemed to take ten minutes to start the engine, as if the man was endlessly pulling the cord, and it appeared it might yet be my fate to drown because an internal combustion engine refused to start. My sense of time was shattered: it actually took only a few pulls to start the engine, and though I thought I'd been in the water not much more than five minutes, I later learned it had taken twenty minutes to launch the skiff.

At last the engine started, and the skiff came slamming across the water. After grabbing the gunwales, strength left me completely. Two deckhands pulled my dead weight up over the side, leaving me hanging on my balls, in true agony, but I couldn't move to help them. I flopped into the skiff like a huge catfish.

"Goddamn!" said one of them. "What the hell happened to you?"

"Run down," I gurgled.

"Jesus," said the second man. "You're lucky to be alive. I never heard of anything like this before, let alone seen it!"

I gurgled again. We came up to the tow, and they handed me aboard like a sack of potatoes. I lay on the deck for a while, flopping around, spitting water. About ten men had gathered around, and about half of them were talking. I remembered Thor and climbed up on my knees.

"Anybody seen a dog?" I said. "My dog's out there!"

An older man who was clearly in charge and several more times agitated than anybody else shoved through the crowd. "Was there anybody else on that boat?"

"No," I said. "Just me and the dog." I got to my feet and looked out over the water. The river was littered with broken wood, rags, papers, jugs, and I could even see my guitar case floating like Queequeg's coffin. I staggered back to the fantail looking for Thor, but all I could see was splintered garbage. The two guys in the skiff went after the guitar case but found it empty.

The old man came up again and took me into the messroom. The black cook handed me an army blanket and took my clothes—all I had left were my Levis, an undershirt, socks, and boots—so he could dry them. They took me to a narrow room, just forward of the engines, furnished with a TV and a couch. I collapsed onto the couch. My head was still spinning. "I'm alive," I thought. "I'm alive."

The old man stepped out of the cabin and left me alone. A young guy with long hair came in, clutching something in his hand.

"Take this," he said. "The cook found it in your pants. Get rid of it. We don't want you to get in any trouble." He handed me a baggie of marijuana. "Throw this in the river," he said.

I took the baggie and hauled myself out of the cabin. The sight of the rushing river scared the hell out of me. I threw the seeds in the flood and then vomited up buckets of bloody Mississippi River water.

The towboat had been backing water, and now she tied her load of barges to a soybean silo dock. The towboat came about and turned upriver toward Helena. The pilot—Captain Joseph Hazard Van Gale, the man I'd talked to on deck—returned and started asking questions. He asked if I wanted to go to a hospital or at least go ashore and have a doctor look me over. I said no. My head had that expansive feeling a mule must get after being hit on the head with a two-by-four, but I was not banged up except for some lacerations on my back and legs. I was in no pain. I did not want to hang up a whole towboat and crew so some doctor could tell me I was all right. And lucky to be alive.

The towboat was the *Olinda Chotin* out of Baton Rouge. Captain Gale was a big man in his mid-sixties. White hair fringed his balding head. He'd worked towboats all his life and was a legend on the river. Gale had been at the helm when I was run over and almost seemed more shook up than I was. Afraid it would make trouble for him, I told him it was my own damn fault and none of his. This didn't calm him down much.

"What the hell were you doing out there in a rowboat?" he asked.

I didn't say anything. And what could I have said? I was out there looking for knowledge? In a rowboat? On the Mississippi River?

Gale filled up the silence. "What kind of business did you have out there in a rowboat? You knew about towboats, didn't you? You'd seen towboats?"

"Yes, sir."

"Well, then, what the hell ..."

"Like I said," I said. "It was my fault." And it was; you just naturally had to expect that a man in a rowboat would see something as large as a towboat before you could expect a towboat to spot something as small as a rowboat.

"You could have been killed," said Gale. "By all rights, you *should* have been killed."

Once more, I was speechless.

"All right," he said, calming down some. "What was that boat worth?"

"It wasn't worth hardly anything," I said.

"No," he said. "You've got to tell me how much it was worth—your boat and gear and everything—so I can make a damage report."

So, still stunned with my watery spiritual experience, we cataloged all my late material possessions. I gave bargain basement prices on the stuff because I didn't want to cause Gale any more trouble than I already had. The damages totaled up to $450. Gale radioed company headquarters in Baton Rouge and very quickly a deal went down: the Chotin company would pay me $450 cash money and give me a free ride to Baton Rouge if I'd sign a legal release. That sounded fine to me. *Olinda Chotin* started downriver.

I went back to the couch and lay there in my army blanket. My brain was overwhelmed, while every molecule in my body seemed to vibrate with intense energy and glow with the pleasure of being alive. Everything seemed to make sense: I was literally born again. I meditated until the cook brought dry pants and the soggy boots that had nearly scuttled me. Captain Gale gave me a white shirt and showed me the guest cabin. I took a shower and then lay on the bed a while. My head was still spinning, my mind kept going back to that awful moment when I turned and saw that line of barges rushing down the river. I was restless and got up to explore the boat.

Olinda Chotin was two years old, 154 feet long and 48 abeam, and the flagship of the Chotin family line. The engine room filled the belly of the boat, reaching below the waterline, and took up most of her lower deck. Machinery that could generate 5,400 horsepower jammed this hot, throbbing cavern and resounded with thunderous noise. Above the engine room you could cross from the galley to the TV room on a catwalk. A long table dominated the mess hall, located aft of the engines, where the officers and crew ate in two shifts at the changing of the six-hour watch. Forward of the engines, the TV room was an open hallway that led to a couple of the deckhands' cabins. The two upper decks contained quarters for the rest of the crew, which were fitted out exactly like motel rooms. The pilothouse perched atop the entire assembly.

The large glass box of the pilothouse had a sweeping view of the river. I asked the first mate for permission to enter it. The pilothouse was fitted out with brass and leather and wood and housed engine throttles and controls, searchlight levers, a chart table, two large swivel chairs, a green radar screen, and a set of gears that served as the steering wheel. I sat in one of the chairs and surveyed the vast expanse of barges plowing south. The bow was incredibly far away. It would have been hard to see a rowboat beyond them even if you were looking for it.

The crew were good old boys, mostly in their late twenties or early thirties, tough, single working men, a lot like the kinds of guys you'd meet in construction fields or jails; my kind of folks. I talked to most of them, and they all said, "Jesus, I don't see how you got out from under there."

"I don't either," I replied.

"What did you do?"

"I swam like hell."

"Jesus." They'd shake their heads. "You're goddamn lucky to be alive."

"I know."

A tall, rangy, weather beaten deckhand named Rex told me he was the one who spotted me in the river.

"What were you doing?" I asked.

"I was sweeping out the pilothouse and brushing it out over the catwalk when I saw the river was full of trash. All I could see of you was your back."

"What'd you do?"

"I went in the pilothouse and told Cap'n Gale."

"What'd you say?"

"I said, "Cap'n, there's a body in the river.""

"You saved my life," I said.

"Hmm. I still don't see how you got outta there. I knew a fella once fell off the bow, and when he came out the other end there weren't even any pieces to pick up."

The pilot who had the afternoon watch was in his late thirties, taciturn and quiet, with the intensity of a wound-up spring you regularly encounter in southern workingmen. I sat in the pilot-house through the afternoon, watching him handle the towboat with the natural ease of a trucker driving a diesel. He said he'd once been on a towboat that found an empty skiff adrift. They hauled it aboard and saw it was stocked and equipped for a long trip. There were notebooks and letters with a guy's name on them and his kin from Chicago eventually came and reclaimed the boat, but the young adventurer vanished without a trace.

By evening my head had cooled down enough so that my stomach was working—in fact, I was starved and ate a vast number of pork chops and biscuits and gravy and potatoes and a wide array of vegetables. The crew kept up riotous conversation and joked all through supper, tales mostly about drinking and whoring. The boat's old engineer was a natural comic who told long stories that kept everybody howling as they tried to eat.

I felt sheepish and stupid and kept my mouth shut except to put in food, but nobody seemed to hold it against me that not only was I fool enough to be in a rowboat on the Mississippi but enough of a fool to put that rowboat directly in front of nine empty petroleum barges and one full towboat.

"You about give out on the rowboat business?" the engineer asked me.

"I'm retired," I said.

And I was. I was also scared to death of the river. I don't believe I stepped out onto the deck once during the rest of my ride on *Olinda*; even standing in the door looking out at the river gave me the shakes. The Mississippi looked entirely new. I had no desire to get any closer to the river than the pilothouse. It was as if I'd just figured out that the river was made of water, or maybe I realized at last the fierce and uncaring nature of the Old Devil. He was as ruthless as time or nature or God; he did not give one damn for any man or for the whole of humankind. Looking at the wide, muddy water gave me a kind of vertigo, as if I would fall in or more exactly some invisible, magnetic force would suck me into the swift-flowing river.

I went to bed about ten but was still too buzzed to sleep. In the dark my mind kept going over and over the wreck, starting with a vivid image of those long, high bows as they swept down until they rolled relentlessly over Thor and me. It would click then back to the image of those bows, so clear that it was like seeing them again. I turned on the light and tried to read a detective magazine but couldn't get those bows out of my mind. I got dressed and went up to the pilothouse.

Captain Gale was standing his night watch. The pilothouse was dark except for the luminous green glow of the radar and the reflected light of the river-sweeping searchlights. The *Olinda Chotin*'s command center consisted of throttles, rudder controls, engine gauges and RPM indicators, radar scopes, a fathometer, radio-telephones to communicate with other pilots, and an array of whistles and lights. It was quiet, except for the intermittent crackle of the radio and the constant throbbing of the engines. After a while Captain Gale asked me why I didn't turn in.

"I tried, but I keep seeing what those bows looked like coming down on me."

Gale took this as if he'd been hit. "Listen," he said with real concern. "Take a couple of aspirin and get some sleep and you'll be okay. Forget about it. It's all over now." I stayed on long enough to acquire an enormous amount of respect for Captain Gale, who had held his pilot's license since 1946 and got his master's license five years later. His fellow pilots admired him enormously. He explained that there were about 3,500 navigation lights between New Orleans, Minneapolis, and Pittsburgh, and the pilot's examination required naming every one of them, and answer about 150 other questions. That summer Gale later told a reporter, "The Coast Guard makes it tougher all the time. Even boys with a college education have trouble."

The next morning I ate a huge breakfast of hotcakes and sausage and eggs. I spent most of the day up in the pilothouse, watching the river. From that perch the river seemed distant and safe, much more like a winding highway than the river I'd come to know. The pilots talked to other tows coming upriver, negotiating how they'd pass each other before the other boat was even in sight. The pilots all knew each other, and they'd shoot the breeze and trade insults. Through the day we visibly rolled deeper into springtime, past Natchez on its high proud bluff and deeper into the lush delta jungle.

I still felt weird as hell, both stunned and enlightened, my very skin electric, but mostly I felt good, awed, joyous, the way I felt the day after I lost my virginity. I also seemed to be hornier than I'd ever been in my life. I couldn't keep my mind off women, and when my mind was on women, it was like that electric skin had caught fire. Lord, it was strange. Maybe it was a natural reaction to coming close to death, but whatever it was, it was powerful.

I felt terrible about Thor, dragging him across country to meet a watery grave under about the lousiest possible conditions. Thor was a damn good dog, and his master betrayed him. There'd been no sign of him in the river, and I hated to think about what could and probably did happen to him. The only thing Thor would know under all that hideous steel was that it was horrible. I talked to a deckhand who said he thought Thor might have made it. He'd seen deer swimming across the river get run over by towboats and come out all right. I hoped, but knowing Thor, he probably never figured out what had hit him.

The day rolled away up in the pilothouse, and *Olinda Chotin* churned into the lower river past the Old River Control Structure where the current slowed as it approached the sea. We passed into a new and different climate. The banks had already exploded into the full bloom of spring and the air was starting to settle into the liquid southern heat of summer. In the evening there were all the T-bone steaks you could eat (I ate a few), and with the last fading of the thick twilight we rounded the wild and desolate bend above Baton Rouge, coming around the point and into the roadstead as it grew dark.

The city was lit up for Saturday night. The mooring lights of the huge sea-going ships riding at anchor began to blink on. The refineries that littered the shore shot blue flames high into the air to become part of the hot, blood-colored sunset. *Olinda Chotin* left her load of barges for the harbor tugs to handle and turned immediately back upriver to dock at the Chotin company boat store where the crew burst into frenetic activity, taking on food and water and fuel and replacements for the men whose thirty-day tour of duty was up.

A couple of Chotin executives and their lawdogs awaited us when *Olinda* docked. We went upstairs to the company offices where they grinned when I signed the legal release and I grinned back when they handed over the check. They even gave me fifty dollars cash so that I could enjoy the weekend. One of the executives assured me I could get a job on one of their towboats and told me to come back Monday.

As the fuel lines were dragged away, Captain Gale came up and said, "You aren't going to be taking any more rowboats down the river, are you?"

"No, sir," I said. "I'm cured of that."

"Well, you be careful. And listen, if you're ever in New Orleans and you need any help, let me know, all right?"

"Thanks," I said. Then, forty-five minutes after she had docked, *Olinda Chotin* was gone, pushing another load of petroleum up to Cincinnati for the Yankees to burn. I was alone again. The adventure was over.

XVI

ALL THE RIVERS RUN INTO THE SEA

The boat store had pretty much emptied when *Olinda Chotin* steamed away, and frantic activity ceased altogether. There were three guys left killing time around a red-hot TV set: a college kid named Lane who watched the boat store at night; an old Cajun named Dupuis who ran a ferry service out to the ships anchored in the roadstead; and a young Cajun deckhand named Jean who was hanging out. We talked about the river and towboats. Jean told us about being on a towboat that fouled a snag and began taking on water. His father, the pilot, ran the boat into shallow water, and they all stood in the pilothouse while towboat sank deck by deck and settled into the mud. In a thick dialect that was mostly French except for the obscenities, Dupuis told tales about running hookers out to the ships. The TV set periodically went haywire, and Jean would beat on it until it straightened out. As the evening wore on and the stories got crazier, the TV got worse and so took quite a pounding, until the frustrated crazy aging Cajun kicked it, killing it stone dead.

The boat store was built on a worn-out barge moored next to the cobblestones of the Baton Rouge waterfront. An oily stretch of water separated the barge and the shore, and Lane and I crossed the gangplank and smoked a reefer. Lane told me the story of the woman who wanted to die.

He'd been working late one Saturday night when a drunk black woman had crossed the gangplank yelling, "I'm gonna kill myself, I'm gonna kill myself!" Lane and Dupuis looked out of the store to see her leap into the backwater. The two or three feet of stagnant, dirty water succeeded in getting her wet but did not drown her at all. Lane and the Cajun dragged her out of the murk and onto the boat store, but she was hysterical and cried that she wanted to die. Dupuis pulled the woman around to the end of the barge and showed her the dark flood of the real river, vast and menacing in the night. He told her that unless she got off the boat store *très rapide* he was going to throw her into the river. The woman screamed and fled, running off the boat and up to town, crying murder all the way. It took me years to realize it, but what had happened to that poor lost woman that night was exactly what had happened to me.

At midnight I went out and walked through the streets of Baton Rouge. It was Saturday night, but now the streets were deserted except for an occasional cab or cop. I came to a department store window and got horny looking at the mannequins. It was awful. I started thinking about my future, wondering especially how long it would take to get laid. I wanted to get a job on a towboat, but this horniness was more than I could endure for thirty days. I decided to go to New Orleans in the morning and see what I could do.

Lane let me sleep on the floor of his apartment. The next morning, sure enough, I met a beautiful blonde from Arkansas. We went to New Orleans and drank a lot and walked out on the levee and made out. But she would not sleep with me. "I've known sailors before," she said. It about drove me nuts. I started thinking hard about going back to California.

Monday morning I talked to the personnel officer at Chotin. He said he'd guarantee me a job if I hung around for a week, but I gave in to loneliness and lust—and yes, fear too, for I was now properly scared of the river—and caught a ride to the New Orleans airport where I spent most of my windfall fortune on a plane ride to California. I told myself I was going back to Lone Star to write the true tale of my adventures, but for three years I hardly picked up a pen. In my expanded state of mind, I was convinced that whatever course I chose was the right one, as inevitable and unavoidable as the bows of *Olinda Chotin*, because, after all, character is fate.

I had learned a lot on my oddball odyssey:

- It's better to be warm and dry than cold and wet;
- humans carry their troubles with them;
- folks who have to worry about work and family and money have troubles that keep their minds from inventing other discomforts;
- and people are basically good.

Those who have had near-death experiences often say, "It changed my life forever." Looking back from the perspective of decades, I have to say my encounter with eternity changed my life for a while. It did teach one profound lesson: it's infinitely better to be alive than dead. My experience filled me with the simple joy of being alive. After the passage of years and decades I have an abiding appreciation of the wonder and worth of life.

This is the end of the predictable fable of the fool in the boat. As the westbound jet lifted off the runway, I looked down at the silver thread of the Mississippi stretching to the blue horizon. I thanked the river for sparing my life. The river would be there for more time than human minds can comprehend. I promised someday I'd be back; now it was California. Ah, why did I pass up a Mississippi River job to return to Santa Cruz? I should've known better: I'd been there before.

Coda

Two last questions and tales: What became of the *Olinda Chotin* and her intrepid commander, Joseph Hazard Van Gale? Some six weeks after my close encounter with Captain Gale in April 1972, John Ed Pearce, a gifted staff writer for the Louisville *Courier-Journal & Times Magazine*, put Gale and the *Olinda Chotin* at the center of his compelling article on the "Hazards of Barging." Pearce described the disaster that destroyed the *Thomas W. Hines* near Cannelton, Indiana. Gale's friend Captain Rolland Griffin disappeared before dawn on April 20, 1972, after the swollen Ohio swept his towboat over a dam and two of its three barges exploded. Griffin was a respected riverman. Many believed his towboat "had a power failure; he was too good a pilot to have gotten caught in that current otherwise." A deckhand saw Griffin's burning life jacket in the churning water before he disappeared. Many assumed he had vanished forever, but in early June the Ohio released his body about a hundred miles downstream. Pearce's article said nothing about my encounter with Captain Gale. Little wonder; Griffin lost his life less than a week after the *Olinda Chotin* almost ended mine.

Captain Gale told Pearce about his fifty years working as a river pilot and spoke of retiring in March when he turned sixty-five. A decade later in 1982 Clarke "Doc' Hawley, former captain of the *Delta Queen*, was master of the New Orleans tourist paddle-wheeler *Natchez*. He invited Captain Joe to join a ten-day, 1,240-mile excursion to Kentucky to race with the *Delta Queen* and the *Belle of Louisville*. Journalist Ward Sinclair talked with "Capt. Joseph Van Gale, a stoic fellow who piloted towboats between New Orleans and Louisville for 30 years" and "Capt. Lexie Palmore, a regular pilot on the *Delta Queen*" and one of the first women to become a licensed river pilot.

"Capt. Gale put the river ahead of all else," Sinclair wrote. After Gale retired from the Chotin line he piloted the *Mississippi*

Queen, which joined the *Delta Queen* hauling tourists up and down the river in 1976. His wife ordered him to quit. "Wife doesn't want to stay home alone. Can't much blame her, I guess," he told Sinclair one afternoon. Gale "took a job piloting the excursion boats around New Orleans and sleeping at home each night."

Captain Gale was born in March 1908 and probably set sail on the Big Sky River long ago. What became of the *Olinda Chotin*? She was sold to Midland Enterprises of Cincinnati in 1973 and renamed the *Olinda C.* in 1994. Midland sold her to JAR Assets of Mandeville, Louisiana, and they dubbed her *Jerry Jones* in 1999. She sailed under that name until December 2016. Since January 2019, the Strait Marine Group of Paducah, Kentucky, has owned this wonderful towboat, now known as the *Mabel C. Etheridge*. Somewhere the beautiful Madame Chotin is still rolling on the rivers of America.

Journalist James Ney took a photograph of "Modern Huck Finn and Crew" at Rock Island's Sunset Marina on the morning the soggy adventurers set sail on the Mississippi, September 24, 1969. Artist Curtis N. Jensen converted the grainy online image to a publishable sketch. Ney wrote the group up in "Mark Twain Inspiration of Raft Trip," for the *Des Moines Register*. Left to Right: Bill Bagley, Suzy Snyder, Eric Wood, Mario Marioncelli III, Diana Harvey, and Ward Stanger.

AFTERWORD

In a 1979 interview with Cameron Crow, Joni Mitchell mentioned the "terrible opportunity" people have when "they discover to the tips of their toes that they're *assholes*." You have plenty of terrible opportunities to make Mitchell's discovery and learn a lot when you begin a book in 1969 and finish it half a century later. You learn about the deceptive nature of memory and how, when the mind forgets something, it often creates recollections to fill the void. You even forget how much you forget over fifty years. I don't like writing about myself but love telling stories, so I thought writing this memoir would be easy. Wrestling with the memory bear and trying to summarize an unexpectedly long life proved harder than I had imagined.

Thanks to Dave Brinks, David Roe, and the wonders of YouTube and Dr. Google, I've recently learned a lot about 912 Toulouse. Its colorful history is a tribute to the endurance of a community. The resident Suzy and I met there on Halloween 1969 was poet and drag queen Randi Ray, who had been living there long before Ramblin' Jack visited. Ray had helped ruth weiss find a place to live after she hitchhiked from Chicago to New Orleans in July 1950. She still refuses to capitalize her name as a symbol of her rejection of "law and order," a logical response for a poet, playwright, performer, and protester who spent her childhood leaving Berlin, Vienna, and the Netherlands before reaching New York as an eleven-year-old refugee in 1939. After ruth settled in New Orleans, poet and saxophonist Bruce Lippincott asked her if he could publish her poetry in his *Old French Quarter News,* which launched her legendary literary career. She was the girl with green hair who danced around the banana tree with Jack Elliot in 1953. Ms. weiss became one of the French Quarter's most beloved poets, "not only for her amazing poetry and sure-fire spirit, but also for the notorious parties that took place almost nightly at her place." She moved west to San Francisco and Big Sur in 1952. Herb Caen, who coined the term beatnik in June 1958, called ruth the "Goddess of the Beat Generation." In 2019, she still is.

Drafts of this book avoided mentioning I was enrolled at the University of California at Santa Cruz from 1968 until I graduated in June 1971. (Suzy took a leave of absence from UC Berkeley to make the raft trip and then transferred to Santa Cruz.) I got credit for writing three independent study papers about the field trip— and more credits from Page Stegner for writing that awful novel. Professors John Dizikies, Laurence Veysey, and John Jordan boldly sponsored the project in what Dizikies called the "immensely bureaucratic and conventional" University of California system. Despite UCSC's pass/fail grades and radical reputation, professors were far from free to do whatever they wanted at Santa Cruz, and faculty from other UC campuses considered them unusual. In late 2011, Dr. Dizikies recalled that a faculty member at a Berkeley meeting told him, "You know, I heard the wildest thing about something going on down there"—a "project to sail down the Mississippi as an independent study, or something." Dizikies replied, "That's great. I'm the person who's sponsoring that," and defended the student who wrote "a wonderful paper about it." Wasn't it odd,

Dizikies wondered, that his colleague considered it "a wild kind of enterprise and notion"?

Even as the 1960s ended, the raft trip *was* a wild enterprise and crazy idea. Personally, the venture seemed to prove if I had a dream, I could make the dream a reality. I've spent fifty years testing the limits of this wild notion. My romantic attachment to the nineteenth century was the driving force behind my youthful adventures as I sought to experience what life was like long before I was born. Did it work? I don't know. I'd like to believe that going down the Mississippi on a raft, peddling a bicycle and riding box-cars across half a continent, building a log cabin in the woods, and raising a tobacco crop on shares gave me insights into the lives and times of the people I've written and thought about so often. This sounds like wishful history, and the world has all it needs of that.

Anyone who survives decades of life's strange events can recall being many different people. *River Fever* described my youthful incarnation as a wanderer, which continued after my near-death encounter with the *Olinda Chotin*. I will wonder until an ice age engulfs hell what would have happened had I gotten a job as a deckhand. I know what happened after I returned to California. That spring, I met Donna Jean Henry of Kingston, Jamaica, who claimed to be the world's only white Rastafarian. D. J. decided to move into Lonestar Peak. That summer we headed east with my musical pal Andy Fuhrman and his sweetheart, Kitty Rose. During an awful August, D. J. and I stayed in New Orleans at a rooming house on Royal Street, while she danced at Lafitte's Boudoir to earn money to fly us to Kingston. There we stayed briefly with her artist mother, camped at her friend Boppo's shanty on Hope Road opposite Queen's House, smoked ganja and drank Red Stripes, hitchhiked across the island, and slept on the beach at Ocho Rios and Negril, circumnavigating the island with our thumbs. We wound up back in Florida. From there we hitchhiked to Spring Creek, North Carolina.

That winter I worked construction in California and bought a coral 1957 Chevy Hydramatic pickup with a sweeping back window. After Ms. Henry left me, I settled for three lost and lonely years in the Smokey Mountains. I built a ramshackle locust log shack overlooking the foundations of Pearl Ponder's cabin with a spectacular view of Bluff Mountain. I learned to play guitar, badly. I wrote and sang dozens of songs, loudly. Rather than give up prose after earlier failures to write a decent novel about the Mississippi, in 1975 I drafted this book as a "non-fiction novel." I got arrested hitchhiking to Atlanta and wrote a song about it called "Hell in Georgia." That fall I chased dreams of publishing fame to Boston, where my brother Kevin was going to law school.

When I visited Kevin recently, he recalled my gift for blowing once-in-a-lifetime opportunities. Bob Dylan began touring New England in 1975 with roadshow circus that included Joan Baez, Roger McGuinn of the Byrds, Allen Ginsberg—and Ramblin' Jack Elliott. A camera crew tagged along to film concerts and random events. By chance, on November 19, they played Worcester Memorial Auditorium, a mere twenty miles from my brother's apartment in Brookline. I hitchhiked to Worcester. Ramblin' Jack, who is as kind as they come, got me inside to see the show. The review had been playing for three weeks and that night really came together to deliver its best show so far. After it was over, Jack invited me to visit the next day at the Sheraton hotel in Boxborough. I showed up in the late morning to find Jack finishing breakfast in the hotel's atrium restaurant with guitarist Mick Ronson and Dylan at his table. Somebody asked what was in my guitar case. I showed off my respectable Gibson J-50, and Dylan said, "Play us a song, play us your best song."

This required a snap decision. Rather than play a rousing

version of my rabble-rousing crowd pleaser "Groundhog!" I picked "Hell in Georgia," with its heroine's haunting chorus, "Who is doing this, who is doing this to me?" The atrium had great acoustics, but I can't say my booming baritone rocked the place, for stone (or relieved?) silence filled the space when I stopped.

"How long you been playing guitar?" Dylan eventually asked.

"Four years," I said.

After breakfast, everybody returned to their rooms, and I hung out with other hangers-on. So far, so good, I thought. Someone on the film crew asked me to stick around because they might need me. I was pretty full of myself and pressed myself on several people while they were eating dinner. When the tour headed for Harvard Square Theater that evening, we hangers-on filled two buses: I rode on the lower-level hangers-on bus and saw another great show. After it ended, I asked the film guy where I should go. "We don't need you anymore," he said.

This derailed my dream of rocketing to fame as a singer-songwriter, but my dreams of a musical career died much harder. By 1976 I realized I would never be at home in the American South and returned to my native Utah, where I started another life working construction and singing in bars and restaurants. While busking at Trolley Square, a shopping mall located in Utah Light & Railway Company's old trolley barns, I met local musicians who taught me how to play country rock. With my hard-won wages, we recorded a dozen songs unleashed on YouTube in 2018 as "Crows Will Pick Our Bones." We consumed copious amounts of youthful energy playing in bar bands at dozens of dives from Rock Springs, Wyoming, to Elko, Nevada. In 1979 I recorded and released a thousand copies of a long-playing record and song cycle, "The Legend of Jesse James." Before acknowledging my lack of musical talent, I sold almost all of them.

On April 15, 1978, I married Janis Johnson. The Wasserman

test required for marriage at the time revealed I had Type 1 insulin-dependent diabetes. I continued to chase my foolish musical dreams while working as a carpenter, cabinet maker, and member of the United Brotherhood of Carpenters and Joiners. Children change their parents' lives profoundly, as did Cassandra Marie, when she arrived in October 1980, and Jesse Miles Lynn, who appeared in January 1984. I became less of a restless dreamer and focused more on being worthy of their unconditional love. Except for singing "Groundhog!" at their birthday parties, I pretty much abandoned my dream of becoming a professional musician.

Cabinetmaker Bob Adams helped to launch another dream when he revived my interest in history. Bob was probably in his fifties when we worked as benchmen at WoodTech in the late 1970s. He sprang from a southern Utah pioneer family and helped me understand how central our tribe had been to so much western history. Bob lent me *Mormonism Unveiled; or the Life and Confessions of the Late Mormon Bishop, John D. Lee.* He offered to sell me his impressive collection of Mormoniana for $500, which would have been the book deal of the decade, but it was $500 more than I had at the time: I would be thirty years old before I made $5 an hour. I think Bob introduced me to Jerald and Sandra Tanner, whose Utah Lighthouse Ministry sold photocopies of early Mormon classics at low prices. I ate them up.

When I grew up, Mormonism was still rural, folksy, and provincial. In those days any member could wander into its dark and dumpy Greek Revival Church Administration Building at 47 East South Temple, visit the Church Historian or an apostle, and ask about whatever was on his or her mind. My raising included marching in the 1956 Pioneer Day children's parade, which contributed to a lifelong fascination with trails, overland emigration, and the dark secrets of American expansion. Western films and television shows dominated popular culture during my childhood;

Nothing topped Fess Parker's Davy Crockett, but Zorro, Paladin, and Maverick played a role. In Mrs. England's third grade class, I picked Magellan after being assigned to do a report on an explorer. The class's encyclopedia had a picture of brave Filipinos terminating the steel-encased explorer's life; the image inspired a need to know more about the brutal conversions and conquests that followed the "discovery" of New Worlds.

I have fond memories of my childhood in East Millcreek during the 1950s, before the religion became what Juanita Brooks called "Reubenized." She resented lawyer J. Reuben Clark's Mormon Republican reformation of the faith she loved. Clark had vast influence on twentieth-century Mormonism. Brooks, the bravest of the generation of historians that included Dale Morgan and Fawn Brodie, stuck with Mormonism but disliked the "dictatorship of Brother Clark." She rejected the growing tendency of "the Church to control all elements of Mormon life" and the regimentation Clark promoted with his "Correlation" policy. "By 'Reubenized,' I mean the writing out of every program, every speech, whether for Sunday School conference, Mother's Day Program, or what not," Brooks wrote, "—the attitude that he gave out to the Seminary teachers that 'you are not hired to think. You are hired to teach.'" In addition to her sharp awareness of how Brigham Young and his northern Utah aristocracy had exiled her ancestors to the "ragged edge of the Mormon frontier," what aggravated Brooks was the transformation of a folksy faith into a vast corporate real-estate empire.

Clark's brand of Mormonism affected my own family. My paternal grandfather was a corporate lawyer, but he shared my other grandparents' rural roots on the farms in East Millcreek, Holladay, and Grantsville, while their children became thoroughly modern Mormons. All remained "active" Latter-day Saints, but my aunts shared my mom's approach to Mormonism: "I know it's all a lot of hooey," she told me, "but I like it anyway."

I knew I wanted to be a writer at age six. My love affair with books hit early and lasted a lifetime. Rambling reading of the story of the American West extended across decades, and during the 1980s I began writing history; after all the wild dreams I had chased, becoming a historian didn't seem impossible. While working construction, I read all eleven volumes of Will and Ariel Durant's *The Story of Civilization* while Cassie and Jesse crawled up into my easy chair. My ongoing survey of western history began at Santa Cruz with a 1970 independent study of the Rocky Mountain fur trade, using Dale L. Morgan's 1953 *Jedediah Smith and the Opening of the West* as its foundation. Mass consumption of popular history and biographies followed. Self-education lacked the discipline of graduate studies but inspired an enduring affection for good storytelling. In 1997 I told Martin Ridge of the Huntington Library I thought graduate school would have made me a better historian. "If you'd have gotten a PhD," Martin said, "they'd have beaten whatever writing talent you have right out of you."

My career in the trades bottomed out while working at Wood-Tech and for a crew of Scientologist remodelers. Thanks to publisher Paul Swenson, every Utah writer's friend, in November 1979 I broke into print with a *Utah Holiday* article, "Country Blues on the Cowchip Trail," which led to my first writing paycheck. A year after IBM released its first personal computer, at about the last possible moment someone who knew virtually nothing about technology could have landed a job in the industry, Evans & Sutherland, the world's first computer graphics company, hired me as a technical writer in 1982. So began my new life as a dad, computer pro, and buff who dreamed about writing history.

These dreams led to a new hobby, historical research. I considered writing a biography of a book, Fawn Brodie's *No Man*

Knows My History. Brodie had died in 1981 and left her papers to her alma mater, the University of Utah, and they told her story. The 1970s were tumultuous times for all who studied the past, especially for progressive historians of the American West who launched the New Western History. It was Camelot for chroniclers of the Mormon past as Leonard J. Arrington introduced academic professionalism to the LDS Church Historian's Office. As a golden age of Mormon history, Arrington's Camelot was every bit as mythical as King Arthur's court; Leonard was a wonderful human being, but as a historian, he was a company man whose mildly liberal policies offended several of the patriarchs who ran the show. (Brodie's papers included a rather craven letter in which Arrington asked her to keep their friendship secret.) With the aid of a few embedded undercover Mordreds, in 1982 the church hierarchy exiled Leonard and his round table to darkest Provo.

The transition enabled Mark Hofmann, predatory Mormon conman extraordinaire, to systematically monetize and corrupt history with a forgery scam that extended beyond Utah. At age ten, Hofmann made his own nitroglycerine in a Salt Lake City suburb. He began faking history in junior high school, electroplating a mint mark on an ordinary dime to boost its appraised value by 98 percent. Deceiving people apparently gave him a sense of power. He served an LDS mission and dropped out of college to become a dealer who produced rare Mormon books and documents to order. His forgeries sometimes cast dark shadows on the faith's official happy history of inspired visions. His faked October 1830 "Salamander Letter" credited Mormon origins not to an angel but to an amphibian. A few observers, including Mormon critic Jerald Tanner and LDS Church Education System instructor Rhett S. James, warned that Hofmann's documents appeared bogus, but Hofmann ran rings around many of the faith's "New Mormon Historians," who sought to integrate his forgeries into a faithful narrative that "did not undermine Joseph Smith's image or the church's divine origins." In June 1984 Jerald Tanner identified the sources Hofmann had used to compose his notorious Salamander letter, proving W. C. Fields was right: "You can't cheat an honest man."

One morning in May or June 1985, I awoke as usual, read the *Salt Lake Tribune,* kissed the kids goodbye, and drove to work at Evans & Sutherland. I couldn't get an article by investigative journalist Dawn Tracy out of my head about purported recent document discoveries. Ms. Tracy, who now uses her maiden name, Dawn House, quoted LDS Church Librarian Earl Olson insisting that a purported Oliver Cowdery early draft of Mormon history didn't exist. What caught my interest was the article's claim that someone (Hofmann) had been inside the First Presidency's vault, a legendary repository for generations of the faith's secrets. Veteran *Tribune* religion reporter and Porter Rockwell biographer Harold Schindler described it to me as "the green safe" he had long seen in Church Historian Joseph Fielding Smith's office in the old church headquarters, where Joseph Smith's great-nephew had served as an apostle since 1910. (Hal suspected it contained an autobiography Rockwell dictated to Elizabeth Roundy in his old age.) It turned out Smith had filled the green safe with random oddities, some embarrassing but many not secret or even interesting.

I had paid tithing as a paperboy and thought, "Hey, I'm still a Mormon." At least, in theory, Brother Olson worked for me. I called up the LDS Church Historical Department and asked to speak to Earl. To my surprise, Olson answered. I asked if there was an Oliver Cowdery history in the vault. "No!" he said. Was there was an inventory of the contents of the First Presidency's vault? "No!" said Olson. "And there never will be!" (Actually, there already was.) If I wanted to ask for access, Olson suggested I write to Francis M. Gibbons, secretary to the First Presidency. I did. Gibbons replied, saying the church "does contain a handwritten

20-page document, probably in the handwriting of Oliver Cowdery, which covers the history of the church from 1829 to 1831." I also asked Brother Gibbons if the LDS Church had a history written by church founder Joseph Smith. "Inasmuch as some information may be published in the future which will touch upon these matters," Mr. Gibbons wrote, "no response to your query will be given at this time."

As I was getting started as a history buff, Hofmann made the past a lethal hobby. Entrepreneur Steve Christensen picked up a package in front of his Judge Building office on October 15, 1985; it exploded and killed him. That afternoon, Hofmann left a second bomb in a driveway and murdered Kathy Sheets, wife of Christensen's partner in a swiftly sinking financial services enterprise. Loyalty and a tendency to trust made easy targets of Mormons like Christensen, who had purchased the Salamander Letter from Hofmann for $40,000 and donated it to the Mormon Church. Kathy Sheets was collateral damage in Hofmann's scheme to divert attention from his own imploding finances and collapsing forgery scam.

Within a year of the bombings, Salt Lake Police Department detectives had closed in on Hofmann and developed a theory of the case that exposed his forgeries and motives. On Thursday, October 16, 1986, a Mormon Church press release denied there was any substance to "widely circulated rumors that the church owns a very early history of the church written by Oliver Cowdery." Secretary Gibbons's 1985 letter had said exactly the opposite. I shared it with Dawn Tracy, who was exposing the tangled web church bureaucrats had spun. She quoted Brigham Young University professor Michael Quinn, who noted "one historical reference that suggests the church may own a secret history" written by Joseph Smith himself.

Memories of the whole sorry history of the Hofmann affair— especially the serial half-truths two high-ranking church leaders trotted out for the press on October 23, 1985; Hofmann's plea deal, which a Mormon prosecutor had tailored so apostles could avoid being held to account for their efforts to hide the Mormon past; and the way the saintly high-and-mighty shifted blame onto less exalted shoulders than their own—affected my view of the modern Mormon theocracy. The church's response raised what became a defining question throughout my career as a professional historian: Who owns the Mormon past? I became convinced it belonged to the Mormon people, not to the Mormon corporation or to the highest bidder.

An engineer at Evans & Sutherland asked me how our brilliant project manager could believe in a religion as weird as Mormonism. For years I considered that the hardest question about the faith. Eventually I realized a person's religious feelings are precisely that—feelings. What separates the many flavors of Mormons—true blue and post-Mormons, conservative Iron Rodders and liberal Liahonas—is emotion. People either love being Mormon or they don't. Having never formed an emotional bond with the Brighamites, I don't. I never found any aspect of social Mormonism attractive but still consider its history among the greatest stories ever told.

While living in Appalachia, I was happy to let my neighbors search for the horns hillbillies believed grew on Mormon heads. I was proud to be a member of the Mormon tribe, which included most of my beloved relatives. One of the tests of being a writer is figuring out how to express an idea well. One of the joys of being a practical historian is finding a voice from the past that does so precisely. On his way to California in July 1852, Edward Kitchell stopped in Great Salt Lake City. He had heard all the evil tales about the Saints, but he found the city to be "really a beautiful place—laid off with a great deal of regularity & taste" and "well watered by the mountain streams that flow through every part of the city." He "took a lounge in the bar-room—sat in a real chair & read a reply to remarks on Mormonism, and came very near being a convert." Kitchell concluded, "The Mormons are not such a bad people after all—They are a remarkable tribe. No other set of people from the United States, would have made the improvements that now are made in ten years—They seem to thrive under persecution." It was true they believed in polygamy, "but did not Solomon, & many more good old fellows that we read of in the Bible?" On Sunday he went to a 10 a.m. meeting at the Tabernacle amid "a perfect sea of heads & bonnets—Heard one good Sermon & some infernal slang & rant from [Heber C.] Kimball & Brigham Young—my idea is (& 'I know it,')"—here Kitchell quoted a favorite refrain of Mormon orators and common audience response—"that the leaders of the Saints are a regular organized set of scoundrels."

I began attending Utah Westerners meetings in 1985 and became a member of this distinguished chapter of Westerners International in 1987. Fawn Brodie called them Jack Mormons— meaning non-observant Mormons—after she spoke to them in January 1976 about Thomas Jefferson, but when I joined, they were an interesting mix of Masons, devout Mormons, Jewish gentiles, heretics, and agnostics. Almost to a man—and until 2002, all Utah Westerners were men—they considered Dale L. Morgan the greatest chronicler of the American West. During his too-short life, Morgan had published more than forty books, including masterworks such as *Overland in 1846* and *The West of William H. Ashley*. Despite losing his hearing to meningitis at age fourteen, Morgan graduated from the University of Utah during the Great Depression with a degree in art, but his first love was history, a passion he developed working with the Utah Writers Project. By age thirty, Morgan's writing talent and command of the history of American West and the Mormons (he was a great-grandson of original apostle Orson Pratt) had won him a national reputation and several book contracts. To escape the "sundry kinds of hack work" he did between 1947 and 1954, Morgan took a job at the Bancroft Library: he never wrote another popular work like his only Utah history, *The Great Salt Lake*, but he produced a long series of meticulously crafted documentary studies on all aspects of the frontier. After he received a rare second Guggenheim Fellowship, cancer killed him at age fifty-six in 1971.

Morgan's reach as a historian exceeded his brief grasp on life. By the time of his death, he had hoped to undertake a comprehensive survey of the American fur trade, a multi-volume history of the Mormons, an edition of William B. Lorton's journal (which he called "the finest Forty-niner diary I have ever laid eyes on"), a documentary history of the Stansbury Expedition, an edition of the American journals of British botanist Joseph Burke he had already titled "From Hudson Bay to the Great Salt Lake: The Journal of Joseph Burke in the Canadian and American West, 1843-1846," an annotated edition of Nelson Slater's "rousingly controversial" *Fruits of Mormonism* (which, he noted, would have been his first book on "my original field of specialization, the Mormons"), updated versions of *Jedediah Smith and the Opening of the West* and his 1950 monograph *West from Fort Bridger*, a frontier chronology that Louise Barry eventually published as *The Beginning of the West*, a study Chad Flake, the head librarian of BYU's Special Collections, finished in 1978 as *A Mormon Bibliography 1830—1930*, and a collection of the papers of fur-trade mogul Robert Campbell to be called *The Rockies and the Yellowstone*, designed to serve as "the companion book to my giant Ashley book," *The West of William H. Ashley*.

Greg Thompson, Dean of Special Collections at the University of Utah's J. Willard Marriott Library, arranged underwriting and persuaded the Bancroft Library to catalogue Morgan's vast papers, which filled up eighty reels of microfilm when the Bancroft completed the task in 1992. Spending Sunday afternoons at the University of Utah's Marriott Library with the microfilms of Morgan's papers helped to make me a historian. I have always been extraordinarily lucky, but that luck reached extravagant levels when it came to finding allies, role models, and mentors.

I learned the term in the computer biz, but "interrupt driven" describes my historical career, which has careened from one project to another in pursuit of an income. In about 1986 I visited the old Oquirrh School building where a new publishing enterprise, Signature Books, had its offices and had what proved to be the first of many conversations with Ron Priddis. I already doubted the wisdom of writing about Fawn Brodie, so I asked Ron what he thought would make a good book. What the world needed, Ron suggested, was a biography of Sam Brannan, the Mormon preacher and promoter who brought the first boatload of American settlers to California in 1846 and became San Francisco's first millionaire. It was a fantastic idea and led me to read Dale L. Morgan's *The Humboldt, Highroad of the West*, where I met Abner Blackburn, whose adventures led deeper into my love affair with the history of the American West. By 1989 I had tracked the manuscript to the Nevada Historical Society, and in 1992 it became my second published book, *Frontiersman: Abner Blackburn's Narrative*.

After my job at Evans & Sutherland ended in 1989, I went to work for Dayna Communications, manufacturer of DaynaFile, which wanted to network Macintosh computers. Dayna had offices in the Key Bank Tower in downtown Salt Lake City, across the street from the Salt Lake temple and a short stroll from the LDS Church Historical Department archives on the second floor of 50 North Temple. I began spending my lunch hours at LDS Archives transcribing sources related to Abner Blackburn, Sam Brannan, Indians, and overland emigration. I made many friends, notably Lyndia Carter, who was well on her way to becoming the leading authority on the handcart disaster, and her husband

Robert, the bard of Utah County. I did not share the staff's love of religion, but Ron Barney, Randall Dixon, Bill Slaughter, Chad Orton, and Ron Watt, shared my passion for history. Michael L. Landon, a graduate of Sacramento State's public history program, introduced me to his advisor, Kenneth N. Owens, who was hoping someone could determine whether someone had forged Abner Blackburn's narrative. In July 1991 Mike alerted me to Thomas Bullock's copy of the Lansford W. Hastings "directions from Bridgers Fort to the Settlements in California also a map of the route," which Hal Schindler and I incorporated in our update of Dale Morgan's *West from Fort Bridger*.

After I submitted the Blackburn manuscript to the University of Utah Press in April 1991, I learned about several 1848 diaries at LDS Archives relating to the opening of the Carson Pass road. This was a hot topic, because Utah Westerner David L. Bigler had recently published his great-uncle's account of the opening of the wagon road in *The Gold Discovery Journal of Azariah Smith*. Bigler showed he could pack more facts into a five-line footnote than most historians can squeeze into five (or 500) pages. His work provided a template for organizing Blackburn's narrative, and everything I've written since.

I wanted to show a university press how quickly it was possible to publish a book in the digital age. In ten weeks I transcribed, photographed, designed, and laid out *A Road from El Dorado: The 1848 Trail Journal of Ephraim Green* in QuarkXPress and had printed copies delivered to the Oregon–California Trails Association convention in Sacramento when it opened on August 8, 1991. The project taught me a vital lesson about vanity publishing: Don't do it. Excellent reasons and centuries of book-making tradition show it takes years to produce a quality book.

At Sacramento I met Robert A. Clark, the third generation of Clarks to lead the Arthur H. Clark Company, America's oldest and most respected publisher of Western History. (I first met him in 1968 when he was playing guitar in the dorm room of his friend John McNicholas at UC Santa Cruz.) In between peddling paperbacks in the convention's book room, I got to know Bob and subscribed to Kenneth L. Holmes's *Covered Wagon Women*, the latest of the Clark Company's legendary series of documentary histories.

One of the research challenges of Blackburn's narrative was the Indian romance that interrupted his 1847 trek from Salt Lake to Monterey with Sam Brannan. Richard Grant of Fort Hall provided the Mormons with a French-Canadian guide, Louis Devon, who told a campfire love story about Sinute Kota—Leaping Faun—his Mandan wife.

Writing biographies forces you to deal with subjects no narrow specialist would touch. Abner Blackburn introduced me to the late fur trade, steam boating on western rivers, the march of the Mormon Battalion, the Gold Rush, and Plains Indian ethnography. Historical research leads deep into endless rabbit holes, but you learn something new every day and make fantastic friends on the way, even if you never find the rabbit. This chase introduced me to the Hudson's Bay Archives at Manitoba and Richard Grant's letters from Fort Hall, which provided invaluable insights into the late fur trade and early overland emigration. Blackburn's stories led to an article, "Lou Devon's Narrative: A Tale of the Mandans' Lost Years," in *Montana The Magazine of Western History*, which it was and still is. Editor Charles E. Rankin put it through a rigorous peer review that introduced me to much better historians than I will ever be. If wedlock entailed the same strains that complicate author–publisher relations, all marriages would end in divorce, but somehow my friendships with Bob Clark and Chuck Rankin have endured for decades.

Western history has always been my first love. History and her story encompasses humanity and so is never simple. I became intrigued with the schemes surrounding James K. Polk's acquisition of New Mexico and California from Mexico. The three critical decades of America's explosive expansion between 1840 and 1870 tell an epic tale of triumph with a cast of some 500,000 white heroes (mostly women and children) and scoundrels (all white men). During their long and perilous journey across the west, they wrote some of the nineteenth century's greatest prose. What storyteller could resist such a saga, especially with its tragic counterpoint: the fate of the million or more native inhabitants of the plains, mountains, and deserts who had blood-thirsty invaders seize their ancient homelands and destroy the resources that had sustained them for some twenty millennia?

Dale L. Morgan's ghost pitched in, for his letters and papers provided detailed instructions on how to approach Abner Blackburn's unpublished memoir, write a Sam Brannan biography, investigate the Mountain Meadows massacre, or undertake a multi-volume history of the Oregon–California Trail. Long ago I considered completing Morgan's unfinished projects as a life project, but as Dale proved, life is too short.

Wallace Stegner's masterful study of Mormon overland emigration, *The Gathering of Zion*, revealed that Thomas Bullock's official journal of Brigham Young's 1847 trek to Salt Lake was still unpublished. (The defenders of the church's vaults had refused to let Stegner review it.) Not even *Deseret News* editor Bill Smart could see it when he wanted to trace the trail from the Weber River to Salt Lake with his Boy Scout troop. Perhaps hoping to soften up A. William Lund, who served for forty years as the "primary gatekeeper of the records" in the old Church Historian's Office, Smart wrote an article with a picture of the Assistant Church Historian gently cradling the two handwritten volumes of Bullock journals shortly before Lund's death in 1971. As he was taking the photo, Bill told me, the ancient Lund croaked, "Someday I'm going to edit these."

The spectacularly successful 1993 Oregon Trail sesquicen-
tennial made me realize the 150th anniversary of the Mormon
Pioneer trek was four years away. Utah Westerner Robert Hoshide
and I applied on July 20, 1993, to the Copyrights and Permis-
sions Office of the Church of Jesus Christ of Latter-day Saints
"for permission to publish the following items from the Thomas
Bullock collection (MS 1385) in the LDS Archives": his 1846
"Poor Camp" and west and eastbound 1847 diaries. Much to my
surprise, the office authorized us to publish a crown jewel of Mormon overland journals, Thomas Bullock's official "Journal of the
Travels of the Pioneer Camp of the Saints, from Winter Quarters,
in search of a location for a Stake of Zion." (Hoshide and I later
parted ways over missed deadlines but collaborated on the book's
biographical appendix.) I had always dreamed of publishing a
book with the Arthur H. Clark Company and knew Bullock's epic
would be perfect for them. In August 1995, I drove the trail with
Dave Bigler from Salt Lake to Grand Island to attend the Oregon–
California Trails Association convention. On our Mormon Trail
tour, Dave shared his encyclopedic knowledge of the land and
its history. I had dinner with Bob Clark in Grand Island, and he
welcomed considering Bullock for publication.

Sheer dumb luck let me become a full-time historian in May
1995. Bob Hoshide alerted me to a help wanted ad in the *Salt
Lake Tribune*: "Inquisitive Research Manager needed for 1 to 2 yr.
full time project on the Fancher Wagon Train Party of 1859 [*sic*].
Generous salary plus expenses. High energy, enthusiasm, resource-
fulness, and self-discipline must be proven via a resume of your
qualifications." I tossed my resume into the ring with some thirty
other historians. Two factors distinguished my application: it did
not list a PhD as a credential or include an assurance that Brigham
Young had nothing to do with the crime. At Dave Bigler's request,
in 1991 I transcribed the 1857 diary of Young's Indian interpreter

and brother-in-law, Dimick Huntington, at LDS Archives. Its contents showed that Young's role was an open question.

So I quit my tech writing job and became an employee of Frank James Singer Jr., Mensa member, swashbuckling entrepreneur, dedicated gun nut, and devoted Republican, who had acquired a consuming interest in western history after converting to Mormonism. He had built a multi-million-dollar insurance business and wanted to apply some of his fortune to his passion for history. Singer decided to sponsor a two-year investigation of the 1857 slaughter of 120 Arkansans by Mormon settlers at Mountain Meadows in southwestern Utah, to provide material for a novel and eventually a movie. Our agreement matched my annual $42,000 salary and provided health insurance as an employee of his Eve Insurance agency—an essential requirement for a full-time diabetic.

Singer was mysterious. I worked directly with his executive assistant and never spoke with him on the phone. The paychecks cleared, but I began to suspect Frank might not exist. In late June we finally met when his Lear jet landed at the Salt Lake airport's private terminal and spent the day outlining an aggressive project schedule. I committed to write a report that would summarize and interpret the research and give him my findings as a historian based on the evidence. I told Frank that he might not be happy with my conclusions, but they would represent my best professional opinion. I met Frank again at the 1995 company Christmas party, but he never commented on any of the many reports and documents I sent to Roseville.

Bob Clark liked my Bullock manuscript so much that on February 26, 1996, he invited me to become editor of an Arthur H. Clark Company series, which I considered equivalent to an appointment to historical immortality. During the annual meeting of the Mormon History Association in Snowbird Lodge on May 16,

1996, I handed out a flyer announcing "*Kingdom in the West: The Mormons and the American Frontier*, a new series from The Arthur H. Clark Company," printed in Clark's classic style. The series would "explore the story of the Mormon people and their part in the greater history of the Western Frontier."

"Primary source documents, many of them never before published, will be at the series' core, continuing the publisher's 95-year tradition of historical publishing. The Mormons' frontier experience, their religious vision and political ambitions will be revealed in the words of the pioneers, edited and illuminated by some of today's foremost historians."

The flyer announced Volume I: "*The Pioneer Camp of the Saints: The Mormon Trail Journals of Thomas Bullock*, The first publication of the complete official journal of the 1847 Brigham Young Pioneer company." It listed projected volumes on the Utah War, the Mormon Battalion, Mormons in California, "The Polygamy Papers," and what became David Bigler's *Forgotten Kingdom: The Mormon Theocracy in the American West, 1847–1896*, his reinterpretation of Utah's early and territorial years. The list included two volumes that never came to be: Lyndia Carter's "Tounge nor Pen Can Never Tell the Sorrow: A Documentary History of the Mormon Handcart Experiment" and Michael Landon's "Great Basin Narratives: The Northern and Southern Routes to California." I discussed editing other volumes with eight noted Mormon scholars but nothing panned out. We signed a contract with Lavina Fielding Anderson to edit the Hannah Tapfield King journal, but it fell victim to her packed schedule. The flyer elicited proposals from Kenneth N. Owens, Michael W. Homer, B. Carmon Hardy, and William P. MacKinnon, the leading authorities on Mormons in California, European visitors to Mormon Country, polygamy, and the Utah War. Each editor produced prize-winning volumes. I recruited Polly Aird and Professor Jeffrey Nichols to help edit

"*Playing with Shadows*": *Voices of Dissent in the Mormon West.* Two faithful Latter-day Saints helped to balance the series. Roger Robin Ekins contributed *Defending Zion: George Q. Cannon and the Mormon California Newspaper Wars of 1856–1857*; and Richard Saunders fulfilled my dream of including our hero in the *Kingdom* with his two-volume study of *Dale Morgan on the Mormons.*

Besides the glory of it all, the liberation of the Mormon past played a part in taking on such a vainglorious project. Now that the sixteenth and last volume, *The Whites Want Every Thing: Mormon–Indian Documents, 1847–1877*, is finally published, it sometimes seems a colossal waste of time. Documentary history is yet another victim of technology, for such collections represent a style of history the Internet has made obsolete. I still believe being grounded in primary sources is an essential foundation for becoming a competent historian. Reading all eight volumes of David A. White's *News of the Plains and the Rockies, 1803–1865*, which the Clark Company published between 1996 and 2001, along with the text of thirty-three proposed additions to the Wagner–Camp bibliography in his bonus book, *Plains & Rockies, 1800–1865*, would be the best possible starting point for a student of the American West. David was a petroleum geologist, not an academic, but with the exception of George Miles of the Beinecke Library, I never met anyone who had a more comprehensive knowledge of western history. White compiled the best series in the Arthur H. Clark Company's distinguished history; Bob Clark's superb design skills and its tan-and-red binding made it the handsomest.

Between investigating a massacre and writing a book about it, indexing Thomas Bullock, editing Dave Bigler's *Forgotten Kingdom*, assembling *Scoundrel's Tale: The Samuel Brannan Papers*, editing the last half of *Army of Israel: Mormon Battalion Narratives* with Bigler for the series, and helping to raise two teenagers, while their mother aced nursing school on her way to receiving an RN/ BS from the University of Utah, I was a busy guy as the twentieth century drew to a close.

While researching at BYU's Special Collections, I had a long conversation with D. Michael Quinn. That day Mike outlined the topics he found most interesting about Mormonism—seer stones and magic, doctrinal changes, church hierarchy and internal politics, priesthood, finances, eternal progression, temple ceremonies, and administration—subjects I found totally uninteresting. Mormon approaches to race, theocracy, sex and polygamy, Danites, blood atonement, and religious violence fascinated both of us. What intrigued me about Mormonism most was what did not interest him: the religion's role in American expansion, overland emigration, and Indian relations. Yet Kent Walgren of Scallywags Books hit the mark when he introduced Mike at a December 1998 book event: "I believe Michael Quinn is the most important Mormon historian of the last fifty years." (In early June 2003, the postman attempting to deliver the culmination of Walgren's lifelong scholarly work, Kent's two-volume annotated bibliography *Freemasonry, Anti-Masonry, and Illuminism in the United States, 1734–1850*, found him slumped in his easy chair in his Paris apartment, dead of a heart attack.)

Only brilliant historians such as Quinn, Jill Lepore, Elliott West, and Richard White approach history creatively, and their discipline and hands-on research produces endless insights into our human heritage. My single inspired idea might be realizing Mormonism's vast archives held unexploited sources of Western American history. These narratives and archival data shed light on a range of vital issues: the conquest of native nations, frontier violence, religion, the incredibly swift settlement and transformation of an arid environment, and the origins of the West's dependency on and conflicts with the national government. From where I sit in Zion, the "Sage Brush Rebellion" is merely another chapter in what that cantankerous Utah native Bernard DeVoto nailed as the "Great Land Grab." "The plan is to get rid of public lands altogether, turning them over to the states, which can be coerced as the federal government cannot be," DeVoto wrote in 1947, "and eventually to private ownership." The plot is the same scam western reactionaries use today, but attacks on American government during the 1850s, richly documented in Mormon archives, shed light on who originally declared war on sagebrush.

Sharing that light was not easy early in my career, especially when it involved accessing restricted materials at LDS Archives, notably the enormous Brigham Young collection (CR 1234). I began surveying and transcribing Young's Utah War letters in the summer of 1995 but got distracted before making it through September 1857. When I asked to see the microfilms again, higher-ups had ordered them closed to discourage "fishing expeditions." I was told a person had compiled a "shoot, the sky is full of pigeons" master's thesis based on racial slurs from Brother Brigham's papers. As usual, I had to write a request to access restricted material, which meant anything interesting. It then had to be authorized by a three-member panel consisting of two archivists and Elder John K. Carmack "of the First Quorum of the Seventy of The Church of Jesus Christ of Latter-day Saints" and "executive director of the LDS Church Historical Department." (Like several of its senior officers, Carmack was a lawyer, not a historian. He and his wife "contributed $3,000 each to the anti-ERA organization of Mormons in Florida" that helped to scuttle the Equal Rights Amendment.)

Most of my LDS Archives requests got a 2 yes to 1 no vote, but Carmack's cancelled out the other two. This game of "hide the salami" went on throughout the Mormon world for decades. As Juanita Brooks told Asael C. Lambert in 1954, "They still try to hold things out on me, but I have nailed them on so many things that I'm not afraid of them anymore—and that's an interesting feeling to have—it makes quite a difference in my inner life." She didn't quarrel, fight, or criticize them: "I can just laugh at them for many of the silly little things they do."

A friend I often saw at LDS Archives was Bill Hartley, one of the Arrington historical department veterans who had taken refuge at Brigham Young University's Joseph Fielding Smith Institute for Latter-day Saint History. Among the gentry who populated the Institute, Bill distinguished himself by publishing interesting books, while the Institute's director published only a handful of articles in the *Ensign*, the church's official magazine for adults.

On March 29, 1999, the *Salt Lake Tribune* printed what struck me as a quintessential Mormon history puff piece: "Brigham Young Likened to Abraham" based on a BYU conference, "Brigham Young: Images and Realities." It quoted Carmack saying the church's "historical documents show Young was a practical and holistic leader involved and concerned with the lives of his people." Historians had "drawn upon tainted and distorted records instead of church archives," BYU historian Ron Esplin claimed, so Young had been systematically vilified. "Brigham Young was erroneously painted as being ruthless and scheming," Esplin said. "The reality is not only softer but something we can admire."

The Brethren had teed up the ball, so I swung at it on ldsbookshelf, a Mormon book collector email list. The *Journal of Discourses* gave me the notion Young was a bigoted misogynist who was devoted to ruthless scheming, I wrote, while restrictions made working in the Brigham Young papers "about as easy as figuring out what an elephant looks like while blindfolded and handcuffed." If they wanted to glorify Young, I fumed, "fine. But they should avoid ridiculous statements that make them appear to be paid liars" and not "outrageously misrepresent the actual record."

Hartley told me they read the post at a Joseph Fielding Smith Institute staff meeting, which resulted in an invitation to meet with them on May 18 and exchange news about our publication plans. So I showed up at the Institute's offices in the Knight Building on the BYU campus at the appointed time, and Bill took me to meet with the male staff members, who included the very kind Dean Jessee and James B. Allen. Hardliners waited in ambush. "I yammered on about Kingdom in the West," I wrote at the time, "and never got around to asking what they were up to until way too late." After I had spilled all my beans about plans for the *Kingdom* the series and approach to Mountain Meadows, I asked about their plans. One of them dourly noted he had submitted a publishing proposal to "the administration"—which at BYU could mean the Quorum of Twelve Apostles—but since it had not yet been approved, he could not discuss it.

I left the Knight building feeling entirely hornswoggled. I could not imagine having to kowtow to some holy Mandarin for permission to pursue one's scholarly interests. Running your own history circus doesn't pay much, but at least you get to be your own monkey. As he escorted me from the sacred precincts, a sheepish Hartley said, "Guess you felt sort of sandbagged."

"Bill, said I, "I *was* sandbagged."

Butting heads with institutional Mormonism meant this was neither the first nor the last time I was similarly deceived. By the turn of the current century, I had been engaged in a war for the liberation of Mormon history for more than a decade. "I love it when they censor stuff," the distinguished scholar Brigham D. Madsen once told me, "because then I know where the good stuff is hidden." It isn't hard to perceive the motive for refusing to let the Mormon people have open access to their own history: the powerful potentates of the priesthood feared that the deception and vicious behavior so well documented in the faith's records would surely destroy their beloved church. Mormonism's princes failed to understand a fundamental truth: Mormons are Mormons for many reasons, and history would not even make a top ten list. Many faithful families had a long legacy of putting up with the behavior of the bullies above them who kiss up and kick down. For my money, "Be not afraid" is the best advice in the entire Bible.

I was a year from turning fifty and close to completing my Mountain Meadows book when the brethren sandbagged me, but I had already been financing the project for two years as a freelance researcher and writer. On June 10, 1997, Frank James Singer walked out of his offices in Roseville, California, and vanished without a trace. In March 1999, a federal grand jury indicted him on four counts of tax evasion. The vast majority of people who try to disappear eventually give up, but he is still missing and probably dead. A California Superior Court judge agreed and declared Singer dead on February 7, 2014.

The turn of the twenty-first century was the most important time of my life. At Floyd and Shawna O'Neil's 1999 New Year's Eve party, Floyd introduced me to his former editor and American West Center veteran, Miss Laura Bayer. Dr. O'Neill had already set me up. On the way to lunch one day, he asked, "Do you know Laura Bayer?" I had heard of her, but we hadn't met, I replied. "She's the best editor in Utah," Floyd said. "Floyd," says I, "you know I've always said John Alley was the best editor in Utah." (I had worked with John at Utah State University Press.) Floyd gave me his contemptuous "you idiot" look. "Laura taught John everything he knows about editing," he said.

In March 2000 I had the submission manuscript of *Blood of the Prophets: Brigham Young and the Massacre at Mountain Meadows* sitting on my desk. "Maybe I should take this down to church headquarters and tell them for a cool million I will forget I ever wrote it," I thought. That was not going to happen; too much was riding on it. I also realized I had achieved my major life goal, which was to write a book that would long outlive me. Like it or not, I suspected the book would change my life—but that's another story for another time.

The saying it takes three years to get a new business off the ground proved true for the Prairie Dog Press consulting operation I launched when Frank Singer disappeared. It also coincided with the collapse of my first marriage, which had been dead for years. We agreed to live apart in the same house until our son Jesse graduated from high school in 2002. Jan gave up and issued an ultimatum as summer 2000 began: either get a "real job" or move out of the home we had remodeled in 1994. I moved out in July, at the start of the best financial years of my life.

With the Mountain Meadows book in production, I pondered what to tackle next. During the late 1990s, I had worked on several freelance projects with Superintendent Jere Krakow of the National Park Service's Long Distance Trails Office in Salt Lake City. I consulted with interpretive specialists Kay Threlkeld and Lee Kreutzer, two of the finest public servants and historians I have ever known, on the Comprehensive Management and Use Plan for the Oregon, California, Mormon Pioneer, and Pony Express National Historic Trails. This led to a job writing draft text for the California and Pony Express accordion brochures, which are not only the two best trail maps ever created but became my biggest hits, since the NPS handed out hundreds of thousands of free copies. In May 2000 I signed a Cooperative Agreement with the Park Service to write "a Historic Resource Study (HRS) on the California and Oregon Trails, with supporting bibliography, photographs, maps, etc.," to "provide basic historical information on the two trails and their significance in the settlement of the American west." The arrangement was to last two years with possible extensions until 2005.

Hal Schindler died on December 28, 1998, at age sixty-nine, leaving an enormous hole behind at the *Salt Lake Tribune*, where he had worked since 1945. Editor Jay Shelledy recognized his newspaper had a huge appetite for the history he exploited with Schindler's great talent. In April 2000 he asked if I would be interested in filling the gap Hal had left behind. I submitted a sample article on James Ferguson, Salt Lake County's first sheriff, and Jay put it on the front page. On the Sunday before Utah's Pioneer Day holiday, the *Tribune* launched a new weekly history column, "History Matters." "It works either way you read it," Jay wrote.

"Brother Pat [Bagley] is the *Tribune*'s infamous political cartoonist," Shelledy added. I have long accepted the reality that my much younger brother is smarter, funnier, better looking, more hated and passionately beloved than his elder brother, not to mention being a 2014 finalist for a Pulitzer Prize, but it kills me that Pat is several inches taller too. That said, being Pat's older brother is probably my noblest if least merited accomplishment.

The same month my first weekly column appeared, my daughter Cassandra gave birth to my first grandchild: Noah Barrett. Megan Cassandra followed in 2003. She was conceived when a Mormon Kahuna married Laura to her first husband, me, on Black Rock Beach in Maui. Laura likes to note she experienced the joys of being a grandparent without having to raise children.

I inherited a fair intelligence, received a first-rate public education, and my culture taught me to work hard, but I never felt I accomplished much beyond what any historian willing to put in the time and effort could have achieved. I failed to learn repeated lessons, such as it's easier to begin a project than to complete one. I submitted the first part of the trails HRS in 2003 for review and began working on the gold rush. Rather than meet the terms of the contract and deliver a one-volume narrative history of the trails from 1840 to 1870 in a timely fashion, I decided this national

epic deserved an epic multi-volume history. I had forgotten Dale
Morgan's warning: "Anything connected with the Gold Rush is best
begun when you're young; you may see the end of it when your
beard has turned snow white." I now have the whiskers to prove it. I
published prize-winning volumes in 2010 and 2012. The final two
are already written in my head but are a confounded mess.

I can point to dozens of similar dumb and distracting career decisions. In 2007 I was fortunate to participate in the PBS
Frontline episode of Helen Whitney's brilliant documentary, *The
Mormons*. Thinking I could exploit this golden opportunity to land
a big advance for a biography of Brigham Young, I decided to try
to get an agent. Any idiot would know that the proper subject for a
page-turning proposal about Brother Brigham would be his fifty-six
wives, but this genius decided that an exposé of the Old Boss's
handcart scheme was the royal road to the Big Casino. I devoted
the next two years to chasing the handcart rabbit down the endless
research tunnels available online at the Mormon Pioneer Overland
Travel website. The handcart catastrophe proved especially dark,
since the suffering of its victims was entirely unnecessary.

Taking a cold, hard look at a beloved historical fairy tale is
never easy and seldom profitable, especially when a comforting
myth leaves uncounted hundreds of starved and frozen corpses
in its wake. I learned about Brigham's brutal instructions regard-
ing his beloved steam engine. I thought President Young put the
welfare of a piece of machinery ahead of saving a thousand starving
and freezing people, whose deep and abiding faith he had betrayed,
but the more I discovered, the worse it got. In April 1856 Young
sent Salt Lake's Mayor, Abraham O. Smoot, to haul missionaries
east and take charge of a church freight train that included three of
the governor's personal wagons. By late October when he reached
Fort Bridger sandwiched between the last two handcart companies, Smoot informed Young he had "a broken-down set of teams,

with which I shall be unable to move all my train any farther." He decided to "leave the Books, Thrashing machine, your Engine & fixtures & a part of the nails, glass & groceries & perhaps a portion of the Dry Goods" at the fort." Three days later Young ordered Smoot "to bring all the goods in and if he had not enough teams to call upon the brethren who were out in the mountains with ox teams to assist the hand cart emmigrations."

This posed a mystery: what cargo was so important it could not wait till spring? Why did Young direct Smoot to divert teamsters and oxen from the starving, freezing Willie Company, while the starving, freezing Martin Company was still trapped far behind at Devils Gate? It wasn't the machinery or the books or the glass that so concerned Brother Brigham; it was the "groceries," which Webster's 1845 *American Dictionary* defined as the goods a grocer sold: "tea, sugar, spices, coffee, liquors, fruits, &c." According to Smoot's clerk and commissary, Caleb Green, Young's wagons "contained about six tons of freight which was for the use of his family," notably "a large supply of Tobacco, Rum, Whiskey, Brandy, and other liquors, also tea and coffee."

When Young tried to foist responsibility for the catastrophe on John Taylor, the ethical apostle would not stand for it. "The Hand-Cart system was to me, and to us all a new operation," Taylor wrote. "I considered that the utmost care and prudence was necessary. I wanted if a train started, to know that it would go through. I knew of the weakness and infirmity of many women, children and aged persons that were calculated to go, I did not consider that a few dollars were to be put in competition with the lives of human beings." Like all bullies, when confronted with a brave and honest man, Young folded.

After putting all this together, I knew I could never write a biography of someone I despised. Fortunately, John Turner is a better and more even-handed historian than I could ever hope to be, and his *Brigham Young: Pioneer Prophet* is definitive. My work on handcarts exposed the depths of Brother Brigham's inhumanity, but in terms of making a living, it was a total bust. But it inspired climber-historian David Roberts to call me the "sharpest of all thorns in the side of the Mormon historical establishment."

Mormon Church leaders' "grab-and-stash" strategy to suppress controversial history energized "the independent sector of Mormon culture, which had an abiding interest in the Church's restrictions on historical research," prize-winning *Deseret News* journalist Linda Sillitoe observed in 1987. As faithful untruths unraveled, she warned, there was a "temptation to belittle those who 'should have been' smarter, better trained, more inspired," which only continued the damage. As someone who fell for a Mountain Meadows forgery Hofmann sold to the Utah State Historical Society, I am among those who need to "search for our own reflections" in the scandal's shiny surfaces and accept "the vulnerability that makes all of us human."

I have no affection for any form of organized religion. Faith does not move mountains, but as a historian, I know it moves people. "Faith is a very personal thing, and is unassailable except from within the mind of the person who holds it," my friend and antiquarian book dealer Rick Grunder wrote in 1999. He noted how often religious authorities "try to deceive by altering history. When they do so, they are on devil's ground, and they force even the most believing scientists and historians who have any integrity at all" to act as Devil's Advocates. "This is not because these scholars wish to harm anyone's faith. It is because they distrust the kind of faith which begins to build on foundations of rock mixed with sand." As Harvard professor Gautam Mukunda observed in 2016, "The most powerful force in the universe is to believe what you want to believe."

Historians of my generation were born at the right time. When

I began practicing the craft, if my small book collection could not answer a basic question, I had to visit a library to track down the answer. I lived to see search engines profoundly alter what Brig Madsen called "the craft of history." Since LexisNexis released the world's first dynamic search engine in 1974, technology has transformed how lawyers, journalists, and then everybody practiced their professions. Increasingly capable computers and networks have put exponentially more powerful tools into historians' hands as they simultaneously destroyed American enterprises seemingly essential to any writer's survival—publishing, book selling, and newspapers. None of this was unforeseen: On November 14, 1990, Jerome S. Rubin, president of the American Association of Publishers, explained "Life After Print" to the organization's annual conference at Redwood City, California. The creation of electronic publishing was as important as the invention of movable type. "Indeed, the impact of the computer is likely to be even more profound than that of the printing press," he said. Rubin spoke from his experience as the driving force behind the development of Lexis. Print was dead, he proclaimed. The mighty publishing industry was responding like the buggy makers who ignored the impact of the automobile. Within twenty years, he prophesied, most people would do their reading on handheld computers. Rubin's apocalyptic vision was scary, a law librarian observed, for he delivered the speech "to a group of *publishers*." This is tough news for someone who has devoted his life to writing and the making of books, but events proved Rubin was right.

For years I boasted about being the world's luckiest historian, which may or may not be true. Simply surviving three decades as a professional historian without even having a master's degree is damn lucky, perhaps miraculous. If anyone ever learned anything from history, America would not be in Afghanistan. I hope seven decades have taught me *something*, but if forced to say what, not being as smart or as good a writer as I long thought would lead the list. I know I have been blessed to spend most of my time doing what I love. I like to think I had some hand in the liberation of my people's history. At every opportunity I reminded Church Historians and their assistants that their restrictive policies confirmed that they had something to hide. I constantly called on the Church of Jesus Christ of Latter-day Saints to "open all of its records." Much to my astonishment, it did.

The process was subtle. In about 2001 I was denied access to a thoroughly innocuous George A. Smith letter describing his 1856 meeting with Sam Houston. The archives turned around and almost immediately provided the letter to a faithful Mormon historian. This pretty much ended my pursuit of the truth at LDS Archives. I had already noticed flocks of volunteers capturing screen shots of restricted documents I could not access and suspected something was afoot, but the change crept up and surprised me. In late 2002 to early 2003, the Brethren published *Selected Collections from the Archives of the Church of Jesus Christ of Latter-day Saints* as seventy-four DVDs lumped into two volumes. At the time, I dismissed this sudden disclosure of about 400,000 manuscript pages, mostly in full color JPG files, as a copyright ploy, a way to avoid the consequences of January 1, 2003, when legal changes caused most of the church's unpublished manuscripts created before 1923 to enter the public domain.

The release repeatedly asserted the church held copyrights to other people's work—a flimsy claim, especially when the church could not prove it had formally transferred copyright from the writer to the Church Historian's Office. After the church let the camel's nose into its archival tent, it faced every censor's problem: What exactly is it you are trying to hide? The onslaught of the Internet democratized access to Mormon history, which led some life-long Saints to feel they had been misled about their church's history. This led to a rise in defections, especially among young women. Ten years after it released *Selected Collections,* corporate Mormonism ran out of thumbs to plug its leaky dikes of doubt. The attorneys who ran the Historical Department realized hiding critical sources proved they had something to hide. In 2013 they reversed direction: instead of trying to restrict access, they opened the vaults. The Historical Department, rebranded as the Church History Library, released thousands of JPGs of hundreds of collections: a year later they began providing patrons with multi-page PDF files via the Internet. I once told a friend I would continue the war to liberate Mormon history until the Brethren cried "Uncle"— and they did. Or perhaps it was a legal strategy to bury people like me in paper. The new access made *Kingdom in the West's* last volume, *The Whites Want Everything: Indian-Mormon Relations, 1847 to 1877* possible, but also made it immensely harder to create.

Rehashing these memories forced me to wonder about the road not taken and raised pointless questions about "what if" too many times. The worst aspect of being a historian is you cannot change anything; the past is immutable.

Growing old is revealing; you finally have to admit what's always been true. Aging is painful and alternates between being humbling and humiliating. After diverticulitis almost killed me in 2007, I began exercising every other day and set about trying to cure what ailed me. I got treated for sleep apnea, which renewed my flagging energy. I had cataract surgery in 2005, but my vision soon deteriorated dramatically. Turns out the surgery caused my vitreous humor to cloud up. On September 18, 2008, I had laser surgery in both eyes and awoke to a glittering world. Some ills are unconquerable. Sacroiliac osteoarthritis, perhaps due to all the sitting on my butt that writing demands, has kept me in constant pain for more than a decade. I've waited—forty years now—for the cure for Type 1 diabetes physicians have predicted would come within five years since 1978.

Looking back at an unorthodox professional career spanning three decades and two centuries, I have no right to complain about anything. I was born in the right place at the right time, an astonishing era when technology transformed modern life and my chosen career, changing how historians have worked for centuries. I have written or edited more than two dozen books on Indians, overland emigration, railroads, mining, violence in the American West, and computers. I have won many awards and have had fellowships at two great universities. I am a member of the Oceanside High School Hall of Fame and a fellow of the Utah State Historical Society. I have made hundreds of friends and know thousands of accomplished acquaintances. I am as famous as I want to be. I have found and lost love only to find the love of my life again.

Writing this old man's recollection of a young man's adventures drove home how, since April 14, 1972, every day of my life has been a gift. This fool has almost completed his spin on the wheel of life and knows the human journey from infancy to childhood to youth to adulthood to old age, and may live to great age. "As we keep our watch and wait the final day," Sophocles wrote, we should "count no man happy until he dies, free of pain at last." No one knows the hour our earth shall pass away, another of life's puzzles that pose an unanswerable question: Would we be better off if we knew how much time we have left?

Many who write history are seeking some version of immortality. We hope our names will live as long as books endure. We see the limits of being human all around, but we are creatures who cannot comprehend huge numbers, let alone eternity. Being a parent or grandparent is as close to heaven as any of us deserve, so a foolish desire to live forever merely confirms what an Old

Testament existentialist wrote thousands of years ago: "Vanity of vanity! All is vanity."

As with all my friends who do creative work, when the job is done, all you see are its flaws. I joke about retiring after "my work is done," but making books is all I ever wanted to do, and I expect to keep doing it until I can do it no more. I'm still dreaming and hoping those dreams come true. When I told that old drunk in Osceola, "I am Huck Finn," I wasn't kidding. I still am.